Think Like a CISO

Cristian Ruvalcaba, CISSP,
CCSP, MFA

Saluca Prints

Book Cover by Cristian Ruvalcaba, CISSP, CCSP, MFA

First edition 2026
Print ISBN: 978-1-972152-00-3
eBook ISBN: 978-1-972152-01-0

For you.

For you.

Contents

Preface

After an over twenty-year journey in cybersecurity, stepping into and out of many interesting and challenging roles, learning what I could and carrying that knowledge forward, I decided to take a bit of a break, the first real break I've had since the first day I stepped into the office wearing a temp badge. During this time, I've begun playing chess, finally picked up the guitar and learned some chords, and began to ponder about the next path I can explore to continue to build upon my career. To that end, I wondered. 'What would I need to know, as a CISO?'

From that question stemmed research, AI and non-AI assisted, followed by a systematic building of a relatively comprehensive manual, capturing my knowledge and conceptual understandings, along with the detailed research and compiling of information which have ultimately led to this book. It has been a fun experience that included frying my mother-board in the process.

I have always used the tools at my disposal in my various endeavors. While the frontier we face does place several new concerns before us, I find it critical to understand those tools to the best of my ability, even they are not one of the frontier threat landscapes we have yet to fully understand... in this case, with what has become ubiquitous: AI. I used AI in my research, aiding my thought processes, fact checking, making the various components of the cover art... and at the end of the journey, to write the "Key Takeaways" at the end of each phase. I have found it an invaluable tool and believe it accelerated my timeline in completing this project.

At some point, the paths of chess strategy and the strategic nuances of the offensive and defensive cybersecurity merged... and I asked AI to tell me which chess piece each role within a comprehensive organization would be.

One AI tool provided me with this assessment for CISO:

The Queen is the most powerful piece on the board — versatile, far-reaching, and dangerous in any direction. The CISO operates across every security domain simultaneously: identity, network, cloud, data, application, and governance. No other security role covers as much ground or wields as much strategic influence.

Phase 1: Foundational Risk and Control Architecture

Introduction

Cybersecurity leadership has evolved into a multidisciplinary executive responsibility that spans governance, technology, risk, operations, and resilience. This handbook provides a comprehensive, end-to-end blueprint for building, modernizing, and leading a security program aligned with modern enterprise and cloud-first environments.

Across the following chapters, readers will find a structured, deeply detailed, and actionable body of knowledge covering identity, cloud architecture, network security, data governance, threat detection, application security, incident response, metrics, compliance, platform security, and more.

1.1 The Scope of Modern Security Leadership

The security leader, at the Director, Senior Manager, Architect, or CISO level, must operate effectively across technical depth, organizational influence, and risk governance. This handbook prepares leaders to:

- Build and manage enterprise-wide security programs
- Integrate security strategy with business objectives
- Lead across cross-functional technical and non-technical teams
- Design and govern scalable, cloud-aligned architectures
- Oversee detection engineering and operational monitoring
- Communicate clearly with executives, boards, and regulators

The chapters that follow present a unified operating model built on principles of Zero Trust, contextual identity, telemetry-driven detection, resilience, and data-centric security.

1.2 Zero Trust as an Architectural Foundation

Zero Trust principles appear throughout the later chapters, including identity and access management (Chapters 10 and 18), network segmentation (Chapter 19), cloud security (Chapter 9), and detection engineering (Chapter 8), and form a structural approach to modern security architecture.

Core principles reflected across the manuscript include:

- Never trust; always verify
- Identity and device as primary control points
- Continuous evaluation and context-aware authorization
- Segmentation of networks, identities, applications, and cloud resources
- Assume breach and design for a constrained blast radius

Zero Trust in this handbook acts as a guiding philosophy, woven into authentication models, network overlays, cloud guardrails, and detection strategies.

1.3 Security Architecture Across Identity, Cloud, Network and Applications

Chapters 9, 12, 18, 19, and 22 form a cohesive architectural blueprint:

- Identity-first access and governance
- Cloud security guardrails, entitlements, posture management, and workload protections
- Modern network design using Zero Trust Network Architecture
- Application security models including API protection, WAF telemetry, secrets management, authorization models, and AppSec lifecycle
- Security engineering and architectural principles for scalable environments

1.4 Governance, Risk, Compliance, and Security Management

Covered in Chapters 15 and 20, the governance and risk management coverage includes:

- Policy development and governance structures
- Enterprise risk identification and tracking
- Integration of security into organizational risk programs
- Regulatory alignment for common frameworks (NIST CSF, NIST SP 800-53, ISO, SOC2, PCI, HIPAA) as discussed in later chapters
- Security steering committees and oversight models
- Vendor/supply chain governance as identified in Chapter 16

1.5 Detection Engineering, SIEM Modernization and Operational Monitoring

A modern operational detection program includes:

- Telemetry design and logging strategy
- SIEM modernization principles (cloud scalability, ATT&CK mapping, identity-centric detection)
- Detection engineering lifecycle and behavioral analysis
- EDR, NDR, DSPM, CIEM, and cloud-native signals
- Validation, tuning, drift management, and regression testing
- Threat-hunting models aligned with ATT&CK (as referenced across chapters)

1.6 Security Operations, Incident Response and Threat Management

In Chapters 13 and 14, this handbook provides:

- SOC roles and workflows
- Threat-hunting maturity
- IR processes, containment, communication
- Incident lifecycle operations
- Executive and cross-functional coordination requirements
- Tabletop exercises and preparedness models

1.7 Data Security, Application Security & Cloud Governance

Chapters 9, 11, and 12 cover:

- Sensitive data identification
- Access patterns, DSPM-aligned alerts, and lineage events
- Data movement monitoring
- API security detections
- Application lifecycle security controls
- Cloud posture management and entitlement governance

1.8 Vendor Risk, Supply Chain Security and Third-Party Controls

Chapter 16 of this handbook includes:

- Third-party assessment models
- Contractual and regulatory obligations
- Ongoing vendor monitoring
- Supply chain risk factors
- Risk classification and remediation workflows

1.9 Resilience, Continuity and Operational Stability

Chapter 17 provides the foundation for:

- Disaster recovery planning
- Business continuity models
- Operational resilience controls
- Testing and validation approaches

1.10 Measuring Security Performance

Chapter 21 incorporates:

- KPI/KRI/KCI models
- Governance metrics
- Identity, endpoint, cloud, and network telemetry-based measurements
- Reporting structures that map directly to the subsequent content

1.11 Outcomes

By following the models, architectures, processes, and frameworks presented in the remaining chapters, readers will be equipped to:

- Build or modernize enterprise security programs
- Operationalize Zero Trust principles
- Develop architecture and engineering strategies
- Mature identity, data, and application protections
- Establish and run SOC, IR, and operational monitoring programs
- Navigate compliance, audit, and risk governance
- Strengthen resilience through continuity and recovery planning
- Produce executive-ready dashboards and communications
- Lead multidisciplinary security teams

This handbook serves as a **strategic, operational, and architectural reference** for modern cybersecurity leadership.

NIST Security Framework

The NIST CSF 2.0 is one of the most widely adopted cybersecurity frameworks globally, serving as a foundation, and aligning across program development through regulatory requirements. The initial release in 2014 has been followed up with the latest version in 2024, adding new domains and modernizing the understanding of core challenges: cloud security, supply chain risks, and AI threats. This chapter provides a deep dive into CSF 2.0 in a format appropriate for security leaders tasked with implementing or maturing cybersecurity programs.

2.1 What's New in NIST CSF 2.0

1. **New Function "GOVERN (GV):"** Govern becomes the *anchor function,* ensuring leadership, strategy, policy, and organizational alignment precede technical execution.

2. **Expanded Coverage of Supply Chain Risk**: Vendor oversight and third-party cyber risk management are now explicit requirements.

3. **Alignment with Modern Architectures**: Includes guidance consistent with Zero Trust principles, cloud-native architectures, and identity-centric security models.

4. **Integration with Enterprise Risk Management (ERM)**: NIST emphasizes that cybersecurity cannot operate separately from business risk.

5. **Stronger Outcome-Oriented Structure**: Focuses on measurable objectives rather than prescriptive controls.

2.2 The Six NIST CSF 2.0 Functions

Core functions define families of considerations in a modern secure environment. CSF 2.0 defines **six top-level Functions.**

Functions

1. Govern
2. Identify
3. Protect
4. Detect
5. Respond
6. Recover

Each represents a lifecycle stage of a mature cybersecurity program. These should not be seen as stand-alone functions, they work as a unit to help with security posture.

2.2.1 GOVERN (GV): The New Core

Governance ensures adherence defined policies. Govern defines *how* the organization establishes:

- Approach
- Priorities
- Roles
- Responsibilities
- Resources
- Policies
- Oversight
- Accountability

Governance Categories

- **GV.OC**: Organizational Context
- **GV.RM**: Risk Management
- **GV.RR**: Roles, Responsibilities and Authorities
- **GV.PO**: Policy
- **GV.SC**: Supply Chain
- **GV.OV**: Oversight

Key Governance Deliverables

- ***CISO Charter:*** Defines the role of the CISO, including scope, authority, purpose and responsibilities within a given organization.
- ***Cybersecurity Steering Committee:*** A group of high-level stakeholders that help guide an organizations cybersecurity strategy, including policy and risk management.
- ***Security Policy Framework:*** The structured and documented guidelines, standards and procedures used by an organization to protect its assets, aligned with best practices.
- ***Risk Appetite Statement:*** The documented level of tolerance for risk an organization is willing to bear while achieving its overall strategic goals.
- ***Vendor Risk Management Program:*** A program designed to assess the risk associated with working with third parties for core functions to limit the risk of operational disruption.
- ***Security Budget and Investment Strategy:*** An approach to assessing the optimal spending allocation in order to align cybersecurity programs to risk appetite in conjunction with organizational strategic goals.
- ***Board Reporting Model:*** A framework used by, in this context, cybersecurity leadership, to report relevant information to a Board of Directors, typically including data on performance, risk and opportunities for strategic decision making to occur.

- ***CISO Metrics and KPIs:*** The set of data leveraged by technical and non-technical leadership to assess efficacy of the cybersecurity programs and the personnel behind them.

Govern is the foundation for all downstream security functions.

2.2.2 IDENTIFY (ID)

Resource awareness and controls around those resources allows for appropriate management and risk tolerance. Identify establishes organizational understanding to manage cyber risks to:

- Assets
- Data
- Systems
- People
- Vendors
- Cloud environments

Identify Categories

- **ID.AM**: Asset Management
- **ID.RA**: Risk Assessment
- **ID.IM**: Improvement

Identify Key Factors

- ***Enterprise Asset Inventory (IT, OT, cloud, SaaS)***: Maintaining a current understanding of assets allows for a better-defined risk assessment and security strategy. Shadow IT concerns can hinder security posture as they often do not comply with organizational security technical requirements.

- ***Business Impact Analysis (BIA)***: The process to assess the potential negative outcomes associated with disruption in business operations while prioritizing recovery activities.

- ***Risk Register***: A compiled list of risks for a given organization, or project, that include risk description, likelihood, ownership, and mitigating factors. This should be updated regularly.
- ***Security Architecture documentation***: The framework that incorporates risk management into an organization's security design in order to provide necessary protections to IT and non-IT assets.
- ***Data Discovery and Data Security Posture Management (DSPM)***: Often the primary target of malicious actors, it is important to understand the value of an organization's data as well as its location, classification and protective security controls.
- ***Threat Modeling (product + enterprise)***: The process for evaluating an entity's, organization or product, viable threats, their likelihood, and the possible mitigating factors.

Identify answers the question: **"What are we protecting and why?"**

2.2.3 PROTECT (PR)

The ability to enforce authorized use is a core pillar of a security program. Protect defines safeguards to ensure:

- Identity is trusted
- Access is authorized
- Data is protected
- Endpoints are secure
- Applications are hardened
- Configurations are enforced

Protect Categories

- **PR.AA**: Identity Management, Authentication and Access Control
- **PR.DS**: Data Security
- **PR.PS**: Platform Security

- **PR.IR**: Technology Infrastructure Resilience
- **PR.AT**: Awareness and Training

Key Protect Outcomes

- ***Strong identity fabric:*** A well integrated set of technologies allowing for contextual understanding of valid users and their authorized access. (SSO, MFA, JIT, PAM)
- ***Data classification + encryption:*** A framework for assigning importance and confidentiality attributes to data in order to align them to access controls.
- ***Patch management:*** A process for ensuring IT systems are up-to-date to minimize their risk profiles.
- ***Secure configurations:*** A documented set of standards applied to assets designed to reduce risk while maximizing their business operations use.
- ***AppSec / Secure Software Development Life Cycle integration:*** The framework integrating security at each stage of the software development lifecycle and controls for validating security at each stage.
- ***Zero Trust policy enforcement:*** The technical implementations for security controls that align to an organization's Zero Trust policies in a continuous fashion.
- ***Cloud guardrails and baseline configuration:*** The security controls implemented in cloud environments to ensure that an organization's security policies are implemented and followed.

Protect implements the heart of Zero Trust in practical terms.

2.2.4 DETECT (DE)

The ability to respond to incidents relies on the ability to know an incident has taken place. Detect establishes capabilities to identify cybersecurity events with minimal dwell time.

Detect Categories

NOTE: Some categories and subcategories from CSF 1.1 Detect have been moved to other functions or categories.

- **DE.CM**: Continuous Monitoring
- **DE.AE**: Anomaly and Event Detection

Key Detect Activities

- ***SIEM Modernization:*** The program or process around implementing the latest in SIEM technologies or stepping into the latest from legacy tools.
- ***Log Baseline Standards:*** A set of minimum requirements for activity monitoring within networks, systems and applications, in context, for the purposes of security monitoring.
- ***Cloud Telemetry Ingestion:*** Ensuring the consumption of an organization's cloud based activity for a more comprehensive understanding of security posture.
- ***Behavioral Analytics:*** The assessment of an entity's activity patterns base-lined with the ability to alert for anomalies to that baseline.
- ***MITRE ATT&CK-Aligned Detections:*** Configured alerting tied to the MITRE ATT&CK framework of tactics and techniques, in use since 2013.
- ***Data Exfiltration Alerts:*** Detection and escalation of unauthorized events of data leaving an organization's approved data residency and use.
- ***Threat-Hunting Program:*** A systematic approach for seeking out and identifying unknown risks and threats within an environment.
- ***Health and Drift Monitoring:*** The continuous process of ensuring systems and data do not not deviate from permitted configurations or use over time.
- ***DSPM Anomaly Alerts:*** Configured escalations for anomalous use, storage or classification of data.

Detect answers: **"How quickly do we know when something goes wrong?"**

2.2.5 RESPOND (RS)

Limiting the impact of an incident relies on well defined processes, technologies and communication standards. Respond defines the ability to contain and mitigate confirmed incidents.

Respond Categories

NOTE: Some categories and subcategories from CSF 1.1 Respond have been moved to other functions or categories.

- **RS.MI**: Incident Mitigation
- **RS.CO**: Incident Response Reporting and Communications
- **RS.AN**: Incident Analysis
- **RS.MA**: Incident Management

Key Respond Activities

- ***Incident Response (IR) Plan and Playbooks*** – Documented plans for reacting to and recovering from security events.
- ***SOAR or Automation-Assisted Containment*** – Technologies used in the incident response process to aid in rapid and repeatable actions following defined playbooks.
- ***Threat Intel Correlation*** – The use of threat intelligence reports and indicators for assessing incident severity and threat actors.
- ***Communications Workflows*** – Documented steps for sharing necessary incident related information with relevant teams at appropriate times during the incident response process, for example: PR, Legal, Executive Leadership.
- ***Regulatory Notification Processes*** – Documented steps for sharing necessary information to the appropriate audience based on regulatory requirements at any level.
- ***IR Tabletop Exercises*** – Regularly conducted incident and response

simulations meant to train and reinforce plans and playbooks while identifying opportunities for improvement in a non-critical situation.

Respond determines how effectively an organization limits impact during an attack.

2.2.6 RECOVER (RC)

Returning to standard business operations in a secure way is the final direct step in an incident's lifecycle. Recover defines capabilities to restore operations and reduce future risk.

NOTE: Some categories and subcategories from CSF 1.1 Recover have been moved to other functions and categories.

Recover Categories

- RC.RP: Incident Recovery Plan Execution
- RC.CO: Incident Recovery Communications

Key Recover Activities

- ***Business Continuity Planning (BCP):*** The framework, including policies, standards and procedures, for reducing or eliminating business disruption caused by an incident or event. These can include security incidents, power disruptions or natural disasters.
- ***Disaster Recovery Planning (DRP):*** The framework, including policies, standards and procedures, for returning to 'business as usual' status following a major business disruption in as short a time frame as possible.
- ***Resilience Strategy:*** A plan designed around preparing for possible business disruptions with the goal of maintaining core business operations functional while adjusting to the unplanned changes.
- ***Workload Restoration:*** The process of returning to normal operations in a given context: IT, physical or business.
- ***Process Improvement Cycle:*** The continuous approach to assessing current processes, identifying opportunities for improvement and integrating solutions to those opportunities into the given process.

Recover enables organizations to return to normal operations with minimal downtime.

2.3 Mapping CSF 2.0 to Enterprise Security Programs

The NIST Framework provides a foundation of **what** needs to be done. Cybersecurity leadership, often the CISO, will define **how** it needs to be done, within specific business parameters. This chapter maps each CSF 2.0 function to:

- Zero Trust domains
- Modern security org structures
- Cloud-native security practices
- Compliance frameworks (SOC2, ISO 27001, PCI, HIPAA)
- Risk management lifecycle
- Security engineering capabilities
- Security operations maturity

The Cybsersecurity Framework becomes a living process, continuously assessed for applicability and improved upon for efficiency and coverage. Threat actors evolve constantly, enterprise defenses must also evolve.

2.4 Using CSF 2.0 for Strategy and Roadmap Development

CISOs and other high level security practitioners may commonly use NIST CSF 2.0 to:

- Assess Current Maturity
- Identify Gaps
- Prioritize Investments
- Build short, medium and long term roadmaps
- Communicate with executives
- Provide measurable outcomes

2.5 CSF 2.0 and Zero Trust Alignment

Zero Trust does not replace CSF 2.0, it *reinforces it* through its core principles of explicit verification and least privilege access, while assuming that a breach is around the corner or has already taken place.

Alignment Highlights

- *GOVERN* anchors Zero Trust governance
- *IDENTIFY* supports data-centric Zero Trust
- *PROTECT* implements identity, data, and application ZT controls
- *DETECT* powers adaptive trust decisions
- *RESPOND* integrates with Zero Trust enforcement engines
- *RECOVER* closes feedback loops to improve guardrails

CSF 2.0 and Zero Trust work hand in hand in providing protection for organizations.

2.6 CSF 2.0 and Cloud and SaaS Environments

With the addition of the Govern function, and its incorporation of categories from other functions from CSF 1.1, CSF 2.0 supports cloud forward models, as well as traditional on-premise models, ensuring a process based set of principles. Several security models align under governance principles:

- Governance of multi-cloud environments
- Cloud-native logging baselines
- API-first system inventory
- CIEM and cloud IAM governance
- Cloud workload protection (CWPP)
- Cloud posture management (CSPM)
- SaaS security posture management (SSPM)

Cloud implementation requires tighter alignment between governance, engineering, and operations.

2.7 CSF 2.0 for Executive Reporting

Executives require clarity, not technical depth. Too much data or a lack of clarity may impede strategic decision making that is critical to meeting business goals.

The NIST CSF 2.0 enables:

- Board-ready domains
- Measurable KPIs
- Heatmaps
- Risk narratives
- Breach preparedness scoring
- Maturity-based progress tracking

This chapter's deeper sections will support your reporting frameworks (in Chapters 20 and 21).

2.8 CSF 2.0 Maturity Model

Achieving CSF 2.0 maturity involves arriving at a Zero Trust principled environment with measurable controls

Level 1: Ad Hoc

No defined structure or governance. This is often times where organizations start and at times fall into the pitfall of a single point of failure with regards to people or technology.

Level 2: Basic

Policies exist, limited implementation. At this point, risk for a single point of failure is reduced, but not eliminated. Policy implementation must be expanded to improve security posture, and considerations must still be made to allow for exemptions where business critical assets cannot yet align to policy.

Level 3: Intermediate

Identity, cloud, and endpoint controls in place. With policies and controls in place, a solid baseline is established, but this may still necessitate a high degree of manual intervention, both in implementation as well as in monitoring and incident response.

Level 4: Advanced

Automated guardrails, Zero Trust program in motion. Adding automated countermeasures and incorporating the principles of Zero Trust, an organization provides an elevated security posture with regards to technology, but also in established process.

Level 5: Optimized

Continuous monitoring, adaptive trust and automation. At this stage, process and technology are regularly evaluated. Opportunities for improvement are incremental and regularly implemented.

2.9 Chapter Summary

NIST CSF 2.0 can be a **foundational** element in building an enterprise security program.

This chapter translates the high-level framework into actionable, modern, Zero Trust-aligned guidance suitable for CISOs and senior security leaders.

NIST SP 800-53

NIST SP 800-53 SERVES as a fairly comprehensive security controls catalog and is used across federal agencies, regulated industries and enterprises adopting strong security and governance frameworks. Revision 5.2.0 was released in August of 2025 with 5.0.0 released in 2020. Revision 5 adjusted its focus toward outcome driven controls whereas revision 4 had focused on impact. With revision 5, and subsequently 5.2.0, the framework expanded its control set dramatically. Updates to the controls include items that align towards:

- Zero Trust
- Cloud-Native Architectures
- Supply Chain Risk
- Privacy Engineering
- Automation
- Continuous Monitoring
- Modernized Identity and Access Management
- Resilience and Cyber-Physical Security Needs
- Agile / DevSecOps Environments

This chapter provides a CISOs-level, **consulting-grade, deeply expanded** interpretation of the framework, with guidance on how to operationalize 800-53 inside enterprise programs.

3.1 Purpose of NIST SP 800-53

NIST SP 800-53 provides a **unified catalog of controls** to enable:

- Security Architecture
- Policy and Procedure Development
- Governance and Compliance
- System Design and Engineering
- Continuous Monitoring
- Risk management (RMF)
- Zero Trust Implementation

As a strong set of controls, it is often used as a checklist but would more accurately be described as a blueprint for building a resilient security program.

3.2 NIST 800-53 Structure

The catalog consists of **20 control families**, grouped logically for governance, technical implementation, privacy, supply chain, and resilience.

Control Families

- **AC**: Access Control
- **AT**: Awareness and Training
- **AU**: Audit and Accountability
- **CA**: Assessment, Authorization & Monitoring
- **CM**: Configuration Management

- **CP**: Contingency Planning
- **IA**: Identification and Authentication
- **IR**: Incident Response
- **MA**: Maintenance
- **MP**: Media Protection
- **PE**: Physical and Environmental Security
- **PL**: Planning
- **PM**: Program Management
- **PT**: Personally Identifiable Information Processing and Transparency
- **PS**: Personnel Security
- **RA**: Risk Assessment
- **SA**: System and Services Acquisition
- **SC**: System and Communications Protection
- **SI**: System and Information Integrity
- **SR**: Supply Chain Risk Management

Control Family Attributes

- Base Controls
- Control Enhancements
- Parameters
- Assignment Statements
- Implementation Guidance

3.3 Major Enhancements in Revision 5

Revision 5 modernizes several aspects of privacy, supply chain and development considerations.

Integration of Privacy Engineering

Security and privacy are now first-class, integrated disciplines.

Stronger Supply Chain Controls (SR)

- Software Supply Chain
- Vendor Risk
- Provenance

Zero Trust Alignment

- Identity-Centric Access
- Continuous Assessment
- Risk-Based Access

3.4 Deep Dive into Key Control Families

Below are the most critical control families for modern Zero Trust and enterprise-grade cybersecurity. Each includes implementation insights, pitfalls, and strategic guidance.

3.4.1 Access Control (AC)

Access Control defines **who** can access **what** under **which conditions**. Below are items to consider in enterprise environments when considering implementing these controls.

Key Zero Trust Themes

- Least Privilege
- JIT/JEA Elevation
- Identity Attribute-Based Access (PBAC)
- Device Trust
- Session Controls
- Risk-Based Authentication

Enterprise Practices

- MFA Everywhere
- SSO Across the Organization
- Elimination of Shared Accounts
- Automated Group/Role Membership
- Periodic Access Reviews
- Privileged Access Policies

AC directly supports Zero Trust's identity pillar.

3.4.2 Identification and Authentication (IA)

Identification and Authentication ensure the **who** is validated before they are permitted to proceed to the **what** they need to do.

IA Covers

- Users
- Services
- Workloads
- APIs

IA Enhancements in Rev 5

- Passwordless support
- Token-Based Service Identity
- Cryptographic Keys Management
- Workload Identity for Cloud-Native Systems

Security Strategy Objectives

- Universal MFA
- SSO Federation
- Machine Identity Management
- Certificate Automation
- FIDO2/WebAuthn Adoption

3.4.3 Audit and Accountability (AU)

Audit and Accountability ensures that actions are tied to the **who** and can be reviewed in real time or retroactively, depending on the review need or audit requirements under which they fall.

AU Focus

- Logging
- Monitoring
- Traceability
- Non-Repudiation

Required Capabilities

- Centralized logging (SIEM)
- Cloud-Native Telemetry
- Immutable Audit Logs (Write Once Read Many, WORM, Storage)
- Time Synchronization
- High-Value Asset (HVA) Audit Policies
- Automation-Assisted Alerting

Beyond policies, the implementation of a mature AU program provides a core pillar of detection engineering.

3.4.4 Configuration Management (CM)

Configuration Management ensures the **how** is followed through knowledge of what tools and settings are used in an environment.

Configuration Management Scope

- Standardization
- Approved Configurations
- Baseline Hardening (CIS Benchmarks)
- Change Control
- Drift Detection

Modern Implementation

- Infrastructure as Code
- Policy as Code
- Continuous Drift Monitoring
- Automated Remediation
- GitOps Workflows

Configuration compliance is mandatory for Zero Trust enforcement.

3.4.5 Contingency Planning (CP)

Contingency Planning allows for reduced business operations disruption.

Resilience Elements

- Backups
- DR/BCP Planning
- Restoration Testing
- Communications Plans

CISO Priorities

- Cloud-Specific Recovery Patterns
- Strategic Recovery Point Objective/Recovery Time Objective (RPO/RTO)
- Immutable Backups
- Geographic Redundancy
- Regular Tabletop Exercises

Rev 5 emphasizes **failover readiness**, not just documentation.

3.4.6 Incident Response (IR)

Incident Response focuses around the reaction to and elimination of active threats to an organization.

The IR Family Mandates

- IR Planning
- Categorized Playbooks
- Communication Workflows
- Training
- Tabletop Exercises
- Evidence Handling

Rev 5 includes enhancements around supply chain IR triggers and privacy incident coordination.

High Maturity IR Integrates

- SOAR
- Identity Disablement Automation
- Cloud Isolation Patterns
- Cross-Team Communications

3.4.7 Risk Assessment (RA)

Risk Assessment helps in identifying where an organization may be vulnerable, how it may be vulnerable and the likelihood of exploitation.

RA Requirements

- Enterprise Risk Register
- Analysis Methodology
- Likelihood/Impact Scoring
- Continuous Reassessment
- Vulnerability Scanning

Modernized RA Requirements

- Integration with DSPM
- API and Cloud-Scoped Risk
- Identity and Access-Based Risk Scoring
- Risk Acceptance and Exception Workflows
- Threat-Based Prioritization (MITRE ATT&CK)

Risk must connect directly to governance.

3.4.8 System and Communications Protection (SC)

System and Communications Protection focuses on secure transfer of information between authorized entities and secure storage of data at rest.

SC Attributes

- Segmentation
- Encryption
- Boundary Protection
- Network Controls
- Service Mesh

Cloud-Native SC Controls

- Zero Trust Network Segmentation
- TLS Everywhere
- Identity-Based Service Access
- Egress Control
- Cloud Perimeter Hardening
- API Gateway Patterns

Security Strategy Drives API, network and cloud security.

3.4.9 System and Information Integrity (SI)

System and Information Integrity ensures securely configured endpoints use approved tools for authorized purposes.

SI Includes

- Endpoint Protection
- Anti-Malware
- Vulnerability Management
- Supply Chain Analysis
- Threat Intelligence
- Anomaly Detection

Rev 5 Expansions

- Real-Time Scanning
- Memory Protection
- CI/CD Pipeline Integrity
- Software Supply Chain Detection

SI forms a large part of detection, prevention, and resilience.

3.4.10 Supply Chain Risk Management (SR)

Supply Chain Risk Management is an expanded control family in revision 5.

New Requirements

- Third-Party Software Integrity
- Secure Development Attestations
- Vendor Security Reviews
- Cloud Service Provider Oversight
- Dependency Scanning

Alignment

- Executive Order 14028
- Zero Trust Supply Chain Security
- Modern DevSecOps Controls

3.4.11 Privacy Controls (PT)

Privacy laws and regulations have expanded globally over the last decade, with consequences for non-compliance becoming more significant along the way.

Privacy Controls Introduce

- Privacy Engineering
- Data Minimization
- Consent Handling
- Collection Limitation
- Retention Requirements
- Privacy Risk Management

These Support

- GDPR
- CCPA
- GLBA
- HIPAA
- Global data protection regimes

Privacy engineering is now integrated into core security design.

3.5 NIST 800-53 in Zero Trust Programs

Control families can be used in conjunction to meet different requirements based on an organization's risk appetite and business objectives.

Identity-Centric Security

Access Control (AC) and Identification and Authentication (IA) are foundational to Zero Trust access control.

Cloud Guardrails

Configuration Management (CM), System and Communications Protection (SC), and System and Information Integrity (SI) map directly to modern cloud posture.

Data Protection

System and Communications Protection (SC), System and Information Integrity (SI), and Personally Identifiable Information Processing and Transparency (PT) align for data privacy and protection.

Automation and Drift

Configuration Management (CM), Assessment Authorization and Monitoring (CA), and Risk Assessment (RA) support automated policy enforcement.

Resilience

Contingency Planning (CP) and Incident Response (IR) build cyber resilience.

3.6 NIST 800-53 and Compliance Mapping

Security leaders can map 800-53 to various frameworks:

- NIST CSF
- ISO 27001
- CIS Controls
- SOC2
- PCI
- FedRAMP
- HIPAA
- FFIEC

3.7 Implementation Roadmap

It may not always be possible to implement all control families within a single project, nor achieve program maturity in short order. By laying a foundation and building upon it, cybersecurity programs can ensure a progress toward a fully mature state.

Phase 1: Governance and Identity

- Access Control (AC)
- Identification and Authentication (IA)
- Planning (PL)
- Program Management (PM)

Phase 2: Cloud and Data

- Configuration Management (CM)
- System and Communications Protection (SC)
- System and Information Integrity (SI)
- Personally Identifiable Information Processing and Transparency (PT)

Phase 3: Operations

- Audit and Accountability (AU)
- Incident Response (IR)
- Contingency Planning (CP)
- Risk Assessment (RA)

Phase 4: Supply Chain

- Supply Chain Risk Management (SR)

Phase 5: Automation and Monitoring

- Assessment, Authorization and Monitoring (CA)
- System and Information Integrity (SI)
- System and Communications Protection (SC)

3.8 Chapter Summary

NIST SP 800-53 Rev 5.2.0 provides a **holistic, modern, and deeply comprehensive** control catalog aligned with today's technologies and threats:

- Zero Trust Implementations
- Enterprise Policy Frameworks
- Compliance Programs
- Risk Management
- Security Engineering
- SOC Modernization
- Cloud Posture and Governance

This chapter provides strategic context needed to apply 800-53 effectively.

NIST 800-207

Zero Trust Architecture (ZTA), defined formally in **NIST SP 800-207**, shifts from a legacy approach of trust permissions based on network or physical location to one of no implicit trust while providing access based on user identity, device, data and context; providing a modern approach for a modern cloud forward and geographically distributed work force:

- NIST 800-207 Foundations
- Modern Extensions (2023–2025)
- Identity, Device, Network, and Application Control Planes
- Data Trust Zones
- Policy Decision Engines
- Enforcement Patterns
- Cloud and SaaS Zero Trust Design
- Microsegmentation
- CIEM, DSPM, API Governance
- SOAR + Automation Integrations
- ZT Maturity Models and Roadmaps

4.1 What Zero Trust *Is* and *Is Not*

A mindset around no implicit trust.

Zero Trust is NOT

- A specific product
- A new marketing label for existing network technology
- A "deny all inbound traffic" rule set
- Identity only
- A "VPN replacement"

Zero Trust IS

- An operating mode
- Continuous verification of every access request
- Minimal implicit trust
- Policy-based access tied to identity, device, data, workload, and context
- Automation-driven enforcement

4.2 Core NIST 800-207 Principles with Zero Trust

Seven foundational tenets

1. **:** Any class of device, data aggregator or SaaS system. **All data sources and computing services are considered resources**
2. **:** No implicitly trusted environment, access to any resource must meet

stringent access controls. **All communication is secured regardless of location**

3. **:** Access is granted on a per use basis and access at a given time point does not imply perpetual authorization for access. **Access is granted on a per-session basis**

4. **:** Policy is based on several factors, with a minimum of identity, device and application. **Access is determined by dynamic policy**

5. **:**All devices are monitored and no device has any implicit level of trust. **The enterprise monitors and measures the integrity and security posture of all assets**

6. **:** Constant reevaluation of the session-based trust. **All resource authentication and authorization is dynamic and strictly enforced**

7. **:** Telemetry and ongoing analytics lead to regular policy improvements. **The enterprise collects as much information as possible to improve posture**

4.3 Zero Trust Architecture Components

NIST defines three major logical components:

1. Policy Enforcement Point

2. Policy Decision Point

3. Resource Systems

4.3.1 Policy Enforcement Point (PEP)

Where decisions are enforced allowing the session to be originated from an untrusted device to the resource system requiring the trust. Some Example PEPs:

- ZTNA or API gateway

- Cloud IAM allow/deny

- PAM elevation workflow

4.3.2 Policy Decision Point (PDP)

Where policy decisions are computed.

PDP Components

- **Policy Engine (PE):** Policy Enforcement Decision
- **Policy Administrator (PA):** Communication Pathway Administration

The PEP queries the PDP; the PDP evaluates policy against context.

Policy Engine Considerations

- Identity Attributes
- Device Posture and Geolocation
- Workload Identity
- Data Classification
- And more...

Common Implementation Stacks

- Cloud Infrastructure Entitlement Management, CIEM, for Cloud IAM
- Identity Providers, IdP, for identity attribute evaluation
- Data Security Posture Management, DSPM, for data context
- Endpoint Detection and Response (EDR)/Managed Detection and Response (MDR) for device posture feeding PEP decisions

4.3.3 Resource Systems

These are the services being accessed and vary depending on the necessary workload or task:

- APIs
- Applications
- Cloud Accounts
- Data Repositories

4.4 Zero Trust Pillars

To operationalize ZTA at an enterprise level, it can be broken into **five pillars,** each corresponding to Operational Planes:

1. **Identity:** Users and Workload Identities
2. **Device / Endpoint:** Posture, Attestation and Compliance
3. **Network / Workload:** ZTNA, Microsegmentation, Service Mesh
4. **Application / APIs:** AuthN/AuthZ, API governance
5. **Data:** Classification, Access, Lineage, Risk

Each plane is controlled by policies, automation, telemetry and risk scoring.

4.5 Identity: The Primary Control Plane

It has been said "Identity-First Security is the New Perimeter." As a biproduct of a cloud forward world, access to resources now often relies on identity. This strategy allows for three high level concepts or ideas for addressing this plane:

1. Identity Governance and Controls.
2. Segmented resources and stringent authorization controls.
3. Awareness of identities and assets in an environment.

4.6 Network in Zero Trust

Following a Zero Trust Network strategy implies the principle of no trust and constant verification. The principle of least privilege is core to the ability to protect resources.

The network plane includes segmentation, microsegmentation, encrypted traffic, egress monitoring and more. Technologies that help in establishing a Zero Trust network model include ZTNA implementations, elevating the idea of a VPN with significantly more stringent controls, and one or more microsegmentation implementations.

4.7 Device Trust

Device Trust is a posture driven authentication model wherein any number of device elemental signals play a factor into its authorization for access:

- OS version and patch level
- EDR presence
- Encryption status
- Configuration compliance
- Certificate presence

These signals feed policy engines to grant or deny access dynamically, ensuring appropriate communication administration.

4.8 Application and API Trust

Applications and APIs are key resources accessed through a Zero Trust model. Stringent controls in place allow for permitted access to go through, while unauthorized access is successfully prohibited.

Common Requirements

- Strong Authentication
- Authorization: Role-Based, Attribute-Based, or Policy-Based
- Secrets Management and Vaulting
- API Gateways
- Policy-as-Code
- Secure Software Supply Chain

API Zero Trust

- Schema Validation
- Token Validation
- Workload Identity for Service-to-Service communication
- Rate limiting and abuse prevention

4.9 Data-Centric Zero Trust

The ability to assess data security posture and enforce appropriate contextual access foundational to Zero Trust. Data is the primary target for malicious actors. As such, it is the ultimate object of protection.

Common Zero Trust Data Practices

- Data classification
- Lineage
- Access governance

- Tokenization/masking
- Encryption (at rest + in transit)
- Key management and rotation
- DSPM for visibility
- Sensitive data zones
- Policy-based access controls

Data Trust Zones

Instead of a simple "sensitive vs non-sensitive," Zero Trust uses dynamic zones based on:

- Classification
- Regulatory exposure
- Business sensitivity
- Required control level

4.10 Example Zero Trust Architecture Models

While there are several architecture models that can be implemented following the core principles of Zero Trust. Below are examples of models, which can be used by themselves or in conjunction with others.

Identity Proxy Model

- SaaS
- ZTNA
- Workforce Access

Service Mesh Model

- Microservices
- Kubernetes
- East-West Encryption
- Workload Identity

API Gateway Model

- APIs
- Services
- B2B Integrations

Microsegmentation Model

- Data Centers
- Hybrid Environments
- Legacy Workloads

Cloud-Native IAM Model

- Cloud Environments
- Serverless
- Workloads using Cloud IAM exclusively

4.11 Zero Trust Policy Evaluation

Appropriate access is limited to the right source, the right destination, the right pathway, the right privileges and the acceptable level of risk.

Policy Decision Considerations

- Subject: who or what is accessing the resource
- Object: the resource being accessed
- Action: what is performed on the resource (read/write/admin/etc.)
- Context: the nuance of the action (location, time, device, behavior)
- Risk: associated with the communication (score-based)

Policy Defining Elements

- Open Policy Agent (OPA)
- Attribute-Based Access Control, ABAC, Rules
- Policy-Based Access Control, PBAC, Rules
- Conditional Access
- Service Mesh Policies
- Firewall/Segmentation Rules

4.12 Zero Trust Automation

Zero Trust fails without automation.

There are myriad moving parts, and the constant access validation prevents manual intervention from being a feasible approach

Automation becomes necessary for:

- Identity Lifecycle
- Drift Detection
- Enforcing IaC/PAC
- Device Posture Evaluation
- Segmentation Enforcement
- Cloud Guardrail Violation Remediation
- SOAR-Triggered Incident Actions

Zero Trust is a **continuous process of checks**, not a set of static controls.

4.13 Expanded Zero Trust Maturity Model

Achieving full maturity leads an organization to secure operations and continuous improvement.

Level 1: Traditional

Flat networks, VPN, implicit trust. At this stage there are no Zero Trust principles in place.

Level 2: Perimeter and Identity Enhancements

SSO, MFA, basic segmentation. This is the start of the Zero Trust journey with identity protection controls in place.

Level 3: Context-Aware Access

Conditional access, device posture and cloud guardrails. This stage includes behavioral analytics, time-based permissions and other key signals in the permitting of context aware access.

Level 4: Full Zero Trust Architecture

PEPs and PDPs integrated across all planes. At this stage, relevant policies and controls have been implemented along with any combination of the models discussed in 4.10, or others.

Level 5: Autonomous Zero Trust

Risk-based adaptive trust, automation and self-healing infrastructure. The highest level of maturity, wherein the process is constantly adjusting based on newly identified risk scores with minimal input from administrators while still granting those administrators the opportunity for continuous improvement of the process.

4.14 Roadmap for Zero Trust Deployment (36 Months)

A well designed Zero Trust environment has several components. A proposed roadmap to that security posture is detailed below.

Phase 1 (0–12 months): Identity + Early ZTNA

- MFA
- SSO
- Identity Governance
- Device Posture Enforcement
- ZTNA Rollout

Phase 2 (12–24 months): Cloud + Application Zero Trust

- Cloud Guardrails
- Microsegmentation

- Service Mesh Adoption
- API Gateway Enforcement
- Secrets Management

Phase 3 (24–36 months): Automation and its Trust

- Policy-as-Code
- Automated Drift Remediation
- SOAR Orchestration
- DSPM Enforcement
- Risk-Based Adaptive Access

4.15 Chapter Summary

NIST 800-207 provides the conceptual foundation for Zero Trust, but enterprise implementation requires far deeper integration across identity, cloud, data, applications, automation, and governance.

This chapter provides a **complete, modernized, blueprint** for operationalizing Zero Trust at enterprise scale.

NIST SP 800-37

THE NIST RISK MANAGEMENT Framework (RMF) defines a repeatable, defensible, and auditable process for managing cybersecurity and privacy risk across an enterprise.

RMF can be found to be in use in:

- Federal Agencies
- Defense Contractors
- Critical Infrastructure
- Regulated Industries
- Large Enterprises that require Structured Governance

While RMF originated in federal environments, modern organizations increasingly adopt the framework because it provides a **complete operating system for cybersecurity governance** through a seven-step process and was most recently updated in August of 2025.

This chapter provides an **expanded interpretation** of RMF meant for cybersecurity leadership, integrating enterprise needs, Zero Trust, cloud adoption, digital transformation, modern DevSecOps, and real-world compliance requirements.

5.1 Purpose of RMF

RMF exists to

- Integrate Cybersecurity Risk into Enterprise Risk Management (ERM)
- Ensure consistent, traceable security decisions
- Define a unified lifecycle for system risk
- Support Governance, Compliance, and Audit readiness
- Ensure accountability for security outcomes
- Enable repeatable processes for high-risk systems

RMF ties together

- System Boundary Definition
- Controls Selection
- Continuous Monitoring
- Authorizations
- Governance Roles
- System Lifecycle Management

The result is a **closed-loop cycle** of risk visibility, decisions, and assurance.

5.2 The Seven RMF Steps (Revision 2)

RMF consists of **seven steps**, each expanded dramatically in Revision 2:

1. Prepare
2. Categorize
3. Select
4. Implement
5. Assess
6. Authorize
7. Monitor

5.3 PREPARE

The Prepare step serves as an expanded governance layer and introduces organization-level activities that were missing from RMF prior to 2018. At this stage, organizations begin their journey in implementing the framework around an enterprise, or a given set of a systems.

Ensures

- Governance Structures exist
- Roles are defined
- Risk Tolerance is documented
- Common Controls are architected
- Repeatable Templates exist
- Data Flows are understood
- Zero Trust strategy aligns with RMF

Organizational Responsibilities

- Define Risk Tolerance
- Align Cybersecurity with Business Objectives
- Establish Governance Boards
- Define Zero Trust Strategy
- Establish Common Control Catalog
- Create Enterprise-Wide Risk Registers

System-Level Responsibilities

- Define System Boundaries
- Identify Stakeholders
- Identify Authorizing Officials
- Identify Data Owners
- Map Data Dlows
- Perform Business Impact Assessments

Prepare is where CISOs may spend the most time when modernizing programs at the organizational responsibility level.

5.4 CATEGORIZE

Categorization determines the **impact level** (Low, Moderate, High) of each system based on the CIA triad: *Confidentiality, Integrity* and *Availability.*

This drives control selection from NIST SP 800-53 in the next stage.

What it Impacts

- Budget
- Architecture
- Risk Prioritization
- Compliance Obligations
- Monitoring Intensity

Common Considerations

- Mapping business processes to data and to systems
- Include cloud and SaaS systems as well as on-premise environments
- Consider API flows, third-party integrations
- Include privacy impact considerations
- Include Zero Trust dependencies

5.5 SELECT

Select is where the organization chooses which security controls apply based on the impact levels identified in the Categorize stage.

Integrated Elements

- NIST SP 800-53 controls
- Control Inheritance
- Zero Trust Policy Structures
- Privacy Requirements

Common Considerations

- Use enterprise-level "Common Control Sets"
- Minimize system-specific configurations into control baselines
- Integrate Zero Trust principles
- Apply automation where possible
- Maintain mapping to ISO, SOC2, PCI, HIPAA where appropriate and/or required

5.6 IMPLEMENT

Implementation creates the **real** security environment. This is the technical execution of the controls identified in the Select stage.

Implementation Activities

- Technical Control deployment
- Configuration Baselines
- IaC / PaC automation
- CI/CD Integration
- Policy Enforcement
- Documentation of Control Implementation
- Architecture Diagrams

5.7 ASSESS

In the Assess step, the implemented controls are validated by either internal or third-party assessors to ensure compliance with selected controls using evidence gathering methodologies and documenting findings to be shared with appropriate stakeholders at the conclusion of the assessment.

Ensures

- Effectiveness
- Completeness
- Policy Compliance
- Consistency across Systems

Common Requirements

- Sufficient technical evidence
- Automation Maturity
- Documented Remediation Plans
- Drift Detection
- Configuration Compliance

5.8 AUTHORIZE

With findings in hand, an authorizing official signs off on the level of risk given the results of the assessment. This is a decision point for more control implementation, acceptance of workarounds in place for given controls or the all-clear, all controls having been satisfied.

The Authorizing Official (AO) evaluates

- Residual Risk
- Risk Acceptance Levels
- Mission Impact
- Compensating Controls
- Business Justification

The output is an **ATO** (Authority to Operate) or **ATO denial.**

ATO Types

- Full ATO
- Interim ATO
- Conditional ATO
- Denied ATO

AOs are often CISOs, CIOs, or delegated executives, but can at times be application owners or business unit leadership.

5.9 MONITOR

Monitor is the longest and most important phase as it ties into the continuous evaluation of security posture and risk. At this stage, a system or application is typically in production and disruption to its operation would have a negative impact on the business.

Continuous Monitoring Components

- Log Analysis
- SOC Monitoring

- SIEM Detections
- Cloud Posture Monitoring
- Vulnerability Management
- Identity Governance
- Configuration Drift Detection
- Periodic Assessments
- Documentation updates

Risk Management Framework Rev 2

- Ongoing Control Assessment
- Automation where possible
- Continuous Authorization
- Integration with Zero Trust Telemetry

5.10 RMF Roles and Responsibilities

At an enterprise level, individual roles may be more granularly defined than at small to medium sized businesses. Below are common roles found within enterprises, in SMBs it is possible that a single individual carries more than one role.

CISO

- Governance Oversight
- Enterprise Controls
- Risk Alignment

Authorizing Official

- Approves/Accepts Risk
- Reviews Systemic Risk Impact

Risk Executive

- Defines Enterprise Risk Tolerance
- Approves Exceptions

Security Architect

- Designs Control implementations
- Ensures alignment with Zero Trust

System Owner

- Defines Operational Needs
- Maintains System Documentation

Control Assessors

- Perform Technical Controls Reviews

Program Managers

- Track Remediation
- Ensure Resource Allocation

5.11 RMF in Zero Trust Programs

RMF and Zero Trust are not mutually exclusive, they are mutually enforcing, requiring:

- Continuous Monitoring
- Identity and Access Controls
- Device Posture Integration
- Automated Policy Enforcement
- Cloud-Native Guardrails
- Dynamic System Boundaries

RMF Provides

- Structure
- Accountability
- Documentation
- Governance Alignment

Zero Trust Provides

- The Enforcement Logic
- Architecture
- Real-Time Telemetry

Together they create a mature enterprise security program, minimizing risk to resources while providing necessary access to them in a continuously monitored approach.

5.12 RMF and Cloud Environments

Cloud RMF Requirements

- Shared Responsibility Models
- Cloud Service Provider (CSP) Control Inheritance
- CIEM Reviews
- Workload Identity
- Cloud-Native Logging
- Multi-Cloud Risk Analyses

RMF Rev 2 Components

- Virtualized Environments
- IaaS, PaaS, SaaS
- Service Provider Dependencies

5.13 RMF Documentation Requirements

Governance

- Risk Management Strategy
- System Security Plan (SSP)
- Roles and Responsibilities
- Boundary Diagrams

Technical

- Control Implementations and Baseline Configurations
- Architecture Diagrams
- Asset Inventories
- Logging Policies

Assessment

- Assessment Plans
- Evidence
- Findings

Authorization

- Residual Risk
- Risk Acceptance
- Authorization Decision

Continuous Monitoring

- Vulnerability Reports
- Incident Reports
- Metrics
- Configuration Drift Logs

5.14 RMF Maturity Model

Level 1: Policy-Only RMF

Documents exist; execution is inconsistent.

Level 2: Project-Based RMF

RMF applied to business critical systems; little standardization otherwise.

Level 3: Programmatic RMF

Common controls, enterprise baseline, central governance.

Level 4: Automated RMF

IaC/PAC, automated evidence, cloud frameworks, CI/CD integration.

Level 5: Continuous Authorization

Security and compliance become continuous, automated, real-time.

5.15 Roadmap for RMF Adoption

Phase 1: Governance and Preparation

- Establish Risk Appetite
- Build Enterprise Control Catalog
- Create Zero Trust Integration Strategy

Phase 2: System Categorization and Architecture

- Identify Systems
- Define Boundaries
- Map Data Flows

Phase 3: Control Selection and Implementation

- Tailor Control Baselines
- Align with Zero Trust
- Implement Cloud Guardrails

Phase 4: Assessment and Remediation

- Perform Assessments
- Remediate Findings
- Document Evidence

Phase 5: Authorization and Continuous Monitoring

- Approve Operational Risk
- Create Dashboards
- Integrate Automation

5.16 Chapter Summary

RMF provides the **governance backbone** for cybersecurity programs. When combined with CSF, Zero Trust, identity modernization, automation, and cloud-native architectures, RMF becomes a powerful **risk-driven security operating model**.

This chapter arms CISOs and enterprise leaders with the frameworks needed to operationalize RMF at scale.

Phase 1: Key Takeaways

Chapter 1: Introduction

- **Paradigm Shift**: Transitioning to a CISO requires moving from a technical focus to a proactive, mathematically sound, risk-based decision-making methodology.

- **Executive Cognitive Restructuring**: Security leaders must be trained to analyze incidents across three simultaneous vectors: technical viability, legal liability, and business impact.

- **Zero Trust as Bedrock**: Zero Trust Architecture (ZTA) is established not as a buzzword, but as the core logical component of modern enterprise risk strategy.

- **Framework Interoperability**: Modern leadership relies on consensus-driven standards (NIST, ISO) that hold weight in legal and regulatory arenas.

- **Mindset over Memorization**: Preparation for top-tier benchmarks (like CISSP) must abandon rote memorization in favor of adaptive, scenario-based evaluation.

Chapter 2: NIST Security Framework

- **Programmatic Outcomes**: Establishes core functions—Identify, Protect, Detect, Respond, and Recover—to organize security outcomes.

- **Executive Alignment**: Serves as a modular ecosystem that treats frameworks as building blocks rather than isolated checklists.

- **Regulatory Vocabulary**: Supplies the precise vocabulary needed to communicate security state to non-technical stakeholders.

Chapter 3: NIST SP 800-53

- **Granular Control Catalog**: Provides an exhaustive catalog of security and privacy controls focusing on the CIA triad (Confidentiality, Integrity, Availability).

- **ZTA Compatibility**: The controls in 800-53 are highly flexible and inherently compatible with Zero Trust models.

- **Bureaucratic Bedrock**: Successfully laying these controls provides the legal and architectural foundation for all subsequent technical chapters.

Chapter 4: NIST 800-207 (Zero Trust Architecture)

- **Resource Focus**: Shifts the defense paradigm from traditional network perimeters to protecting individual resources and logical components.

- **Never Trust, Always Verify**: Mandates an operational posture where all communication is secured end-to-end.

- **Identity as Control Point**: Identity and device state become the primary control points in the architecture.

- **Dynamic Authorization**: Access is granted strictly on a per-session basis determined by dynamic policy.

Chapter 5: NIST SP 800-37 (Risk Management Framework)

- **Continuous Lifecycle**: Dictates the systemic, iterative lifecycle required to authorize, monitor, and assess controls.

- **Operational Management**: Controls are not static; they must be managed within a continuous operational lifecycle to be viable.

Phase 2: Tactical Operations and Threat Detection

CIS Controls and Zero Trust Alignment

The **CIS Controls v8.1** are a prioritized, prescriptive, and highly actionable set of 18 critical security controls designed to provide a well rounded security posture within an organization and go beyond technical controls and dive into the culture of an organization:

- Mid-Size and Large Enterprises, and State and Local Governments
- Managed Security Service Providers
- Organizations with limited resources seeking high-value controls
- Zero Trust Transformation Roadmaps
- Audit and Compliance Mappings (SOC2, NIST CSF, ISO 27001, PCI)

CIS Controls v8.1 emphasizes operational maturity, cloud readiness, identity-centric security, and continuous measurement.

The detailed framework document is freely available and released under creative commons for non-commercial use. This chapter includes interpretations based on the publicly available list of control names and implementation groups outside of the detailed framework document without reproducing the content of the framework itself.

6.1 Structure of CIS Controls v8.1

CIS Controls v8.1 consists of **18 Critical Controls**, divided into three Implementation Groups:

- **IG1, Essential Cyber Hygiene:** When implementing within this group an organization is establishing foundational controls that provide the highest value relative to the quantity of controls in place. Often times, this is where small to medium sized businesses spend their security journey.

- **IG2, Intermediate Controls:** Within this group, an organization is taking things one step forward and defining roles dedicated toward the overall security posture of that organization. At an enterprise size, this level of granularity becomes common place.

- **IG3, Advanced, High-Security Controls:** Within this group, most controls, if not all, are likely to be implemented and specialization within the role definitions are key to the overall success and maturity of the security program. When reaching a point of becoming a high value target with national or global impact, organizations begin to fall into this third implementation group.

By organizing the controls within this implementation group model, the framework provides a roadmap for maturity in security programs while also prioritizing the most common attack vectors for a rapid return on investment.

6.2 The 18 CIS Controls (Expanded)

Below is a detailed interpretation tailored for enterprise leaders.

CONTROL 1: *Inventory and Control of Enterprise Assets*

For an organization to appropriately protect its assets and resources, it must ideally be fully aware of its assets and resources. An inventory of endpoints, physical and virtual, as well as workloads and containers, provides a contextual understanding of the attack surface that must be protected. This may also include IoT devices and OT/ICS equipment.

While many methods exist for identifying assets, some common approaches include network scanning which can include vulnerability scanning, API based cloud discovery, and attack surface discovery tools and services.

Zero Trust principles would necessitate a full inventory as resources would fall under defined policies and any shadow IT resources would either violate standards, or be inaccessible by subjects in certain implementations. For resources to be accessed, the trust decision must be made, requiring the full context of identity, subject and object.

CONTROL 2: *Inventory and Control of Software Assets*

Going one step beyond an asset inventory is an understanding of what lives on those assets. Understanding items like the operating system and its version, software installed and their configurations, container details, API endpoints and versions helps in establishing a more complete picture of the attack surface to be protected and either establish or ensure alignment to an approved software list comprised of tools that have been validated for security posture and deemed necessary for business use. This also provides an organization with the foundation necessary to establish a vulnerability management program accounting for severity of vulnerability, likelihood of exploit and business exemptions that may need to be made to ensure the business goals are met.

With regards to Zero Trust, it is not possible to apply policies to unknown tools or software and have them be used for business purposes while still adhering to Zero Trust principles.

CONTROL 3: *Data Protection*

Data is the backbone of any organization, whether intellectual property or customer information, these data provide the competitive advantages organizations use in the course of business to maximize revenue by providing products and services. The objective behind most malicious actors is data acquisition for financial gain; a gain which comes from selling of the data, using the data directly, or extortion, either to allow for data recovery or a commitment to not release it publicly.

It is important to understand not only what data exists within an environment, but also where it exists. This allows organizations to implement controls around the data with a goal of only permitting the data to be used for authorized purposes. Data classification practices enable organizations to prioritize protective measures while monitoring for unauthorized use.

In Zero Trust, the data can be considered one of the most important resources and policies would apply directly to the context of the data through classification, workload and identity.

CONTROL 4: *Secure Configuration of Assets and Software*

Software is vulnerable. Full stop. Secure coding practices have evolved over the years, but this does not account for the myriad variables that can take place within an IT system. Configuration adjustments to limit the attack surface for individual tools and for their underlying systems are needed and often go through rigorous scrutiny to ensure a level of allowable risk for us within an organization's environments. Once specific versions and configuration settings have been sufficiently vetted, organizations begin their standardized use of these tools, often beginning with a golden image and followed up with automated configuration compliance processes.

It is important to keep in mind that golden images, while serving as a primary source for asset configurations, may still need additional testing and validation when new vulnerabilities are published or previously undisclosed malware is identified.

This continuous approach to monitoring for and protecting against unknown issues also applies to the software development lifecycle when building applications. Following CI/CD principles may allow for reduction in attack surface for a given application if newly identified gaps are prioritized through the development process.

Cloud environments are designed for rapid deployment and ease of use. They have security measures that can be implemented, but are not necessarily implemented by default. Establishing policies and implementation standards, and ensuring these are enforced, may be the difference between a secure cloud based workflow and a compromised SaaS application.

For Zero Trust policies to be enforced, the security posture of the software in use may apply to the context used for decision points.

CONTROL 5: *Account Management*

Identity is a cornerstone of a well understood environment. The who behind what is authorized within an environment is important, just as important is when that authorization is no longer in place. User identity lifecycle management plays a critical role in the use of technology systems, at times involving other teams for solid security operations. The provisioning of accounts, paired with attribute and permissions management give users and applications appropriate level of access while proper governance limits the possibility of abuse of that access.

Tying accounts to individual users or services also provides a layer of trackable accountability and provide monitoring tools a relatively accurate way to assign action to account.

Just as important as managing the account and its access through the life of its use, is the deprovisioning stage in the lifecycle. Accounts inadvertently left active with access privileges are another attack vector that can be exploited.

When working within a Zero Trust framework, identity provides one of the pillars for context and as such, appropriate account management is foundational to working within that framework.

CONTROL 6: *Access Control Management*

A major component of use of accounts within an environment is their access. What an account is permitted, or not permitted, to do helps mitigate inappropriate use of resources. Account attributes, user roles, allow or block lists, and permissions elevation are often used to control access. Additional methods for validating account use permissions can be used, such as multi-factor authentication.

It is important to limit access to the minimum amount needed for further risk reduction, following the principle of least privilege.

In the context of Zero Trust, enforcement of access depends on policy definitions that take identity into account, policy administration exists to define the permitted access.

CONTROL 7: *Continuous Vulnerability Management*

Vulnerability scan results paint a picture of a snapshot in time. Patching for identified vulnerabilities does not guarantee systems and software are invulnerable. Vulnerability Management Programs help organizations establish a process for patch roll out based on severity, potential impact, likelihood of exploit and risk to business operations.

Certain organizations weigh the risk to business operations against the other factors to create temporary exemption policies, usually requiring approval from an Authorizing Official, often within a dedicated security leadership role, a business unit leader or an application owner.

These programs include regular scanning, reporting of findings and patch management. The frequency of scans may be defined by regulatory compliance requirements or in conjunction with a security steering committee's guidance.

A subject's or resource's vulnerability posture plays a factor in decision making for policy enforcement in a Zero Trust environment.

CONTROL 8: *Audit Log Management*

Accountability, the ability to tie activity to a subject and a resource, plays a major factor in the ability to properly assess interactions and monitor for unauthorized activity leading to more in depth investigations. These investigations necessitate the ability to review events that have taken place in the past.

In a successful audit log management program, anomalous behavior sends alerts to investigating analysts for further review and may lead to deeper event analysis for a full forensic understanding of the events that led to a breach. For this to be viable, logs must include relevant details, often defined in policy, and must also be immutable when accessed for investigative purposes. In addition to these factors, a comprehensive understanding of relevant telemetry is required for in depth analysis to get a complete understanding of all elements at play.

Organizations may use technologies paired with frameworks to establish their anomaly detection programs, often SIEM with a detection framework like MITRE ATT&CK, discussed in the next chapter. Continuous monitoring is a foundational component of the Zero Trust framework.

CONTROL 9: *Email and Web Browser Protections*

Some of the most common attack vectors are those used by most users. Email and browser are technologies ubiquitous in daily life, both in personal and professional contexts. Often times, these contexts intertwine with personal bleeding over into the professional and vice versa. These practices introduce risk, and given a user's practices, can lead to compromise of an endpoint, a user account, or data.

Technology based countermeasures can be implemented at the endpoint to help mitigate the risk. For self hosted email, more secure protocols can be used alongside email assessment tools leveraged to limit risk of unintended action. Isolating the means of accessing outside resources, such as a browser, while also limiting unauthorized changes to those tools, can help reduce risk.

Ideally, these types of resources, email or browsers, are not accessible from systems that do not need them. With more browser based applications in use, even internally, Zero Trust policy enforcement help reduce risk in context.

CONTROL 10: *Malware Defenses*

Malicious actors can act in very targeted ways, but at times may simply create some code and let it loose into the wild to spread and cause havoc. Dealing with SQL Slammer and WannaCry, personally speaking, were no fun. In addition to secure configuration practices, other tools can be implemented to limit risk of malicious code finding its way onto a system, or subsequently executing successfully in a system.

Malware can be introduced via digital communications pathways, as well as through physical means, such as connecting unauthorized or unknown hardware to a system. Malware can be designed with one or more of any number of goals in mind, such as business disruption, data exfiltration and access control bypass.

The presence of malware may lead to the prohibitive enforcement of Zero Trust policies.

CONTROL 11: *Data Recovery*

Data is at the center of an organization works with, whether their own intellectual property, or data belonging to their customers that they may serve as custodians of. Ensuring the data is secure is important, but just as important is making sure that the data is available when needed. Following the C-I-A triad of confidentiality, integrity and availability, the data must be readily accessible at the time it is needed and that it has not been changed in an unauthorized fashion.

Data integrity can be put at risk by any number of factors, malicious and not. Data availability can be put at risk by any number of factors as well, including unforeseen outages caused by third parties. Recovery from these sorts of issues can mean the difference between continued business operations and a resume building experience.

Simply having processes and tools in place is a first step, but ensuring their viability is just as important. Regular testing of data recovery methods, and plans around different reasons behind their need, such as malware or natural disaster, is just as important. This is to make sure recovery from a worst case scenario is possible, whatever that case may be.

CONTROL 12: *Network Infrastructure Management*

Any networked environment is comprised of core elements: endpoints, routers and switches. This includes cloud and on-premise environments. Any security controls begin with these devices being properly configured; in cloud based environments, organizations depend on their cloud providers' ability to properly configure their data center hardware.

Adding layers of security countermeasures involves adding additional functionality, through technologies like firewalls, for access controls around communications and their limits. In cloud environments, organizations can manage their virtual networking and implement controls akin to those they may implement in on-premise environments.

By using microsegmentation practices around assets, services and resources, an organization can align their strategy toward a Zero Trust framework implementation.

CONTROL 13: *Network Monitoring and Defense*

Much like audit logging for tracking user-based activity, it is important to monitor network-based activity. This can include logs from networking equipment and firewalls, but can prove to be prohibitively noisy. Other technologies exist to reduce the noise through analysis, or to monitor for specific types of activity based on known patterns or heuristics. Monitoring networks and implementing controls is performed in on-premise as well as cloud based environments.

When anomalies are detected by these network monitoring tools, they raise alerts that can lead to more in depth investigations of those anomalies. In environments with centralized correlation tools, these logs, in conjunction with audit logs, can paint a more complete picture of the anomalous, potentially malicious, activity; in turn, this can lead to improved security countermeasures being implemented and updated processes.

As part of a Zero Trust enforcement implementation, the communications channel is allowed or disallowed based on policy, but that communications channel still relies on the underlying infrastructure which merits a level of monitoring that would allow for detecting insecure configurations or bypass of Zero Trust policy enforcement.

CONTROL 14: *Security Awareness and Training*

"Security is everyone's responsibility," a mantra that was drilled into me just months into my career. While security practitioners are constantly running scenarios in their mind, non-practitioners may not put much mind to them outside of what they see on TV or in the news. Some government entities have laws requiring regular cybersecurity training for their employees, many organizations have policies in place with similar requirements.

Establishing a culture of security awareness can play a significant factor in reducing risk to an environment. This can span cyber and physical security alike. Regular training and readily accessible tools for notification of anomalies empowering employees to *say something* if they *see something* helps make company culture an important security control.

CONTROL 15: *Service Provider Management*

Organizations running on a cloud forward strategy have a deep reliance on service providers but maintaining much control over their data and how it's stored, used and protected. Organizations that leverage SaaS tools as part of their day to day operations rely on those service providers and those providers' ability to protect the data entrusted to them.

Reliance on third parties goes beyond the digital and into the physical. Employee hardware is often acquired in large quantities, data center equipment from specialized providers; disruption, or interception and manipulation, can lead to significant business impact.

It is important to trust, but also verify, claims of secure practices and processes with third parties. This may involve both technical and non-technical processes evaluating anything from contracts and stipulations, to third party attack surfaces, depending on agreement between parties and level of risk appetite tied to an organization's security requirements.

CONTROL 16: *Application Software Security*

For any software developed in house, acquired, or even hosted within an organization's infrastructure, it is imperative to ensure the software introduces as little risk to an environment as possible.

As part of this, any development should implement a Secure Software Development Lifecycle, SSDLC, and employ application security testing, either static or dynamic. Acquired software should be put through in depth composition analysis, and any further development should employ the same stringent development controls as natively developed software.

Any dependencies these software rely on may also need assessment to validate their integrity as well.

Zero Trust principles necessitate an awareness of software security posture and benefit from a shift-left approach to development.

CONTROL 17: *Incident Response Management*

The bread and butter of a Security Operations Center, SOC, relies on its ability to respond to cyber incidents in a timely fashion, including identification, eradication and recovery. A full suite of tools can be used to aid in these efforts, but they first rely on contextual understanding of normal and abnormal activity. As part of on-going process improvement efforts may include tabletop exercises, individual or group training, as well as maintaining industry knowledge.

Incidents are not limited to cyber infrastructure. Physical incidents, such as natural disasters, power outages or equipment failure also require contingency plans that may be part of a mature incident response program.

Incident response programs often involve teams beyond the analysts investigating the incident itself, bringing in representatives from Public Relations, Legal, and other business units in order to appropriately respond to public release and notification requirements as mandated by industry practice or by law.

The ability to respond quickly can determine overall outcomes.

CONTROL 18: *Penetration Testing*

Circling back to the idea of *trust but verify*, a part of any successful and mature security program includes validating controls are functioning as designed through penetration testing. This can be either physical or network based tests, or a combination of both, including the involvement of human targets, all of which would require full authorization to perform.

Very security mature organizations may have their own specialized teams that plan for, coordinate and execute on this type of testing within their own environments regularly. Many organizations rely on third parties to perform the testing for them.

The scope and depth is defined by the organization needing the testing to be performed and can also plan for assumptions of malicious actor inside knowledge, such as network topology, user account details, or more.

6.4 Roadmap for CIS Controls Adoption

Phase 1: Identity, Inventory, and Data (Controls 1–6)

Establish baselines and focus design around Zero Trust principles.

Phase 2: Detection and Defensible Architecture (Controls 7–13)

Build out the segmentation models and monitoring infrastructure.

Phase 3: Resilience, Engineering, and Validation (Controls 14–18)

Spread the culture of security, ensure incident response readiness and ensure constant validation is in place.

6.5 CIS Controls in Enterprise GRC Programs

Governance, Risk and Compliance Programs serve as an umbrella program meant to aid in managing strategy surrounding each of these areas and their interconnected dependencies. CIS controls can help simplify the implementation of an organization's GRC Program, its strategic direction, and the various functions therein.

6.6 Chapter Summary

CIS Controls v8.1 provides a **practical, prioritized, and highly actionable framework** for rapidly maturing enterprise security programs. Used in conjunction with elements, where appropriate, of other frameworks and concepts, they can provide a solid foundation for an organization's security operating model.

MITRE ATT&CK Framework

THE **MITRE ATT&CK FRAMEWORK** is one of the, if not the, most comprehensive frameworks focused around adversary behaviors, tactics, techniques and procedures (TTPs), organizing the ways malicious actors operate across a full attack and provides a solid foundation for several areas of cybersecurity, making it suitable for security teams of all kinds to leverage in to accomplish their organizational goals and mission statements.

This framework is often used for detection engineering, red and purple team operations, adversary emulation and tabletop exercises, and SOC modernization, among other uses. This chapter provides a **high-level interpretation**, focused on operationalization rather than theory, connecting adversary tactics and techniques, along with common knowledge, into a broader security strategy.

7.1 Purpose of ATT&CK

MITRE ATT&CK helps organizations understand the behavioral processes, tactics and techniques, that malicious actors actually do in practice. Unlike the frameworks discussed in previous chapters, focused primarily around best defensive approaches meant to limit impact, this framework is focused around offensive approaches, meant to maximize adversarial impact while also limiting defensive awareness or detection. By leveraging this framework, organizations can better understand how attackers may breach their assets, and use that understanding to design and implement better defenses. When used in conjunction with the understanding of their own organization's data and infrastructure, it is a formidable foundation for a risk management program.

7.2 ATT&CK Structure

Tactics > Techniques >> Sub-techniques

The framework is organized into tactics, representing objectives at each stage of an intrusion effort. Each tactic is host to a group of techniques, each with sub-techniques. Attackers will use any combination of techniques across the various tactics in their efforts to achieve their goals allowing for extensive attacker behavior modeling.

The 14 Tactics

- Reconnaissance
- Resource Development
- Initial Access
- Execution
- Persistence
- Privilege Escalation
- Defense Evasion
- Credential Access
- Discovery
- Lateral Movement
- Collection
- Command and Control (C2)
- Exfiltration
- Impact

7.3 Foundation for Detection Engineering

ATT&CK can serve as a foundation for detection engineering by providing likely approaches as models for creating detection and alerting rules in detection and correlation tools.

Detection engineering focuses on behavioral analysis and telemetry evaluation focused on hypothesis-based assumptions to implement those detection and alerting mechanisms. These mechanisms are often tied to response procedures and playbooks allowing for closing the loop on proper incident response management.

ATT&CK Helps Define

- What to detect
- How to detect it
- What telemetry is needed
- Which gaps need remediation
- Which mitigations to prioritize

ATT&CK therefore becomes a **roadmap** for building mature detection and response capabilities.

7.4 Threat-Informed Defense

With an understanding of adversary behaviors, organizations can align detection and response processes to likely methods of attack. They can also take steps to improve their architecture to reduce their risk of compromise:

- CTI Alignment with ATT&CK techniques
- Mapping Adversary Groups
- Understanding Toolkits and Malware Families
- Building Detections for Specific TTP Clusters

7.5 Data Sources

ATT&CK provides a mapping of each technique to appropriate **data sources**. The data provided by these sources are used in conjunction with other telemetry in order for correlation tools to escalate alerts when anomalous behavior is detected.

Data Source Examples

- OS Event Logs
- Cloud Audit Logs
- Container Logs
- Network Flow Logs
- DNS Logs
- Authentication Logs
- Logs From Security Tools

This list is not comprehensive.

This mapping is essential for building a telemetry strategy. Without the right logs, detection is impossible.

7.6 SIEM Modernization

Modern SIEMs require more sophistication than traditional correlation rules. The use of behavioral analytics in SIEM strategies has become more common place, and some security vendors have begun to incorporate artificial intelligence into their detection approaches, enabling for a more dynamic approach for detection engineering design.

ATT&CK Helps Define

- Relevant log sources
- Detection logic
- Enrichment data
- Threat hunting hypotheses

Detection Coverage Maps

- Which ATT&CK techniques are covered with currently implemented detection logic?
- Which are missing?
- Which require additional telemetry?

Detection and Prevention Maturity Ratings

- Prevented
- Detected with Enrichment
- Detected with Correlation
- Detected but Noisy
- Not Detected

ATT&CK helps transform SIEM from a log and alert collecting machine to a veritable behavioral detection engine.

7.7 Threat Hunting

In the course of their operations, threat hunters leverage ATT&CK as roadmap for their investigations, often in stages.

ATT&CK Benefits

- Build Hunting Hypotheses
- Design Proactive Hunts
- Search for Behaviors rather than Specific IoCs
- Integrate Behavior-Based Analytics
- Uncover Long-Term Undetected Activity

Hunts are structured around the likely behaviors used by attackers, not correlation rules.

7.8 Red, Blue, and Purple Teams

Red Team

Uses ATT&CK to structure offensive simulations in conjunction with their in-depth knowledge of the environments in which they work.

Blue Team

Uses ATT&CK to build and test defensive measures, leveraging all relevant and available telemetry, while prioritizing for the highest value potential targets.

Purple Team

Bridging Red and Blue team responsibilities, Purple teams use ATT&CK to align their detection strategies with common tactics and techniques and provide a continuous improvement process around detection logic and incident response.

ATT&CK becomes the **shared language** enabling collaboration.

7.9 ATT&CK and Zero Trust

Zero Trust assumes breaches will occur. With this in mind, security strategy can be guided through use of the ATT&CK framework:

- Designing segmentation boundaries
- Enforcing least privilege
- Building behavioral detections
- Enforcing identity and access controls
- Validating device trust requirements
- Detecting lateral movement attempts

Zero Trust is validated through ATT&CK-aligned detection patterns.

7.10 Use Case Development Framework

Modern detection engineering teams use ATT&CK-driven workflows and use case development.

Phase 1: Identify TTPs

Based on threat intel, compliance needs, or risk. This is tailored to an organization's environment although industry verticals may share common TTPs across organizations.

Phase 2: Map Required Telemetry

Ensure collection of relevant log sources. A good logging strategy can help inform a baseline from which to build upon while identifying additional sources from which to collect data as an organization's security program matures.

Phase 3: Build Detection Logic

With the right data collected and the right TTPs identified, correlation rules and behavioral models can be built to detect suspicious activity deserving of investigation. Statistical anomalies and deviations from baseline expected behavior can also serve for identifying patterns of interest.

Phase 4: Validate Through Red/Purple Teaming

Run simulations. Testing scenarios to confirm detection capabilities provides a sanity check on the use-cases and can help identify gaps in detection methodologies or in data collection.

Phase 5: Tune and Deploy

Minimize false positives. This can be done through traditional tuning, or through data enrichment allowing for a higher likelihood of true positive detection while reducing the noise that can cause alert fatigue for analysts.

Phase 6: Automate Response

Leverage technology for stepping through the investigative and response processes. SOAR can be an aid in ensuring investigations are performed in a repeatable way and issues addressed in a timely manner. This can also enable for automated or human aided rapid response in stopping malicious activity so as to limit impact.

7.11 Cloud, SaaS, and Container Environments

Modern ATT&CK matrices include specialized platforms. Tactics now include techniques specifically tailored to a cloud native world. Creating behavioral models for cloud only or hybrid, cloud and on-premise, environments is possible with the ATT&CK framework. Telemetry would still be needed from the relevant environments.

7.12 ATT&CK and Incident Response Plans

As identification is one of the pivotal component of any incident response plan, the ATT&CK framework, through its use in detection engineering, can be foundational to incident response plans across the preparation and identification stages, as well as in understanding the approaches for containment and eradication while providing possible strategy considerations for implementing mitigating controls.

7.13 ATT&CK Maturity Model

Level 1: Technique Awareness

SOC is familiar with ATT&CK concepts. At this stage, analysts begin piecing together data, with tools or in a manual way, and compile incidents into likely related tactics in use.

Level 2: Mapping and Gaps

Detections mapped to techniques; gaps identified. With mapped detections, a better understanding of an environment's security posture comes into focus. Gaps, when identified, can lead to mitigation efforts, through better baseline configuration, more tools, or improved processes.

Level 3: Threat-Informed Defense

Threat hunts, SIEM rules, and CTI aligned to ATT&CK. At this stage, a proactive approach to finding previously undetected breaches helps organizations catch what was already missed. At the same time, SIEM detection rules leverage telemetry, and threat intelligence, to have a more tailored defensive posture.

Level 4: Purple Team Integration

Continuous validation, iterative improvement. Repeatable processes help teams improve their incident response while also allowing for consistent improvement in security posture.

Level 5: Autonomous Behavioral Defense

Machine learning, identity, and posture-driven automatic response. At this stage, regular assessment outputs lead to adjustments in controls while limiting the risk of human error.

7.15 Roadmap for ATT&CK Adoption

Transitioning into full use of the ATT&CK can take time and can lead to very nuanced conversations across the organization. Teams can begin with understanding where they are today and how it aligns with the framework, at the same time, the larger conversations can begin to take place to ensure shared vision across business units leading to successful implementation of detection tools, and with that, data collection.

Phase 1 (0–6 Months): Build Foundation

- Adopt ATT&CK Navigator
- Map current detections
- Assess telemetry gaps

Phase 2 (6–12 Months): Build Detections and Hunts

- Build TTP-based detection use-cases
- Integrate with SIEM / EDR
- Create hunting program

Phase 3 (12–24 Months): Automation and Validation

- SOAR playbooks
- Purple team operations
- Detection regression testing

7.16 Chapter Summary

The MITRE ATT&CK Framework provides the **behavioral foundation** for modern detection engineering, SOC operations, purple teaming, Zero Trust validation, and threat-informed defense.

It ensures organizations build defenses aligned with real-world adversary behaviors, not theoretical controls.

Detection Engineering SIEM Modernization

Detection engineering and SIEM modernization form the backbone of modern security operations. Traditional SIEM implementations relied heavily on static correlation rules and siloed teams, but today's environments must deal with ever evolving challenges. To meet those challenges organizations must now work with:

- Behavioral Detections
- Real-Time Analysis
- Cloud-Native Telemetry
- Identity-Aware Detections
- Automation-Driven Response
- Data Engineering Capabilities
- Continuous Tuning and Regression Testing

Along with these approaches, frameworks like MITRE ATT&CK and strategies like Zero Trust help form a well-rounded and modernized approach to detection engineering and SIEM use.

This chapter provides a blueprint for building and sustaining a modern detection engineering program and high-performing SOC capability.

8.1 From Traditional SIEM to Detection Engineering

SIEM technologies have existed for over two decades. Since their inception, they've focused on log collection and event correlation using Boolean, search or context-based logic to tie together events using common data points. They provided alerts to analysts, allowing them to perform further investigative steps, often requiring more searching.

Traditional SIEMs

- On-premise Logs
- Network Perimeter Monitoring
- Signature-Based Detection
- Manual Investigation
- Basic Correlation

Modern Security Operations Require

Big-Data Scale

- Cloud Logs
- SaaS Logs
- Endpoint Telemetry
- Traditional Log Sources.

Behavioral Analytics

Identity, device and workload behavior models. After establishing a baseline, deviations can be indicative of compromise.

Threat-Informed Defense

MITRE ATT&CK alignment paired with tailored threat intelligence assures relevant detection coverage.

Automation

SOAR-driven triage, containment, and enrichment provide rapid response in repeatable and predictable ways.

Cloud-Native Architectures

Cloud native architectural design considerations incorporated into detection strategies.

Detection Engineering as a Discipline

Not "SIEM administration." This goes further into specialized process lifecycle management.

8.2 Detection Engineering Defined

Detection engineering is the applied science of designing, building, validating, and tuning threat detections focused on given targets and likely attack vectors.

Detection Engineering Considerations

- Log Source Requirements
- Data Pipelines
- Detection Creation
- Signal Analysis
- SOC Integration

- Data Enrichment Strategies
- Threat-Hunting
- Performance Tuning
- Red and Purple Team Feedback Loops

Detection engineering is centered around precision, measurement, automation, and reliability.

8.3 The Detection Engineering Lifecycle

A mature detection engineering program follows a structured and continuous lifecycle.

1. Requirement Gathering

Identify risk scenarios leveraging ATT&CK techniques and tailored intelligence to meet compliance needs and protect against targeted threats.

2. Telemetry Evaluation

Identify necessary data, their sources, and requirements. Address gaps if possible and ensure normalization of data.

3. Detection Design and Development

Design and implement the detection logic with appropriate thresholds, providing data enrichment where possible to aid in more attuned correlation.

4. Validation

Red and purple team testing processes established and executed upon. Simulating prioritized scenarios to confirm acceptable levels of alerting when moving to production.

5. Deployment

Transition from any staging status or environment to full production and operational use. Route alerts to appropriate analysts, typically SOC team. Assign severity to alerts and prioritize investigative efforts.

6. Tuning and Optimization

Assess production use of alerts for excess noise and false positives. If gaps in coverage, data collection or detection logic are found during investigations, address them.

7. Lifecycle Review

Regular review of detections to sunset those no longer needed, update those needing changes with version control. Automate regression testing where possible.

This framework ensures detections remain relevant and reliable.

8.4 SIEM Modernization Core Principles

Principle 1: Telemetry Quality Before Quantity

Poor telemetry leads to poor detection. Quality matters.

- Completeness
- Consistency
- Contextual Fields
- Timestamp Accuracy
- Identity Correlation
- Device Posture Info
- Cloud Audit Logs

Principle 2: Behavior Over Signatures

Attackers bypass signature-based detection. Behaviors allow for a better contextual understanding.

- Process Lineage
- Statistical Anomalies
- Identity Behavior
- Cloud API Call Patterns

Principle 3: Cloud-Native Scalability

Traffic patterns can be unpredictable, as such, events and their log volumes can be unpredictable. Limitations to any capacity needed may lead to missed compromises.

- Big Data Scale
- Low Latency
- Low Storage Cost

Principle 4: Mapped to ATT&CK

Detection coverage must be tied to known adversary techniques.

- Relevant Technique Families
- Prioritized on Likelihood

Principle 5: Integrated Automation

SOAR orchestration becomes part of the SIEM workflow.

- Rapid and Repeatable Response
- Automated Containment, where appropriate

8.5 Telemetry Strategy Foundation

A mature telemetry strategy necessitates clear logging policy. This includes families of logs, such as identity, network and application logs. This also includes relevant data points, such as host, account, timestamp, process.

Identity Logs

- SSO (SAML/OIDC) and MFA attempts
- Conditional Access Decisions
- Account Changes
- Privileged Activity

Endpoint Logs

- EDR Alerts
- Process Events
- Script Executions

Network Logs

- DNS
- Proxy
- Firewall

Cloud Logs

- SaaS
- IaaS
- PaaS

Application Logs

- Session Creation
- Privilege Changes
- API Usage

Data Logs

- DSPM Alerts
- Access to Sensitive Data
- Lineage Events

Telemetry integrity drives detection integrity.

8.6 Detection Engineering for Identity Threats

Identity has increasingly become an attack vector of choice for malicious actors.

Common Detections

- **Impossible travel**: An account used in two geographic locations within a time frame making it impossible to be the same user
- **MFA fatigue attacks**: Repeated MFA confirmation requests received on a device whose user confirms access so as to stop the alerts.

- **Password spraying**: Authentication attempts using common passwords across small batches of usernames.
- **Service account compromise**: A service account being used for actions beyond the scope of its intended purpose.

Key Tools

- IdP logs
- CIEM telemetry
- Anomalous login patterns

Identity detections are the backbone of Zero Trust monitoring.

8.7 Detection Engineering for Endpoint and EDR

Endpoints can serve as data stores or proxies into environments where data reside.

Modern EDR Detections

- **Process injection**: Execution of malicious code in the address space of legitimate processes
- **Credential dumping**: Extraction of authentication credentials
- **Remote thread execution**: Creating threads running in virtual space of a separate process.
- **Persistence mechanisms**: Approaches to maintain undetected access to systems
- **Ransomware behaviors**: Patterns of file encryption en-masse, often times sequentially

EDR + SIEM Enable

- Alerts
- Behavior sequences
- Timelines

8.8 Detection Engineering for Cloud Environments

Cloud-native threats differ from on-premise, controls and detection strategies can as well.

Common Critical Cloud Detections

- **Anomalous IAM Role Assumption**: Unusual behavior associated with using a given identity role.
- **Privilege Escalation Chain**: The series of steps taken to elevate privileges toward an administrative account.
- **Unauthorized Region Usage**: Unauthorized resource deployment.
- **API Key Exfiltration**: Theft of API credentials that can grant malicious actors privileges.

Cloud Requirements

- Continuous Posture Checks
- Cloud Infrastructure Entitlement Management, CIEM
- Cloud Security Posture Management, CSPM

8.9 Detection Engineering for Network Threats

All communications happen over networks; detecting anomalies in network traffic can aid in identifying an existing breach or attempts at compromise.

Key Areas

- **Lateral Movement**: Malicious actors moving from one compromised system to another post compromise.
- **Abnormal Internal Traffic**: Patterns in network traffic that deviate from expected behavior.
- **C2 Traffic Patterns**: Indicators of communication with possible command and control servers.
- **DNS Tunneling**: Abuse of DNS protocol to establish channels of communication
- **Encrypted Malicious Traffic**: Malicious traffic passed through protocols making detection difficult.
- **Port Scanning**: Reconnaissance for detection of active services.
- **Beaconing Behaviors**: Indicators of successful and active compromise sent to a designated destination controlled by the malicious actor.

Modern Network Defense Components

- NDR
- Flow logs
- Behavioral analytics

8.10 Detection Engineering for Data Security

Data, and their appropriate use, are core to successful business operations. Any risk to their confidentiality, integrity or availability introduces the possibility of business disruption. It is important to monitor for any activity that can compromise any of these elements of the **CIA triad**.

Example Data Centric Detections

- **Anomalous Large Downloads**: Unauthorized data movement or replication.
- **Access Outside Normal Hours**: Unauthorized access.
- **Sensitive Data Access from Untrusted Devices**: Possible malicious or compromised endpoint accessing data.
- **Unusual API Calls for Data Export**: Data exfiltration risk.
- **DSPM Alerts**: Data access beyond the scope of approved actions based on policy.

Data is part of the detection fabric.

8.11 Detection Engineering for Applications and APIs

APIs have become a core element in application design and use. Ensuring the use of secure endpoints and preventing their abuse is key when considering strategy.

Common API-Specific Detections

- **High-Error-Rate API calls**: Indicative of misconfiguration or attempts at abuse
- **Token Misuse**: Unauthorized use of API token.
- **Credential Stuffing**: Using stolen credentials in API calls in an attempt to access resources.

- **Abnormal Endpoint Access Patterns**: API usage patterns that deviate from original data flow design
- **Rate Limit Violations**: Automated processes using API resources in unauthorized ways.
- **Admin Role Assignment via API**: Privilege escalation for further unauthorized actions.

API gateways and Web Application Firewalls, WAFs, become critical telemetry sources.

8.12 Mapping Detections to MITRE ATT&CK

As discussed in the previous chapter, the MITRE ATT&CK framework provides a fairly comprehensive set of tactics and techniques used by malicious actors and allows for behavioral modeling of attacks.

A mature detection engineering program leverages these to understand their detection coverage, identify gaps and continuously improve their coverage by addressing those gaps.

Detection Model Attribute Mapping

- ATT&CK Tactic, Technique and Sub-technique
- Relevant Data Sources
- Response Playbook

Operational Benefits

- Coverage Heatmaps
- Gap Identification
- Strategic Prioritization

ATT&CK becomes the detection atlas.

8.13 Modern SIEM Architecture

Modern SIEM technologies must address challenges at scale with analytic capabilities alongside traditional correlation approaches. Paired with strategic response plans and technologies, they create a formidable defensive posture.

Modern SIEMs Components

Modern SIEMs are comprised of several components, working in unison to provide insights into the activities in the environment

Data Lake Layer

- Blob/Object Storage and Compression
- Cost Optimization

Analytics Layer

- Query Engines
- Machine Learning
- Behavioral Analytics

Correlation and Detection Layer

- Rule-Based Detection
- Baselines
- Anomaly Detection
- Identity-Linked Detection

Automation Layer

- SOAR
- Identity Disablement
- Device Isolation
- Cloud Resource Quarantine

Content Management Layer

- Versioning
- Regression Tests

8.14 Automated Threat Detection and Response

The ability to contain an incident and eradicate the issue quickly can be critical to ensuring proper business operations while limiting impact of that incident.

In a mature detection and response program, authorized activities, endpoints and tools are known entities, any deviation from these would be indicative of unauthorized behavior and can, with appropriate policy in place, be acted upon in an automated way and additional context around the anomalous behavior can be discovered:

- Auto-Disable Compromised Accounts
- Isolate Hosts via EDR
- Revoke Cloud Tokens
- Quarantine Cloud Workloads
- Block Suspicious IPs
- Generate Automated Enrichment

Zero Trust alongside SOAR lead to adaptive trust enforcement.

8.15 Purple Teaming for Detection Validation

Focused on both, offensive and defensive efforts, purple teams can aid in the design, implementation *and* validation of detection strategies.

Purple team workflows ensure detection accuracy:

- **Red team** executes ATT&CK techniques
- **Blue team** observes and verifies detection
- Tuning occurs iteratively

This limits detection blind spots and creates a process for addressing gaps when identified.

8.16 Detection Engineering Metrics and KPIs

As part of any mature cybersecurity program, efficacy must be tracked. The ability to measure process and strategy improvement over time necessitates quantitative data.

Performance Metrics

- Detection coverage as measured against ATT&CK and possible targets
- Mean time to detect
- False positive rate
- False negative findings
- Detection lag

Quality Metrics

- ATT&CK alignment
- Telemetry completeness
- Enrichment sources

SOC Enablement Metrics

- Triage time
- Automation utilization
- Case handling times

While these metrics are not comprehensive, they provide a starting point that empowers security leadership to properly communicate an organization's security posture to executive teams, security steering committees and boards of directors.

8.17 SOC Modernization Framework

Technology modernization does not happen in a vacuum. SOC teams must be prepared to work with modern SIEM and understand the underlying principles that enable those modern SIEMs to alert them of events to investigate. SOCs should modernize alongside SIEM. This is especially true if a SOC is charged with purple team responsibilities.

Phase 1: Telemetry Foundation

- Get logs right
- Standardize collection
- Integrate identity and cloud sources

Phase 2: Detection Engineering

- Build use cases
- Map to MITRE
- Tune continuously

Phase 3: Automation and SOAR

- Automate triage
- Automate containment
- Integrate identity-driven response

Phase 4: Analytics and Behavior Models

- UEBA
- Machine learning
- Risk scoring

Phase 5: Autonomous SOC

- Adaptive trust
- Automated remediation

SOC teams often have a tiered organizational structure and provide a path for career advancement. Working with a framework that enables team members to work with different elements of the detection engineering and analysis lifecycles will help reduce burnout and create a culture of knowledge and skill building.

8.18 Chapter Summary

Detection engineering and SIEM modernization are no longer optional, they are **mandatory** for minimizing attack surface, enforcing Zero Trust, and enabling scalable, resilient security operations.

This chapter provides a *blueprint* for security leaders implementing a modern detection engineering program.

Phase 2: Key Takeaways

Chapter 6: CIS Controls and Zero Trust Alignment

- **Cyber Hygiene**: Bridges basic cyber hygiene with advanced ZTA principles using prioritized implementation.
- **Data-Driven Prioritization**: Prioritization is driven by real-world threat assessments and breach reports.
- **Policy Engine Integration**: Risk must be continuously monitored by a "Policy Engine" to grant or deny access in real-time.

Chapter 7: MITRE ATT&CK Framework

- **Behavioral Taxonomy**: Moves beyond static indicators of compromise to categorize adversarial behavior (Tactics, Techniques, and Procedures).
- **Ground Truth Validation**: Provides the "adversarial ground-truth" needed to validate the efficacy of architectural layers.

Chapter 8: Detection Engineering & SIEM Modernization

- **High-Fidelity Pipelines**: Uses behavior models (MITRE) to build automated alerting pipelines within modern security information systems.
- **Detection Dependencies**: Modern SIEM platforms are fundamentally dependent on behavioral threat intelligence rather than static IP or hash lists.

Phase 3: Asset, Domain, and Application Defense

Cloud Security

Cloud security has become the centerpiece of modern cybersecurity strategy. As organizations migrate infrastructure, workloads, data, identities, and applications to the cloud, security leaders must implement architectures and adopt controls designed specifically for cloud-native and hybrid environments.

This chapter provides:

- A comprehensive understanding of cloud security frameworks
- Zero Trust–aligned cloud security designs
- Identity-Centric Cloud Governance
- Cloud-Native Detection, Monitoring, and Response
- CIEM, CSPM, CWPP, DSPM, API security, and multi-cloud posture models
- Practical enterprise migration patterns
- Pitfalls and anti-patterns

9.1 Cloud Security Realities

The attack surface in cloud environments is vast and presents its own independent challenges as compared to traditional on-premise environments.

The ease with which resources can be rapidly deployed with little to no controls can pose a risk to an organization's data, applications and workloads. Without proper policy, process and culture in place, myriad risks can be introduced through well intentioned efforts or shadow IT resources.

Cloud Breach Vectors

- Overly permissive IAM roles
- Misconfigurations
- Lack of Logging
- Overexposed Storage Buckets
- Missing Network Controls
- Improperly controlled Shared Accounts
- Poor Key Management
- Absent Data Governance

Cloud is ***not i*****nherently insecure.** The danger is **improper use**, not the cloud itself.

Attack Surface Considerations

- Every API is an entrance
- Every identity is a potential threat
- Infrastructure is ephemeral
- Misconfigurations propagate instantly
- Traditional perimeter controls don't provide equivalent mitigating effect

Cloud requires **identity-first, data-centric and automated, where possible,** security.

9.2 Cloud Security Frameworks

Organizations adopt cloud frameworks to align architecture, governance, and controls. Several frameworks can be considered in alignment with industry standards.

1. NIST SP 800-53

Privacy and security controls tailored to cloud systems. For more detail, revisit chapter 3.

2. NIST CSF 2.0 (Cloud-Ready)

Fully compatible with cloud guardrails and modern architectures. For more detail, revisit chapter 2.

3. CSA Cloud Controls Matrix (CCM)

Cloud-specific controls mapped across compliance frameworks. With 17 specific domains of controls, Cloud Security Alliance provides an in-depth matrix and assessment aids to help organizations with their cloud controls.

4. CIS Benchmarks

Hardened cloud configuration baselines. For more detail, revisit chapter 6.

5. ISO 27017 and ISO 27018

Providing frameworks for cloud security and data privacy, these standards provide guidance for organizations and their service providers.

6. FedRAMP

A program that standardizes security assessment, authorization and monitoring requirements for cloud providers seeking to obtain government contracts.

7. CISA Zero Trust Maturity Model

Cloud-integrated Zero Trust guidance consisting of **5 pillars**: identity, devices, networks, applications and workloads, and data. The detailed documentation is readily available.

8. BeyondCorp

Based on Google's Zero Trust model, BeyondCorp follows three guiding principles: perimeter-less design, context-aware access and dynamic access controls. Reference architecture is also provided through their website.

9. Cloud provider best practices frameworks

The top industry cloud service providers each provide frameworks that organizations can leverage to architect secure cloud environments.

9.3 Shared Responsibility Model

Provider Responsibilities

- **Physical infrastructure**: Cloud environments are still composed of traditional data centers.
- **Hardware**: Those data centers are full of hardware used by cloud customers.
- **Core network**: In order for cloud customers to use relevant services, hardware must be able to communicate.
- **Hypervisor**: The dynamic nature of cloud services relies on virtualization capabilities, and importantly, the inability to jump from virtual environments to physical environments.
- **Managed service platform**: The interface that customers use to interact with their cloud services must be accessible and secure.

Customer Responsibilities

- **Identities**: Which users and what services are permitted to interact with cloud services.
- **Data:** While it may reside on cloud service environments, the data is owned by the customer, and they must implement appropriate controls around its security.
- **Configurations**: Given the nature of rapid deployment and ease of use, secure configurations play a key role in securing cloud architecture by limiting attack surface.
- **Workloads**: Ensuring cloud computing resources are used only for authorized purposes will limit risk of abuse and limit risk of unanticipated operational costs.
- **API permissions**: With cloud services leveraging APIs with varying levels of permissions, leveraging the appropriate permissions for the anticipated activity limits risk of unauthorized exposure.
- **Encryption**: Data should be protected, whether in transit or at rest. Proper encryption helps mitigate risks to confidentiality.
- **Logging**: Used as part of development, testing and security monitoring, logging is extremely valuable. Just as important is the ability to keep logs secure.
- **Monitoring**: Cloud telemetry is used as part of a mature detection engineering and cybersecurity program.
- **Network controls**: As part of secure architecture design, some traditional concepts are still in play, in particular network controls. Although virtual, they play a vital part in protecting communication pathways between cloud resources.
- **Application code**: While this code is hosted on cloud environments, it is implemented and managed by organizations for their use. Whether developed in house or not, the code is controlled by the cloud customer.

Misunderstanding this model can lead to inadvertent risk being introduced to an environment, consequences of which can have significant business impact.

9.4 Identity is the Cloud Perimeter

Given the nature of cloud services, access is based on who is permitted and what they are permitted to do, often times with how it is permitted being defined as well. It follows that identity and access management is foundational to cloud security.

Cloud IAM

- Least Privilege Policies
- Role-Based Access
- Permission Boundaries
- Identity Federation (SSO) and MFA Enforcement
- Conditional Access
- Automated Access Reviews
- Service Account Governance
- Workload Identities

CIEM (Cloud Infrastructure Entitlement Management)

- Monitoring Excessive Permissions
- Eliminating Privilege Sprawl
- Enforcing Least Privilege at scale
- Continuous Access Analysis

Identity is *the* line of defense in cloud.

9.5 Cloud Network Security

In cloud environments, network security shifts from perimeter to **micro-perimeter**. We've covered microsegmentation, micro-perimeters are the logical outcome.

Core principles

- Zero Trust Network Access (ZTNA)
- Private Access via Identity
- No broad flat networks
- Limit egress
- Use service endpoints
- Enforce VPC/VNet segmentation
- Implement service mesh
- Encrypt all traffic

CSPs have native tools available. In addition, third party security tools can be integrated providing an additional layer of protection. Network design adapts to ephemeral workloads and API-heavy environments.

9.6 Cloud Data Security

As discussed in 9.3, data security responsibility lives with the data owner, the cloud customer. Measures must be taken to maintain appropriate confidentiality, integrity and availability.

Discovery and Classification

- Sensitive data mapping and shadow data detection
- Lineage tracking

Protection Controls

- Encryption keys and rotation policies
- Tokenization
- Masking/redaction
- Signed URLs
- Least privilege data access

Data Governance

- Data residency
- Retention policies
- Data Leak Protection/Prevention, DLP
- Real-time anomaly detection

Data is always the ultimate target making data security core to Zero Trust.

9.7 Cloud Application Security

As organizations use cloud-based applications and trust those applications with their data, it is important to establish a practice around securing the data, as covered in 9.8, but also in securing the applications they run in cloud environments to limit risk of application abuse or data compromise.

Key Security Components

- API Authentication
- API Authorization
- Serverless Security

- Application Secrets Management
- Dependency Scanning
- Container Image Scanning
- Infrastructure as Code, IaC, Security
- API Gateways

Securing cloud applications relies on strong identity boundaries, validated input and output, patched dependencies, monitored runtime behavior and appropriate secrets protections.

9.8 Cloud Workload Security

Cloud workloads are any collection of cloud computing resources and tasks for running applications or services. Disruption in their ability to run properly can have significant impact to business operations, while improper use can lead to overrun operational expenses.

Workload Examples

- VMs
- Containers
- Kubernetes Clusters
- Serverless Functions
- PaaS Services

Common Workload Protections

- Cloud Workflow Protection Platforms, CWPPs
- Runtime Protection
- Container Isolation

- RBAC
- Service Mesh mTLS
- Workload Identities
- Vulnerability Scanning

Workload-level controls must integrate with identity and network policy, and relevant telemetry should feed into continuous monitoring processes.

9.9 Cloud Logging and Monitoring

Logging is crucial for detection engineering. Telemetry and data enrichment provide security teams with necessary context for investigating anomalous behavior and determining likelihood of compromise and impact.

Required logs

- Audit and Container Audit Logs
- VPC Flow Logs
- DNS Logs
- Application Logs
- Identity Provider, IdP, Logs

Cloud providers provide the ability to send logs to customer hosted log collection points, while also providing cloud native security tools for customers designed to monitor and protect these environments. Cloud security requires **complete, normalized, contextualized** telemetry.

9.10 Cloud Threat Detection

Included in detection engineering programs for organizations that have a cloud forward strategy is a requirement for cloud threat detection.

Cloud environments face unique challenges, but methods attackers use still find their place in frameworks like MITRE ATT&CK. Building detections for cloud specific threats is important.

Common Cloud Threats

- Unauthorized IAM Role Usage
- Privilege Escalation
- Serverless Misuse
- Metadata Service Exploitation
- Credential Theft
- Snapshot Exposure
- Overly Permissive APIs
- Misconfigured Storage
- Container Escapes

The ability to detect threats such as these relies on cloud telemetry integration into SIEM, along with tools like EDR and CIEM where appropriate.

9.11 Multi-Cloud Security Considerations

Cloud providers have built their businesses around their own proprietary models, each having specific competitive advantages. It is common to see customers leverage several providers in the course of business operations. Ensuring consistency in security implementations across providers can help limit risk, policy and strategy should not rely on a given provider's capabilities.

Multi-Cloud Risk Multipliers

- Inconsistent IAM Models
- Fragmentation of Policy Frameworks
- Inconsistent Logging

- Increased Attack Surface
- Duplicated Misconfiguration Risks
- Inconsistent Segmentation Models

Adopting **identity-first, cloud-agnostic interpretations** of Zero Trust can provide the necessary guidance for secure implementations across any number of cloud providers.

9.12 Cloud Security Anti-Patterns

Cloud security *anti-patterns* are security averse common practices that introduce risk, usually at unacceptable levels. They are usually employed for ease of implementation, speed to delivery or intended short term testing.

Common Cloud Mistakes

- Relying on Perimeter Controls
- Hardcoded IAM Keys
- Lack of Logging
- Poor Network Design
- Poor Authentication Enforcement
- Unmanaged SaaS Sprawl

Aligning practices to secure strategy often results in more secure environments and addresses gaps that would otherwise necessitate additional security tools to mitigate.

9.13 Cloud Security Roadmap

Establishing a mature cloud security program may seem daunting but is a necessary journey in our cloud driven world. A sample roadmap to reach that goal is listed below.

Phase 1: Foundations

- Identity and Access Modernization
- Secure Authentication Practices
- IAM Redesign
- Enable Cloud Audit Logs

Phase 2: Architecture

- Segmentation Design
- Cloud Guardrails
- CIEM
- CSPM

Phase 3: Protection

- Workload Protection
- Secrets Management
- Data Governance
- API Security Controls

Phase 4: Monitoring

- SIEM Integration
- Tailored Detections
- Anomaly Detection

Phase 5: Response

- SOAR Workflows
- Cloud Isolation Patterns
- Incident Playbooks

Phase 6: Optimization

- Continuous Posture Monitoring
- Risk-Based Policy Enforcement
- Automated Remediation

9.14 Chapter Summary

Cloud security is a **discipline**, not a set of tools.

This chapter provides a Zero Trust–aligned, identity-centric *blueprint* for designing and operating secure cloud and multi-cloud environments. With this foundation, organizations can modernize their security architecture, integrate cloud telemetry into detection engineering, and enforce governance across distributed cloud ecosystems.

Identity and Privileged Access Management

IDENTITY IS THE **CORE control plane** of modern cybersecurity. Modern business practices leverage Cloud, SaaS, remote work, APIs, containerized workloads, service accounts, and distributed applications; making identity the foundation of Zero Trust.

Attackers increasingly target:

- Identity Stores
- Cloud Roles and Trust Relationships
- MFA Fatigue Weakness
- OAuth Token Hijacking
- Service Account Keys
- API Tokens
- Privilege Escalation Paths

This chapter provides a *blueprint* for IAM governance, identity architecture, privileged access management, and identity threat detection across enterprise, cloud, and SaaS environments.

10.1 Why Identity Is the New Perimeter

Traditional perimeter controls, while still important, no longer provide sufficient protection. With a more distributed workforce and continued transition to cloud environments, focus on identity protection has become paramount.

Identity governs the *who* can access, and *how* it can be accessed. This includes conditions like devices, source networks, privilege levels and more.

Identity is the single strongest enforcement point for Zero Trust.

10.2 The Modern Identity Fabric

Identity Fabric is a term encompassing a framework of interconnected identity and access management tools whose unified mission is to allow the right identities to perform authorized activities.

1. Identity Provider (IDP)

- SSO
- MFA
- Federation
- Session Management
- Authentication Policies

2. Directory Services

- On-premise
- Cloud IAM

3. Identity Governance (IGA)

- Role Governance
- Access Reviews
- Approval Workflows
- Birthright Entitlements

4. Cloud IAM (CIEM Layer)

- Cloud Permission Monitoring
- Excessive Privilege Detection
- Cloud Role Cleanup
- Trust relationship mapping

5. Privileged Access Management (PAM)

- Vaulting
- Session Monitoring
- Privilege Elevation
- Credential Brokering

6. Secrets Management

- Application Secrets
- API Keys and Tokens
- Certificates

7. Identity Threat Detection

- Anomalous Authentication
- Privilege Misuse
- Session Hijacking

Identity Fabric spans human, service and workload identities in a unified trust plane.

10.3 Identity Principles for Zero Trust

Zero Trust principles mandate continuous validation of access privileges, even in session.

In an expanded concept, this also implies an identity lifecycle tied to individual users, devices and workloads, and in our changing world, to autonomous AI agents and agentic workflows.

Strong Identity Proofing

- HR-Integrated On-Boarding
- Identity Verification
- Distinct Personas
    - Workforce, Volunteers and Contractors
    - Machines, Wworlflows and Agents

Least and Minimum Privilege

- No standing privilege
- Just-In-Time, JIT, Access
- Role Lifecycle Management

Continuous Verification

- Real-Time Device Posture
- Risk-Based Authentication and Session-Level Evaluation

Policy as Code

- Conditional Access
- Attribute-Based Access (ABAC)
- Policy-based access control (PBAC)

Attack Surface Reduction

- Eliminate Local Admin
- Eliminate Shared Accounts
- Universal MFA
- Remove Legacy Authentication

By aligning strategy to these principles, organizations help reduce risk associated with identity misuse.

10.4 Identity Governance and Administration

IGA ensures the right access is granted to the right identity at the right time, based on policy, with the ability to review and revoke those privileges.

IGA Core Capabilities

- Joiner-Mover-Leaver Workflows
- Re-certification Campaigns

- Segregation of Duties
- Access Request Workflows
- Visibility into all Entitlements
- Automated Access Cleanup

Enterprise Best Practices

- Integrate Human Resources Information Systems, HRIS, with Identity Lifecycle
- Build Persona-Based Access Models
- Automate Deprovisioning across all SaaS Apps
- Enforce Separation of Duties for high value teams such as Finance and Engineering
- Connect Cloud IAM Roles to IGA

IGA policy serves as directive structure for proper identity governance.

10.5 Cloud IAM (CIEM): Critical Identity Layer

Cloud Infrastructure Entitlement Management tools can provide visibility into access privileges within cloud and multi-cloud environments:

CIEM Functionality

- Cloud Permission Analysis
- Risk Scoring
- Privilege Reduction Recommendations
- Toxic Combination Identification
- Automated Remediation

CIEM is increasingly required to successfully achieve least privilege goals in cloud environments.

10.6 Privileged Access Management (PAM)

With limited privileges, most identity accounts can only perform so many actions. The higher the privilege level, the more important security controls around identity become. As such, it becomes critical to have strong Privilege Access Management practices in place.

PAM Core Capabilities

- Credential Vaulting
- Session Recording
- JIT Access Elevation
- Brokered Sessions
- Password rotation
- Ephemeral Privileged Accounts
- Least Privilege Enforcement
- Privileged Session Monitoring

PAM for Cloud

- Assume-Role Limitations
- Cloud Admin Boundary Controls
- Session Monitoring for Cloud CLI Usage
- Break-Glass Account Workflows

Privileged access is no longer just for sysadmins. In cloud environments it includes workloads, containers, and applications.

10.7 Secrets Management

Secrets are any unique strings of characters that provide authenticated access to resources. These include tokens, keys, passwords, certificates and connection strings. Proper storage of those secrets limits risk of exposure leading to misuse of secrets.

Common Secrets Misconfigurations

- Hard coded into source code
- Stored on public repositories
- Hard coded into configuration files
- CI/CD variables without protections
- Included in container images

Secrets Management Elements

- Vaulting
- Rotation
- Access Policies
- Just-In-Time Provisioning
- Discovery of hard-coded secrets

A single secret, with the right privileges, can compromise an entire environment.

10.8 Identity Threat Detection

Modern identity attacks often bypass traditional controls. Threats from external actors span authentication attacks and dive into privilege abuse across on-premise and cloud environments.

Insider threats must also be considered. A combination of logs, correlated, are necessary for a more complete detection program:

- IdP Logs
- Cloud Audit Logs
- Device Posture
- Behavioral Analytics

10.9 Zero Trust Identity Architecture

Tools and technologies around identity security are often not deployed alone.

Zero Trust Identity Architecture Components

1. SSO across all applications
2. Universal MFA
3. Passwordless Strategy
4. Conditional Access Policies
5. Least Privilege
6. PAM
7. CIEM
8. Secrets Vault
9. Identity Threat Detection

Identity is the enforcement engine of Zero Trust, ensuring access is only granted when enforcement policy is adhered to.

10.10 Identity Maturity Model

As organizations transition from legacy identity and authentication models toward a more modern and comprehensive approach, they may find incremental improvements can be used as means of showcasing progress and a foundation for successful business justification used to expand their identity programs into maturity.

A sample model in that maturity journey can be seen below.

Level 1: Fragmented Identity

- Multiple Identity Stores
- Inconsistent MFA
- No Governance

Level 2: Unified Identity Foundation

- SSO + MFA
- Basic Provisioning
- Centralized Directory

Level 3: Governed Identity

- IGA Automation
- Periodic Access Reviews
- Role Lifecycle Management

Level 4: Zero Trust Identity

- Conditional Access
- Device Posture and Full Cloud Integration

Level 5: Autonomous Identity

- Continuous Risk-Based Access
- Adaptive Policies
- Identity-Driven Automated Response

10.11 Roadmap for Identity Modernization

With the goal of reaching maturity with a multi-year plan, several phases can be defined to allow for incremental milestone achievement with clearly documented success criteria.

Phase 1: Stabilization (0–6 Months)

- SSO
- MFA
- Disable Legacy Auth
- Eliminate Shared Accounts

Phase 2: Governance (6–12 Months)

- IGA Deployment
- Access Reviews
- Automated Lifecycle Management

Phase 3: Cloud Identity (12–18 Months)

- CIEM Rollout
- Cloud IAM Redesign
- Privilege Cleanup

Phase 4: Privileged Access (18–24 Months)

- PAM
- JIT access
- Session monitoring

Phase 5: Automation and Adaptive Access (24–36 Months)

- Risk-based access
- Identity Threat Detection
- User Behavior Analytics

This roadmap can be adapted to meet an organization's needs, taking into account their current status.

10.12 Chapter Summary

Identity is the **foundation** of Zero Trust, cloud security, SaaS governance, and enterprise cyber resilience. This chapter provides a complete, end-to-end identity architecture model used to protect modern businesses from credential compromise, privilege escalation, insider threats, and cross-cloud identity abuse.

Data Security and Data Governance

Enterprise Data Protection, DSPM, Zero Trust Data Models and Regulatory Alignment

Data is the most valuable and targeted asset in an organization. Attacks increasingly bypass infrastructure and identity layers to directly target data where it resides:

- Cloud Object Storage
- SaaS Data Repositories
- Databases
- Data Lakes

This chapter delivers a complete framework for data security and governance, integrating Zero Trust, DSPM, cloud architectures, identity controls, and regulatory alignment.

11.1 Why Data Security Is Core to Zero Trust

Access policies in Zero Trust focus around permitting access to resources. These resources are data or used to work with data.

This shifts the focus from legacy aspects of protection to Zero Trust:

- Networks to Data
- Location to Context
- Perimeter Defense to Continuous Verification
- Infrastructure Controls to Data Access Controls

The modern enterprise challenge

One of the challenges faced by organizations today relates to awareness. Knowing where data resides is critical to the ability to implement proper controls. Data is not often centrally controlled to begin with and as such may find its way into any number of locations. Data is everywhere:

- Cloud Storage
- SaaS Applications
- Business Intelligence Tools
- Logs
- Backups
- CI/CD Pipelines
- Developer Sandboxes

Organizations must implement a data-centric security strategy that spans all environments.

11.2 Data Lifecycle Security

Value is attributed to data. Fresh data may imply the highest value, stale data less so, but still may still hold value.

To borrow a quote "It's an older code, sir, but it checks out." It becomes critical to define a proper data lifecycle and enforce security controls and processes around it.

Data Lifecycle Stages

- Creation
- Storage
- Processing
- Transmission
- Access and Usage
- Archival
- Destruction

Each phase requires its own set of security controls.

11.3 Data Discovery and Classification (DSPM)

Data Security Posture Management (DSPM) is now critical. The ability to discover data, properly classify it and identify risk to its security posture enables organizations to align towards a Zero Trust strategy.

DSPM Features

- Automated Data Discovery
- Classification of Sensitive Data
- Data Lineage and Flow Mapping
- Exposure Risk Scoring
- Anomaly Detection
- Accessibility

DSPM Detections

- PII
- PHI
- PCI
- Financial Data
- Source Code
- Access Tokens
- Secrets
- Confidential Business Data

DSPM is the visibility engine for data governance and can help enrich context in SIEM detections.

11.4 Data Classification Framework

Along with value attributed to data, the potential impact of disclosure plays a factor in classification. Some data can be high value but merit public classification, where other data may be low value and still garner internal or confidential classification. Organizations often define their own classification framework, where others leverage commonly used models:

Level 1: Public

No confidentiality damage.

Level 2: Internal

General internal documents not meant for public disclosure. Limited impact for disclosure.

Level 3: Confidential

Moderate harm if disclosed. Deserving more access controls.

Level 4: Highly Sensitive

Regulated or critical data. May require specific controls to be implemented to meet regulatory requirements.

Level 5: Restricted

Business critical data, including that whose disclosure could pose a risk to the organization's business operations as a whole: internal-company and customer data; requiring appropriate access controls, monitoring and retention policies.

11.5 Data Governance Program Components

An organization's data governance program defines how data is handled.

Policy

- Classification and Acceptable Use Policies
- Retention/Destruction
- Access Governance

People

- Data Owners
- Data Stewards
- Security Teams
- Legal/Compliance

Technology

- DSPM
- DLP
- CASB
- Encryption Systems

Process

- Classification Workflows
- Access request Workflows
- Data Transfer Approvals
- Incident Rresponse

Data governance gives structure around data ownership, access decisions and enforcement.

11.6 Data Access Governance (DAG)

Controlling who can access what data and *how* is the heart of data governance.

Key Capabilities

- Role and Attribute-Based Access
- Identity-Data Correlation
- Privileged Data Access Approvals and Periodic Reviews
- Segregation of Duties

Data access must be governed across data stores of all kinds, SaaS applications and collaboration tools, logs and analytics platforms.

11.7 Data Encryption and Key Management

Encryption is necessary but not sufficient. A comprehensive encryption strategy is necessary to ensure an adequate level of protection:

- Encryption At-Rest and In-Transit
- Key Management Systems, KMS, and Hardware Security Module, HSM, usage
- Centralized Key Management and Key Rotation
- Key Access Governance
- Mutual TLS (mTLS)

Modern encryption practices include:

- Client-Side Encryption
- Application-Level Encryption
- Hardware-Backed Security Keys
- Secure Enclaves

Key management is a **privileged identity** and should be protected as such.

11.8 Data Loss Prevention (DLP)

Data Loss Prevention systems have existed for decades, monitoring data at rest and in transit through communications pathways. The technology has evolved and expanded capabilities over time.

Modern DLP Coverage

- Endpoint DLP
- Cloud DLP

- Email DLP
- API-based SaaS DLP
- Context-Aware Detection
- Data Fingerprinting
- Inline and Out-of-Band Monitoring

DLP is not about restricting business, it's about preventing accidental leakage or malicious data exfiltration.

11.9 Data Segmentation and Trust Zones

Where data can reside as well as where data can travel are key components in ensuring a secure data posture. Establishing strong segmentation trust zones aligns with Zero Trust concepts.

Trust Zone Examples

- Public Data
- Corporate Data
- Sensitive Data
- Restricted Data

Zone Specific Controls

- Access Restrictions
- Encryption Requirements
- Monitoring Depth
- Retention Periods
- Anomaly Detection Granularity

Data zones may deal with specific requirements beyond data sensitivity, including regulatory requirements, business impact and confidentiality requirements.

11.10 Data Minimization and Retention

Organizations often accumulate data indefinitely, creating unnecessary risk and regulatory exposure while increasing their attack surface. To limit this risk, only necessary data should be collected, and should only be used for explicit purpose for which collection took place and held only as long as absolutely necessary, minimizing data.

Policies Must Define

- Data Minimization Principles
- Retention Periods
- Secure Destruction Workflows
- Archival Controls
- Regulatory Mapping

Minimize data to minimize risk.

11.11 Data Security in Cloud Environments

Data security in cloud environments can present complexity. With several storage models and encryption methods available, proper configuration and data lifecycle management can be the difference between well-guarded data, and inadvertent exposure.

Key Focus Areas

- Cloud Object Storage
- Databases
- SaaS Applications

Implementing proper controls for securing data varies depending on the data storage model. Regardless of how data are stored, Zero Trust data principles must be applied in a cloud-native approach.

11.12 Data Security for APIs

APIs are now a primary data access channel. Privilege levels for that access can vary, as such the accessed data can risk inadvertent exposure if API endpoints are not well protected.

Controls to consider

- Authentication
- Authorization
- Rate Limiting
- Schema Validation
- Logging
- Anomaly Detection
- Input Sanitization

APIs are the gateway to data; they should be treated as high-risk assets.

11.13 Data Security for SaaS

SaaS is the largest blind spot for most enterprises. SaaS tools serve as data storage and manipulation tools, the importance around proper access controls cannot be understated as an elevated level of privilege can lead to improper data access, placing the data at risk. Strict controls around data lineage are also important as unauthorized use of SaaS applications may expose data to residency in insecure environments or unauthorized environments.

SaaS Risks

- Misconfigured Access
- Shadow IT
- External Collaboration
- Ungoverned Data Sharing
- Unmanaged Admin Roles

SaaS sprawl must be managed through identity, governance, and continuous monitoring.

11.14 Data Lineage and Flow Mapping

Understanding how data moves is critical. Even in the late aughts, mapping data flow between data centers across dispersed geographic areas was done to solve for latency issues causing application failures. A web and database server on one end of the country with the application sitting on the other could easily cause timeout failures. In modern workflows, it's more critical to understand where data enters and environment, how it's used or transformed and where it resides:

- Creation
- Storage
- Transformation
- Aggregation

- Distribution
- Consumption
- Deletion

Data lineage limits risk of blind spots in governance and protection.

11.15 Insider Threat and Data Misuse

Insider threats can include malicious insiders, compromised employees or negligent users. Not all insider threats are malicious, but all insider threats should be accounted for. Anomalous behavior, whether outside scope of role or deviating from baseline, can help in identifying potential threats.

Common Detection Indicators

- Unusual Access Times
- Disabled Security Controls
- Irregular Privilege Escalation
- Risky Downloads
- Large Dataset Transfers

Insider threat mitigation requires detection, governance, and company culture.

11.16 Data Security Metrics and KPIs

In order to assess the efficacy of a data security program, an organization needs to collect proper metrics and track them over time. These metrics can, in turn, be used to communicate that program efficacy to security steering committees, executive leadership and boards of directors and thus help in guiding overall security strategy.

Visibility Metrics

- Rate of Data Discovered vs Unknown
- DSPM Coverage
- Classification Accuracy

Access Metrics

- Excessive Privilege Instances
- Approval-to-Access Ratio
- Access Review Completion Rrate

Risk Metrics

- Number of High-Risk Data Stores
- Number of Unresolved Data Exposure Alerts
- Encryption Coverage

Incident Metrics

- Data Exfiltration Attempts
- Insider Threat Cases

KPIs tie data security to measurable outcomes.

11.17 Roadmap for Data Security

Data security begins with understanding what data an organization owns and where it resides. Defining classification of that data permits that organization to begin establishing prioritized controls and monitoring. A roadmap to a mature Data Security program can aid in establishing timelines and milestones to achieving that goal. A sample roadmap can be found below.

Phase 1: Discovery and Classification

- DSPM
- Manual Review
- Data Cataloging

Phase 2: Governance

- Steward Assignments
- Data Policies
- Access Controls
- Retention Policies

Phase 3: Protection

- Encryption
- DLP
- Access Control Models

Phase 4: Monitoring

- SIEM Integration
- Anomaly and Exfiltration Detection

Phase 5: Optimization

- Automation
- Identity-Data Integration
- Adaptive Data Controls

11.18 Chapter Summary

Data security and governance form a core of Zero Trust, cloud security, identity governance, and enterprise risk management.

This chapter provides an end-to-end, modernized framework for governing data across multi-cloud, SaaS, on-premise, and hybrid environments, enabling organizations to reduce risk, enforce controls, and strengthen resilience.

Application Security and Secure Software Development

Modern enterprises rely on applications, internal, external, cloud-native, legacy, and hybrid; to deliver critical business services. Application security (AppSec) is no longer a function of periodic scanning; it is a *continuous discipline* that spanning disciplines and technologies alike:

- Architecture
- Development and Deployment
- Runtime Behavior
- API Security
- CI/CD Pipelines
- Supply Chain
- Identity and Secrets Governance

This chapter provides a blueprint for building a modern AppSec and Secure Software Development Lifecycle (SSDLC) program aligned with DevOps, cloud-native development, Zero Trust, and threat-informed defense principles.

12.1 Why Application Security Is Now Mission-Critical

In an application driven world, breaching a private network's perimeter no longer guarantees access to data of value. Attackers have set their sights on targets of higher value, including IaaS providers and SaaS applications hosting high value data from several organizations.

Common Targets

- APIs
- CI/CD Pipelines
- Open-Source Libraries
- Container Images
- Misconfigurations
- Identity Tokens
- Authentication Flows
- Hard-Coded Secrets

Breach Sources

- Supply Chain Compromises
- Credential Misuse
- API Abuse
- Misconfigured Cloud Services
- Inadequate Authorization Controls

AppSec is not optional. It is a board-level risk requiring architectural maturity.

12.2 The Secure Software Development Lifecycle

Secure coding practices have been at the forefront of proper development for decades. Shift-left principles assure that security is considered at every stage of the development lifecycle. This is characteristic of the Secure Software Development Lifecycle, SSDLC.

SSDLC Elements

- Requirements
- Design
- Coding
- Build
- Testing
- Deployment
- Operations
- Maintenance and Monitoring

Security must be incorporated into **every stage** beginning with defining security requirements, not added afterward.

12.3 Foundational Application Security Principles

An understanding of how attackers determine an application's vulnerabilities and ease of compromise helps in determining how to best design applications to limit that risk.

1. Threat Modeling

Identify attack paths before code is written. This begins with application architecture and data flow mapping.

2. Security by Design

Architect security directly into the application. Validating that the application architecture meets security requirements from the start helps limit risk, but also to prevent the need for layers of additional code to be retrofitted to mitigate issues.

3. Shift-Left Security

Integrate security early in development. The sooner security is considered, the more likely an application will be secure upon release.

4. Defense-in-Depth

Multiple reinforced layers of protection. Beyond just secure code, defense in depth spans to input and output validation, runtime monitoring and regular security testing.

5. Zero Trust for Applications

Zero Trust implies assumption validation. Inputs should meet allowable standards or be discarded: devices, identity, workflow, etc. There are no implicit permissions.

6. Visibility

Continuous monitoring of application behavior should be integrated into workflow behavioral analytics where feasible, and SIEM detection engineering.

12.4 Threat Modeling

Attackers are not concerned with what an application is *supposed* to do, they are more concerned with what it *can* do to meet their purposes. This can mean breaking an application, or simply exploiting designed behavior for unauthorized purposes.

The ability to take on that mindset and build process around it leads to Threat Modeling:

- *What can go wrong?*
- *Why would it happen?*
- *How do we prevent it?*

While organizations may leverage any existing model or their own custom models to meet their purposes based on custom needs, STRIDE and DREAD introduced by Microsoft in 1999 and 2003 respectively, are common and incorporate risk scores.

STRIDE Model

- **Spoofing**: Imitating a legitimate user
- **Tampering**: Modification of components like data, memory, network, etc
- **Repudiation**: True accountability, ensuring an action can be attributed to a specific actor
- **Information Disclosure**: Risk of unauthorized access to data
- **Denial of Service**: Disruption of business operations
- **Elevation of Privilege**: Unauthorized access levels

DREAD Scoring

- **Damage**: What overall negative impact can a threat cause
- **Reproducibility**: Ease of attack and its replication
- **Exploitability:** How vulnerable is a target
- **Affected Users**: The possible user base impacted by a threat
- **Discoverability**: How easy is it to identify vulnerabilities

These are just two examples of threat modeling frameworks. Others exist and components of each can be used to customize an organizations application threat modeling program.

Threat modeling must be continuous, not a one-time exercise, focused around application elements like architecture, API flows, identity boundaries and more.

12.5 Code Security

Many approaches exist to validate code security. Testing and scanning methods aid application security teams to identify risks embedded in code and application design:

1. SAST (Static Application Security Testing)

Full access to code and ability to identify hard-coded secrets, buffer control issues and flaws in logic. Code level vulnerabilities must be mitigated to ensure a secure application.

2. DAST (Dynamic Application Security Testing)

An approach to identifying issues of a fully functional application. This can help identify runtime vulnerabilities such as cross site scripting, misconfigurations and authentication issues.

3. SCA (Software Composition Analysis)

Focused on open-source, third party packages and frameworks, this analysis validates secure components are in use and identifies vulnerable components, empowering organizations to assess their use based on risk appetite.

4. Secrets Scanning

A specific approach to code scanning focused around hard coded secrets, this helps to limit risk of unauthorized use of secrets by malicious actors. Code should not include API keys, passwords, tokens, certificates or other information that can be leveraged to compromise assets.

5. Infrastructure-as-Code (IaC) Scanning

Scanning automated infrastructure management capabilities, Infrastructure-as-Code, and their configurations can help identify risks introduced by improperly deployed infrastructure components that would inadvertently expose the organization to risk. As this can be executed during development stages in the infrastructure lifecycle, it helps limit risk of production concerns.

6. Container Scanning

Libraries of container images abound for all sorts of services, publicly available images help developers with rapid development needs. Ensuring container images are properly configured for use is critical, but just as important is validating the base images are safe for use as well. Packages built into base images, if not well understood or properly vetted can lead to the introduction of unacceptable risk to an environment.

Shifting left ensures vulnerabilities are caught before deployment.

12.6 API Security

API security is both an internal and external, or proprietary and third party, issue. Building secure API endpoints with proper monitoring and controls can mean the difference between well running secure applications and risks to data confidentiality, integrity or availability. When working with third parties, it is important to also ensure that use of their APIs meets acceptable risk appetite.

APIs are the new attack surface.

- Broken Authentication or Token Misuse
- Excessive Data Exposure
- Business Logic Abuse
- Rate-Limit Bypass
- Insecure API Gateways

Controls to ensure strong authentication, authorization enforcement, schema validation and rate limits are critical. The ability to monitor for any deviation from authorized API use is part of a mature detection engineering and incident response program.

APIs often contain an organization's most sensitive data, as such they must follow a full Zero Trust model and validate identity, device, and behavior.

12.7 Web Application Security (OWASP Top 10)

The Open Web Application Security Project, OWASP, was founded in 2001 and is a non-profit centered around secure software design, implementation and maintenance. The organization releases a top 10 list of security concerns for web applications. This list is updated every few years to reflect the latest threats in the ever evolving threat landscape. As of this writing, the release candidate for the 2025 top 10 list is available fo review, and risks are listed below. Ensuring proper controls and processes around this list aligns with industry best practices.

OWASP Top 10 Risks

1. Broken Access Control
2. Security Misconfiguration
3. Software Supply Chain Failures
4. Cryptographic Failures

5. Injection
6. Insecure Design
7. Authentication Failures
8. Software or Data Integrity Failures
9. Logging and Alerting Failures
10. Mishandling of Exceptional Conditions

These represent the majority of exploitable application vulnerabilities.

12.8 CI/CD Pipeline Security

Modern development pipelines pushing for continuous release through CI/CD practices imply a continuously changing code base. Proper continuous review and controls around updates help limit risk of code injection, artifact tampering, supply-chain attacks and credential theft. Several process and technical controls can help mitigate risk.

1. Pipeline Hardening

- Signed Commits
- Static Scanning
- Dependency Checks
- Secret Detection
- Linting
- Artifact Scanning

2. Build Environment Isolation

- Ephemeral Runners
- Containerized Builds
- Restricted Access

3. Identity Controls

- Restricted Service Accounts
- Scoped Tokens
- Short-Lived Credentials

4. Verification

- Signed Artifacts
- Supply-Chain Attestation
- Software Bill of Materials, SBOM, generation
- Vulnerability Exploitability eXchange, VEX, correlation to assess likelihood of exploit

Pipeline compromise can lead to complete organizational compromise, brand reputation concerns and more business impact.

12.9 Supply Chain Security

Organizations rely on third parties, their products and their services. This reliance inherently introduces risk, the process of reducing that risk is the underpinning of supply chain security.

Common Supply Chain Risks

- Malicious Dependencies
- Compromised Packages
- Tampered Binaries
- Poisoned Container Images
- Dependency Confusion Attacks

Mitigating Best Practices

- Enforce SLSA Levels
- Generate SBOM for every release
- Enforce VEX for exploitability
- Sign Artifacts
- Lock dependency versions
- Monitor package registries

Modern breaches often originate from compromised dependencies. Limiting risks around those dependencies is part of a mature supply chain security posture.

12.10 Secure Deployment Patterns

Deploying applications into production places them into regular use and interaction with data whose integrity and confidentiality are paramount for proper business operations.

Deployment must ensure security across several areas.

Infrastructure Security

- Hardened Base Images
- IaC Enforcement
- Isolated Networks

Identity Security

- Workload Identity
- JIT Access
- Secretless Architecture, where possible

Runtime Security

- Behavior Monitoring
- Container Enforcement
- API Security

Observability

- Distributed Tracing
- Application Logs
- Performance Baselines

Mature deployment security is the layer turning DevOps into SecDevOps.

12.11 Runtime Application Security

Runtime protections add another layer. Application performance and behavior must be measured to ensure no unauthorized deviation from baseline takes place. These anomalies can be indicative of system or application compromise.

Controls to Consider

- RASP (Runtime Application Self-Protection)
- WAF
- API Monitoring
- Behavior Anomaly Detection
- File Integrity Monitoring

Runtime Telemetry

- Access and Error Logs
- Exceptions
- Auth Failures
- Request Patterns

Monitoring runtime through access, error, authentication and audit logs. Runtime security provides protection while *in production*.

12.12 Zero Trust for Applications

Following Zero Trust principles, applications must not implicitly trust inputs, users or access requests. Controls must be applied to meet the pillars of Zero Trust.

Identity-Level Controls

- Strong Authentication
- Continuous Session Verification
- Risk-Based Access

Application-Level Controls

- Microservice Identity
- Mutual TLS, mTLS
- Service Mesh Policy

Data-Level Controls

- Attribute-Based Data Access
- Encrypted Storage
- Telemetry Correlation

Session Controls

- Token Expiration
- Device Posture Validation
- Step-up Authentication

Applying these types of controls and monitoring configurations helps provide a more secured approach to use of applications.

12.13 Metrics and KPIs for AppSec

The ability to measure a program's efficacy is critical for an organization to allocate appropriate budget, tooling and personnel while on its journey to its strategic goals. Relevant metrics help track that efficacy over time to ensure continued progress, or identify set backs and thus run mitigating projects.

Code Quality Metrics

- Vulnerabilities per Lines of Code
- Fix-Time SLA Compliance
- Recurrence Rate

Release Quality Metrics

- Release Security Score
- Failed Security Gates
- Dependency Health Score

Operational Metrics

- API Abuse Rate
- Blocked Attacks
- False Positives
- Threat Coverage

Business KPIs

- Reduction in high-risk vulnerabilities
- Time-to-Remediation
- Percentage of apps passing SSDLC checks

AppSec must measure both **technical outcomes** and **business impact**.

12.14 AppSec Roadmap

In order to successfully implement a mature AppSec program, an organization must assess their current state and build a roadmap to reach their maturity goals. That roadmap includes milestones around process and technology. A sample roadmap is included below.

Phase 1: Stabilize

- SAST
- SCA
- Secrets Scanning
- Threat Modeling adoption

Phase 2: Integrate

- CI/CD integration
- Security Gates
- Vulnerability Workflows

Phase 3: Expand

- Runtime protection
- WAF
- API Threat Detection
- Supply Chain Security

Phase 4: Optimize

- SLSA Compliance
- Dynamic Access Enforcement
- Microservice Zero Trust
- ML-based Anomaly Detection

Phase 5: Full Maturity

- Autonomous Security Controls
- AI-assisted Code Review
- Automated Dependency Patching

12.15 Chapter Summary

Application security is a **full-stack discipline** spanning code, pipelines, API security, supply chain, infrastructure, and runtime behavior.

This chapter provides a unified application security strategy enabling resilience against cloud-native, identity-based, and supply-chain attacks.

Phase 3: Key Takeaways

Chapter 9: Cloud Security

- **Ephemeral Environments**: Focuses on securing distributed compute environments where traditional perimeters are completely dissolved.

Chapter 10: Identity and Privileged Access Management (IAM/PAM)

- **Primary Control Plane**: In perimeter-less architectures, identity functionally replaces the firewall as the primary enforcement mechanism.

Chapter 11: Data Security and Data Governance

- **Information Lifecycle**: Categorizing and encrypting sensitive information throughout its entire enterprise lifecycle.

- **Dependency on Identity**: Stringent data governance is practically impossible without context-aware identity enforcement.

Chapter 12: Application Security and SSDLC

- **"Shift Left"**: Integrating security natively and early into the software development lifecycle to reduce remediation costs.

- **Emergent Property**: Security cannot be "bolted on" to applications; it must be an emergent property of the system itself.

Phase 4: Maturation, Response, and Enterprise Resilience

SOC Maturity and Threat Hunting

Security Operations have undergone a profound transformation from traditional log monitoring to a **threat-informed, intelligence-led, detection-engineering- driven, automation-enhanced function** that sits at the center of enterprise cyber defense.

Modern SOCs now integrate:

- Detection Engineering and SIEM + XDR
- Threat Intelligence
- Threat Hunting
- Automation, SOAR and Incident Response
- Behavioral Analytics and Identity-First Detections
- Cloud Monitoring
- CTI Feedback Loops
- Purple Team Operations
- Zero Trust Enforcement

This chapter provides a blueprint for SOC maturity and threat hunting program development.

13.1 The Evolution of the SOC

The first SIEM project I was involved with dates back to 2005, I was intrigued by the correlation capabilities of events using Boolean logic in an automated way. I could finally leave manual firewall log review behind. A few years later, I was one of four designated analysts destined for our organization's first official SOC. Since that time, Security Operations Centers have evolved and expanded their practices. Modern SOC teams have mature incident response programs with well documented playbooks, alongside detection engineering programs leveraging modern frameworks and technologies. They are tasked with ensuring security across an organization and may interact with any team within the organization, as well as third party security or law enforcement organizations in the course of executing their responsibilities.

Legacy SOC (2005–2015)

- Alert Triage
- Signature-Based Detection
- Limited Visibility
- Manual Response
- On-premise Infrastructure

Modern SOC (2016–Now)

- Cloud-Native and Telemetry Driven
- Proactive Hunting
- Identity-Aware
- Automation-Powered
- Threat-Informed and ATT&CK-Aligned

Next-Gen SOC (2026 and beyond)

- Autonomous Containment
- Behavior-Driven Detection
- AI-Assisted Analysis
- Continuous Validation
- Zero Trust Adaptive Access

The SOC has become the nerve center of an organization's cyber operations.

13.2 SOC Core Functions

A SOC has a defined set of responsibilities within an organization, business units within these organizations may also have dedicated security personnel whose primary responsibility is security oversight for their business unit's output and who work closely with SOCs to align towards the overarching security strategy. Even with this structure, the SOC maintains primary security responsibility.

SOC Responsibilities

- Threat Monitoring
- Detection Engineering
- Threat Intelligence Production and Analysis
- Incident Response
- Forensic Analysis
- Threat Hunting
- Security Architecture Validation
- Purple Teaming

Detection and response capabilities must be integrate intelligence and perform validation constantly.

13.3 SOC Tiers - Modern Interpretation

While early SOCs were comprised of a flat org structure and were often a small team within a larger security team, modern SOCs have grown and established a tiered structure, each tier having a set of responsibilities and collaborating with other tiers as needed:

Tier 0: Autonomous Security Controls

Machine-driven blocking, identity containment, and automated enrichment. This is the baseline technology tier.

Tier 1: Monitoring and Triage

Analysts handle:

- Initial Alert Triage
- False Positive Reduction
- Initial Enrichment
- Ticket Creation

Tier 2: Investigation and Threat Hunting

Analysts in this tier typically have more incident experience than Tier 1, they perform:

- Deep Investigations
- Correlation
- Cloud Analysis
- Root Cause Analysis

Tier 3: Incident Response and Advanced Threat Hunting

Tier 3 analysts use their experience to address more complex threats. They handle:

- Active Threats
- Cloud-Native Compromises
- Lateral Movement
- Malware Analysis
- Containment Strategy

Tier 4: Threat Intelligence and Detection Engineering

Tier 4 analysts and engineers incorporate their knowledge of their environments along with understanding of attacker behavior to help define detection strategy and logic:

- Use Cases
- Detection Logic
- Adversary Emulation
- ATT&CK Mapping
- Automation

A modern SOC is a multidisciplinary, intelligence-led, engineering-driven team often necessitating open channels of communication with other teams.

13.4 Telemetry Strategy for SOC Maturity

A SOC's ability to monitor their environment relies entirely on their ability to collect the right data. Telemetry completeness empowers the SOC to execute on their investigative efforts.

Critical Telemetry Categories

Collecting the right logs at the right time is critical.

Identity Logs

- Authentication Events
- Conditional Access
- Cloud IAM logs

Endpoint Logs

- EDR
- Process Creation and Script Execution
- Memory Anomalies

Cloud Logs

- Audit and Gateway Logs
- Cloud Identity Activity
- Serverless Logs

Network Logs

- DNS
- Proxy and Egress Monitoring
- NDR and Flow Logs

Application Logs

- Authentication
- API Usage
- Privilege Changes

Telemetry is the foundation of detection engineering, threat hunting, and incident response.

It plays a critical factor in SOC maturity and success.

13.5 SIEM and XDR Integration Model

Modern SOCs use **SIEM for correlation and XDR for depth**.

This combination provides a wide and deep approach to detection with response capabilities.

SIEM Strengths

- Multi-Source Correlation
- Long-Term Retention
- Compliance Reporting
- Behavioral Analytics

XDR Strengths

- Deep Endpoint and Identity Visibility
- Behavioral Analytics
- Automated Response Workflows

Combined SIEM/XDR Architecture

- SIEM collects and correlates
- XDR enriches with endpoint/identity detail
- SOAR automates triage and containment
- Threat intel drives prioritization
- ATT&CK informs detection logic

This layered model reduces detection time and false positives while accelerating time to resolution.

13.6 SOC Maturity Model

Many organizations begin with small IT departments and shared responsibilities, leaving security as a secondary function. As they grow and security becomes more important to their strategy, they begin to define their tasks and eventually mature into a fully structured and well prepared SOC.

Level 1: Foundational

- Reactive Alerting
- Limited Telemetry
- Ad-hoc Investigations

Level 2: Basic

- SIEM Correlation
- Documented IR Processes
- Basic Playbooks
- Limited Automation

Level 3: Intermediate

- EDR Integration
- CTI-driven Priorities
- Threat-Hunting Program
- Multi-Cloud Monitoring

Level 4: Advanced

- ATT&CK-Aligned Detection Engineering
- Purple Team Operations
- Automation-First Model
- Deep Identity Analytics
- AI-Assisted Triage

Level 5: Autonomous SOC

- Continuous Validation
- Adaptive Zero Trust Enforcement
- Self-Healing Infrastructure
- High-Fidelity Detection Coverage
- Automated Response at Scale

13.7 Threat Intelligence Integration

A modern SOC consumes and produces threat intelligence, whether through freely available sources or through engaging dedicated third parties. This intelligence is integrated into SIEM detection logic, red team exercises, adversary profiling and threat modeling.

Types of Threat Intel

- Strategic
- Operational
- Tactical
- Technical

Cyber Threat Intelligence, CTI, must integrate with ATT&CK to build threat-informed defense.

13.8 Threat Hunting Program Development

Threat hunting is *not reactive*, it is *proactive*. This is where hypothesis meets validation, in a sense. Proposed models are put to the test by searching for evidence to determine if they've already taken place in an environment.

Types of Hunts

- **Hypothesis-Driven Hunting:** ATT&CK techniques, intelligence reports and anomalous patterns.
- **Data-Driven Hunting:** Behavioral trends, statistical anomalies and identity behavior.
- **Adversary Emulation Hunts:** Red and purple team input, specific threat actor TTDs.

Threat Hunting Workflow

1. Define Hypothesis
2. Identify Required Datasets
3. Execute Queries
4. Analyze Results
5. Determine Findings
6. Create Detections
7. Integrate into SIEM/XDR

Threat hunting drives continuous improvement of detection engineering.

13.9 Purple Team Operations

Purple teaming is the **collaboration between red and blue teams**.

This provides organizations with many benefits, including but not limited to validating detection coverage, testing and improving incident response workflows, and evaluating Zero Trust controls.

Purple Team Responsibilities

- ATT&CK Mapping
- Simulation Exercises
- Detection Tuning
- SIEM/XDR Regression Testing
- Threat Hunting
- Threat Modeling

This enables rapid detection maturity growth.

13.10 Incident Response Integration

SOC and IR must operate as one. Incident response processes often take up six stages: Preparation, Identification, Containment, Eradication, Recovery and Lessons Learned. SOC responsibilities include detection of anomalies and triage of alerts, core functions of the Identification stage. When confirmed, these alerts can be escalated to a separate investigative tier or investigated within the triaging tier of the SOC. Incident response teams can also span beyond the SOC depending on the tasks necessary as part of the incident being responded to.

IR Responsibilities

- Contain Incidents
- Eradicate Malicious Presence
- Recover Systems
- Preserve Evidence
- Communicate Internally and Externally

Mature SOCs use any tools at their disposal for their detection and investigation tasks, including SIEM, SOAR, forensics tool kits (FTKs), identity controls and cloud workflows.

13.11 Use Case Development and Prioritization

Use-case development is the primary objective of detection engineering. Prioritizing use-cases enables implementation of the highest value detection logic first, based on several factors. Each use case is composed of logic, relevant data sources, ATT&CK TTPs, severity, response actions and a solid understanding of expected and thus unexpected behavior.

Prioritization Factors

- Business Impact
- Threat Intel

- Likelihood
- Regulatory Requirements
- Coverage Gaps

This ensures focus on high-value detections first.

13.12 SOC Automation and SOAR

Automation is mandatory for reducing analyst fatigue and response times.

This also permits repeatability in investigative steps, accounting for human error or oversight.

SOAR Capabilities

- Automated Enrichment
- Phishing Auto-Triage
- Account Disablement
- Host Isolation
- Network Blocking
- Cloud Token Revocation
- Playbook Orchestration
- Timeline Tracking and Rreporting

Automation frees analysts to focus on high-value investigations and threat hunting. The level of automation may vary based on an organization's needs and requirements for manual validation.

With a higher level of maturity within the organization's overall security culture and practices, more automation is possible, introducing minimal risk of unintended business disruption.

13.13 SOC Metrics, KPIs and Executive Reporting

As the central nervous system of an organization's cyber security posture, SOC performance and efficacy can be at the forefront of Security Steering Committee and Board of Directors' interest.

The ability to properly communicate how the SOC is performing and the value it provides the organization is critical as it can impact budget, head count and strategy.

Operational Metrics

- Alert Volume
- False Positive Rate
- Mean Time to Detect (MTTD)
- Mean Time to Respond (MTTR)

Maturity Metrics

- ATT&CK Coverage
- Detection Precision
- Identity Visibility
- Cloud Coverage
- Automation Rate

Strategic Metrics

- Reduction in attack path exposure
- Dwell time reduction

- Successful detection validation cycles

Reporting must focus on **outcomes**, not alert counts. Trends are more valuable than snapshots in time.

13.14 Roadmap for SOC Modernization

With a focus on SOC modernization, organizations will touch on several elements, including technology, process and intelligence, while improving their incident response capabilities along the way.

Phase 1: Telemetry Foundation

- SIEM
- Network Logs
- Cloud Logs
- Identity and Endpoint Logs

Phase 2: Detection Engineering

- ATT&CK Alignment
- Use-Case Prioritization
- Correlation Improvements

Phase 3: Automation

- SOAR Deployment
- Response Playbooks
- Enrichment Automation

Phase 4: Threat-Informed Defense

- Integrated CTI
- Purple Teaming
- Adversary Emulation

Phase 5: Autonomous SOC

- Identity-Driven Access Enforcement
- Adaptive Controls
- Automated Containment

13.15 Chapter Summary

Security Operations is the operational heartbeat of the cybersecurity organization. This chapter provides a blueprint for developing a modern SOC capability that is:

- Telemetry-rich
- Intelligence-driven
- Automated
- Threat-informed
- Cloud-aware
- Identity-centric
- Continuously validated

Threat hunting, detection engineering, and automation transform the SOC from reactive to proactive, enabling resilience against modern adversaries.

Incident Response Crisis Management and Tabletop Exercises

Incident Response (IR) is the **last line of defense** when prevention and detection fail. It encompasses processes that address and remove the threats, while also providing guidance around necessary communications and steps to limit or prevent future occurrences.

A mature IR function is goes beyond technical:

- Operational
- Strategic
- Legal
- Regulatory
- Executive-Facing
- Customer-Facing
- Board-Visible

This chapter provides a *complete, enterprise-grade IR framework* required for security executives to lead through cyber crises, supported by forensics, detection engineering, business continuity, and communications.

14.1 The Role of the CISO in Incident Response

When the role exists in an organization, the CISO bears the responsibility and accountability for that organization's security posture, guided by industry best practices, security steering committees and business objectives.

CISO Foundational Responsibilities

- Ensure IR Readiness
- Own and Maintain IR Frameworks
- Establish Playbooks and Roles
- Align IR with Legal, HR, and Executive Teams
- Act as Crisis Advisor, not necessarily Spokesperson
- Provide decision support to Executive Leadership
- Oversee Containment and Recovery Coordination
- Report to The Board on incident status

CISO Crisis Responsibilities

- Strategist
- Coordinator
- Translator between technical and non-technical stakeholders
- Risk advisor

A CISO sits in the eye of the storm, remaining calm while troubled waters surround, with the responsibility to coordinate the storm response.

14.2 The Incident Response Lifecycle

Incident response lifecycles are generally comprised of six stages with technical and non-technical components.

1. Preparation

- Policies and Procedures
- Tools
- Playbooks
- Training
- Tabletop Exercises

2. Detection and Analysis

- Alert Triage
- Forensic Logs
- Behavioral Evidence
- Attack-Path Reconstruction
- Threat Intelligence
- Telemetry Correlation

3. Containment

- Short-Term Containment
- Long-Term Containment
- Identity Isolation

- Device Isolation
- Cloud Workload Isolation
- Network Isolation

4. Eradication

- Remove Malware
- Remove Persistence
- Revoke Credentials
- Shut down Attacker Paths

5. Recovery

- Restore Business Services
- Validate Restored Systems
- Reinstate Trust Policies
- Conduct Root Cause Analysis

6. Post-Incident Activity

- Lessons Learned
- Executive Summary
- Control Improvement
- Roadmap Adjustments

The lifecycle is best used as a feedback loop, with post incident outputs feeding into the continuous preparation stage, further refining the detection and prevention capabilities of an organization.

14.3 Preparation: Building an IR Program

Successful IR is rooted in preparation. Aligning to business and security strategies along with an in depth understanding of an organization's on-premise and cloud environments, provides security organizations the foundation for preparing for incidents. With a combination of policies, tools and well trained personnel, the preparation stage is a continuous effort.

Key Components

- IR Policy
- IR Playbooks
- Escalation Paths
- Severity Classification
- RACI Model
- Legal and Regulatory Guidance
- Executive Communication Plan
- External Forensics Partners
- Communications Templates
- Backup and Restoration Strategy

IR readiness determines crisis survivability and is constantly adapting to real world threats.

14.4 Detection and Analysis

Visibility is a key requirement when considering detection capabilities. Telemetry completeness enables tools and analysts to detect, triage and appropriately analyze events and behaviors of interest. This leads to understanding true positive or false positive status, determining known and likely expanded impact, and viable containment strategies.

Incident detection

- SIEM
- EDR
- XDR
- Audit Logs, Cloud and On-premise
- Anomaly Detection
- Identity Analytics
- DSPM Alerts
- Network Telemetry

Analysis Priorities

- Entry Point
- Adversary Behavior
- Privilege Abuse
- Persistence Mechanisms
- Lateral Movement
- Data Exposure

- Affected Business Processes
- Level of Impact

Artifacts to Collect

- Disk Images
- Memory Captures
- Logs, Cloud and On-premise
- Network Traces

A mature SOC and detection engineering team is essential for accurate IR analysis. The IR analysis relies on established process and necessary data collection.

14.5 Incident Severity Classification - Enterprise Model

Any incident has several attributes that guide its severity classification. These attributes include business disruption and impact, data classification and regulatory alignment, impacted infrastructure and recovery cost and timeline. Incident severity classification drives communication requirements, escalation path and resources allocated to the response process. Each organization defines their classification model. A sample model is detailed below.

SEV 1: Critical

- Ransomware Event
- Active Data Exfiltration
- Major Cloud Compromise
- Significant Business Outage
- Regulatory Impact

SEV 2: High

- Targeted Intrusion
- Lateral Movement or Privilege Escalation Detected
- PII/PHI Exposure Suspected

SEV 3: Moderate

- Isolated Malware
- Suspicious User Activity
- API Abuse Indicators

SEV 4: Low

- Unauthorized Scanning
- Commodity Phishing and other minor anomalies

Incident severity classification is a core component of any incident response process, driving escalation paths, communication requirements including executive level involvement, and resource allocation.

14.6 Modern Containment Strategies

Containment steps focus around limiting impact that can include damage to an organization's security posture, public reputation or continued business operations.

Containment Characteristics

- Fast and Surgical

- Identity-Aware
- Cloud-Native, where appropriate
- Minimally Disruptive to Regular Business Operations

Rapid Containment Techniques

- Disabling user accounts and vulnerable services
- Revoking Cloud Tokens
- Isolating Endpoints
- Segmenting Compromised Networks
- Blocking Malicious IPs/Domains

Cloud-Specific Containment Approaches

- Detach IAM Roles
- Disable Compromised Cloud Keys
- Isolate Workloads
- Restrict Cloud Service APIs

Containment must minimize business disruption while stopping attacker movement.

14.7 Eradication and Forensic Validation

When attacker activities are contained, they may still leave compromised artifacts in place.

Returning to standard business operations without eradicating all traces of the attacker's compromise activities may continue the negative impact the attacker had initiated.

Common Goals

- Remove Malware
- Remove Persistence
- Close Exploited Vulnerabilities
- Rotate **all** Compromised Credentials
- Validate System Integrity

Common Forensic Validation

- Validate: No Remaining Persistence
- Analyze: Autostart Locations and Startup Scripts
- Check: Cloud IAM Logs for privilege resets
- Verify: Patching Levels

Eradication without validation can almost guarantee re-compromise. Validation is a critical step before returning systems to production ready state.

14.8 Recovery and Reinstating Trust

Recovery is not simply bringing systems back online after a comprehensive validation. It's also ensuring, with as much trust and confidence as possible, that all appropriate security controls are in place, including those that would prevent the same compromise from taking place again.

Recovery is both technical and trust based.

Technical Recovery

- Restoring from backup
- Reconfigure workloads

- Fully rebuilding compromised systems
- Validating application behavior

Trust Recovery

- Ensuring identity integrity
- Verifying EDR installation
- Revalidating network segmentation

Systems should not return to production until trust has been reestablished.

14.9 Crisis Communications and Executive Alignment

Incidents impact IT systems and data. Technical response is critical in the incident response process. Non-technical response procedures must not be overlooked. Depending on the scope of impact, several stakeholders, internal and external, may need to be informed. Third parties, such as law enforcement or regulatory bodies, may also play a large part in the response process. Incidents can be expansive, proper communication procedures must be in place and followed.

Stakeholders

- CEO
- CIO
- CISO
- Legal
- Regulatory bodies
- Customers
- Investors
- PR/Media

- Law Enforcement
- Cyber Insurance

It is critical to avoid both overreaction and underreaction. Communication should be clear and accurate, devoid of speculatory commentary, align with legal and business appropriate language. The goal is to reassure stakeholders and maintain trust.

14.10 Insurance, Legal and Law Enforcement

With any incident, there may be legal and financial implications. Working with law enforcement, when appropriate, establishes a record of the criminal activities, but limiting information disclosure to the required information is critical. Working with legal teams assures the right information, with appropriate language, is used when communicating with law enforcement or- otherwise disclosing news of the incident. The financial impact may be limited with proper cyber insurance, but note that there are significant requirements to qualify for coverage policies.

Cyber Insurance

- Notify Immediately
- Follow Policy Requirements
- Use Approved Vendors

Legal Counsel

- Ensures Regulatory Compliance
- Manages Discovery and Protects Privilege

Law Enforcement Involvement

- Criminal Activity is confirmed, including ransomware

- Nation-State Activity
- Major Data Theft

Incident response processes must align with legal requirements.

14.11 Forensics and Evidence Handling

Evidence gathering and handling principles apply in proper incident response. Artifact integrity is crucial in criminal investigations, civil litigation, and root cause analysis.

Forensic Priorities

- Chain of Custody
- Integrity-Preserving Imaging
- Artifact Preservation
- Secure Storage
- Timestamp Integrity

Improper evidence handling introduces business and legal risk. The importance of evidence integrity cannot be understated.

14.12 Regulatory and Compliance Considerations

Depending on an organization's business vertical, it may fall under compliance considerations that include levels of implemented security controls, compensating controls and communications requirements.

Major Regulatory Requirements

- GDPR 72-Hour Reporting Rule
- HIPAA Breach Notification
- PCI Breach Protocols

- State Privacy Laws
- SEC Cybersecurity Rules
- FFIEC/FINRA Requirements

Incident response programs must map processes to applicable regulatory frameworks. Non-adherence risks major legal and financial implications.

14.13 Building IR Playbooks

Incident response playbooks incorporate the full scope of potential incident models. The level of detail should suffice to define any step necessary for prioritizing and addressing the incident, communicating with key stakeholders and define RACI roles.

Playbook Components

- Summary
- Scope
- Triggers
- Severity
- Roles and Responsibilities
- Data Sources
- Containment Steps
- Eradication Steps
- Recovery Workflows
- Communication Plan
- Evidence Handling Procedures

Playbooks can be defined around high level incident categories, or specific TTPs.

Common Playbook Categories

- Phishing
- Ransomware
- Cloud IAM Compromise
- Data Exfiltration
- Insider Incident
- Endpoint Malware
- API Abuse

Having well developed incident response playbooks helps organizations handle incidents smoothly and account for communication and regulatory requirements.

14.14 Tabletop Exercises

Simulations and tabletop exercises not only strengthen team capabilities in incident response, but they also help identify gaps or opportunities for improvement in the incident response playbook being run through the exercise. Tabletop exercises validate readiness.

Types of Tabletop Exercises

- Discussion-Based
- Walkthrough Simulations
- Technical and Executive Hybrid Exercises
- Full-Scale Crisis Simulations

Participants include stakeholders from all necessary teams for the given incident. Common participants span teams like security, IT, HR, PR, legal, executive leadership and vendors.

Types of Outputs

- Readiness Gaps
- Improvement Actions
- Timeline Enhancements
- Process Refinements

A mature organization conducts tabletop exercises with a regular frequency.

14.15 After-Action Review and Lessons Learned

Once a compromise has been contained and eradicated and all necessary evidence collected, once business operations have returned to normal production level for applications or incidents involved, it is important to fully understand what led to the compromise and how it can be prevented in the future. Any issues relating directly to the incident response activities and playbooks should also be addressed.

Post-Incident Analysis

- Timeline Reconstruction
- Root Cause
- Control and Detection Failures
- Escalation and Communications Issues
- Staffing Considerations
- Response Delays

Technical and non-technical deliverables are appropriate outputs of this step. They should provide tactical and strategic findings, an appropriate executive summary and guidance for updating roadmap, policies and playbooks helping the security program mature.

14.16 IR Metrics and KPIs

Incident metrics may serve as the most important security metrics gathered by an organization. These effectively measure efficacy of all components involved in a security program.

Operational KPIs

- Time to Detect, Contain, Eradicate and Recover
- Number of affected systems, applications, and users

Quality KPIs

- Detection Accuracy
- Containment Success Rate
- Forensic Readiness Score

Strategic KPIs

- Reduction in Downtime
- Reduction in Regulatory Risk
- Reduced Attacker Swell Time
- Increased Detection Coverage

These KPIs inform board-level reporting and can have important implications for budget, strategy direction and personnel decisions.

14.17 Roadmap for IR Maturity

It is possible to establish a fully mature incident response program from the ground up. It is much more common that organizations find themselves somewhere along that maturity journey with clear vision on achieving full maturity. A sample roadmap is detailed below.

Phase 1: Stabilize

- Create IR Policy
- Build Foundational Playbooks
- Establish Roles and Responsibilities

Phase 2: Operationalize

- Integrate SIEM/EDR/XDR
- Train SOC
- Implement Forensic Workflows

Phase 3: Harden

- Tabletop Exercises
- Supply-Chain IR Plan
- Cloud IR Plan
- Ransomware-Specific Plan

Phase 4: Automate

- Isolation Workflows

- Ticketing and Data Enrichment
- Containment Playbooks via SOAR

Phase 5: Optimize

- Continuous Validation
- Integration with Threat Intel
- Purple Team Validation

Organizations at any stage of their maturity journey can benefit from assessing their readiness. The goal is continuous improvement tracked through measurable outcomes.

14.18 Chapter Summary

Incident Response is the ultimate test of a security program. A mature IR capability is proactive, intelligence-driven, cloud-ready, identity-aware, and deeply integrated into business operations.

This chapter provides an **IR framework** required for modern cyber defense and executive readiness.

Compliance, Audit and Regulatory Frameworks

Compliance and audit functions often get treated as checkbox activities. In a mature cybersecurity organization, compliance operates as a **strategic governance engine** that:

- Protects the business from regulatory risk while strengthening customer trust.
- Aligns cybersecurity with industry standards while enhancing defense posture during incidents.
- Provides structure and accountability while supporting board oversight.
- Drives maturity across people, processes, and technology.

This chapter delivers a **broad-spectrum view** of regulatory frameworks, certification programs, audit readiness, documentation standards, and how an organization integrates compliance into the broader governance and cyber-risk operating model.

15.1 Compliance vs Security vs Audit

While compliance, security and audit functions integrate as part of an overarching governance function, they have very specific purposes and depend on each other in a mature and compliant well governed security focused organization.

Compliance: Required Standards

- External Obligations
- Regulatory Requirements
- Contractual Expectations
- Industry-Standard Frameworks
- Evidence-Driven Controls

Security: Implemented Defense

- Implemented Protection Controls
- Threat-Informed Defense
- Prevention, Detection, Response and Their Maturity
- Secure Engineering Practices

Audit: Validated Controls

- Independent Assurance
- Control Testing
- Governance Validation
- Risk Reduction Verification

A mature organization ensures all three align fostering buy in from stakeholders and a culture of proactive defense.

15.2 Core Regulatory and Compliance Domains

Depending on an organization's products, services or data, it may fall under one or more specific domains of regulatory or industry standard domains.

These obligations often dictate minimum controls, while allowing for viable countermeasures when necessary. They may also define financial or other liability consequences for non-compliance.

The list below, while not comprehensive, provides a starting point for understanding which domains an organization may be subject to.

1. Privacy Regulations

- Europe's GDPR applicable to European residents, and citizens globally
- CCPA/CPRA applicable to California
- Virginia CDPA
- Colorado Privacy Act
- Brazil LGPD

2. Financial Regulations

- SOX, legislation passed in 2002
- FFIEC
- NYDFS Part 500, introduced in 2017
- FINRA
- Office of the Comptroller of Currency Cybersecurity Guidance

3. Healthcare

- HIPAA
- HITECH

4. Government

- FedRAMP
- FISMA
- DFARS / CMMC

5. Payments

- PCI DSS

6. Critical Infrastructure

- NERC CIP
- TSA directives for transit agencies
- ISO 27019 for energy utilities

7. Cross-Industry Security Frameworks

- ISO 27001
- NIST CSF 2.0
- NIST SP 800-53
- CIS Controls
- SOC 2

An organization must map internal controls across multiple frameworks, reducing duplicated work.

15.3 NIST CSF 2.0 in Compliance Programs

The Cybersecurity Framework from the National Institute of Standards and Technology provides an overarching strategic structure for security controls for enterprises and proper governance.

Discussed in detail in chapter 2, a summary of functions and strengths is listed below.

CSF 2.0 Functions

1. Identify
2. Protect
3. Detect
4. Respond
5. Recover
6. Govern

CSF 2.0 strengthens

- Governance
- Supply Chain Security
- Business Alignment
- Metrics
- Risk-Based Decision Making

It is a very flexible framework for large enterprises and provides a solid foundation upon which organizations can establish mature security posture.

15.4 NIST SP 800-53 Stringent Baseline Controls

The NIST Security and Privacy Controls, SP 800-53, provide a set of required minimum baselines for federal systems, cloud organizations intending to do business with government entities and other regulated industries. Some of the control families are listed below.

Control Families Coverage

- Access Control
- Audit Logging
- Incident Response
- Risk Management
- Contingency Planning
- Supply Chain
- Privacy

For organizations that don't absolutely require these baselines, mapping to 800-53 helps ensure completeness of security controls.

15.5 ISO 27001 - International Standard

An international standard, ISO 27001 provides an approach for vetting of policy, technology and personnel. A high-level overview of the benefits of this standard is provided below.

- Information Security Management System (ISMS) structure
- Governance
- Risk methodology
- Control catalog

- Internal and external audits

15.6 SOC 2 Trust Services Criteria (TSC)

A framework from the American Institute of Certified Public Accountants, SOC 2 provides a foundation for security, confidentiality, availability, privacy and processing integrity. Organizations that handle customer data, including SaaS and cloud services providers, should align to SOC 2 common criteria.

Common Criteria

- **CC1:** Control Environment
- **CC2:** Communications and Information
- **CC3:** Risk Assessment
- **CC4:** Monitoring of Controls
- **CC5:** Control Activities
- **CC6:** Logical and Physical Access Controls
- **CC7:** System Operations
- **CC8:** Change Management
- **CC9:** Risk Mitigation

Assessment Types

- **SOC 2 Type I**: a single point in time assessment
- **SOC 2 Type II**: an assessment over a rolling period of time

SOC 2, while not legally mandated, is the most common assurance standard for SaaS and cloud-native companies. It all starts with identifying the proper Trust Services Criteria applicable to an organization.

15.7 PCI DSS

Making its debut in 2004, the Payment Card Industry Data Security Standard, PCI DSS, was modeled after Visa's security program and released under their brand. The goal has been to standardize security measures for payment card processors, merchants and organizations that store, transmit or process cardholder data:

- Data/PII
- Encryption
- Secure Network Design
- Monitoring
- Logging
- Incident Response
- Vulnerability Scanning
- Penetration Testing

PCI has 12 high-level requirements, structured around data protection and monitoring. The amount of stringent audit requirements depends on the annual transaction volume, requiring either self-attestation or third-party audit by a Qualified Security Assessor, QSA.

15.8 HIPAA / HITECH

Introduced in 1996, the Health Insurance Portability and Accountability Act, HIPAA, is legislation centered around protecting people's health information privacy and security. In 2009, the Health Information Technology for Economic and Clinical Health Act, HITECH, expands controls to include electronic health records. This covers entities like health insurance companies, health care providers and organizations that process medical information.

Focus Areas

- PHI Protection
- Access Control
- Audit Logging
- Breach Notification
- Privacy Controls
- Data Handling Policies

There exists a public misconception around disclosure limits and to whom HIPAA applies. It is important to understand who is required to align to these legislations. HIPAA fines can be severe, making compliance essential.

15.9 FedRAMP: Cloud Authorization

Cloud service providers working with US government agencies must align to NIST SP 800-53 with stringent third-party assessments taking place annually:

- NIST 800-53 High Baseline
- Continuous Monitoring
- Standardized Reporting
- Rigorous Third-Party Assessment by Recognized 3PAOs

Compliance takes major undertaking that requires engineering-heavy compliance.

15.10 Cybersecurity Maturity Model Certification

A certification focused on the defense industry, the program requires defense industrial base and contractors to demonstrate capabilities around protecting Controlled Unclassified Information, CUI. With requirements spanning three tiers, it builds from basic access controls to advanced threat protection:

- NIST 800-171: focused on protecting CUI in non-federal systems and organizations
- Access Control
- Auditing
- Incident Reporting
- Supply Chain Protection

Released in 2024, CMMC Revision 2.0 simplifies levels and expands compliance alignment timelines but retains strong control requirements.

15.11 Privacy Regulations (GDPR, CCPA, etc.)

Privacy regulations have defined jurisdictions geared toward protecting citizens and residents of those jurisdictions, regardless of the service provider's location. These regulations specify levels of security goals around data protection, at the same time, often establish customer rights and compromise notification requirements.

Privacy Framework Goals

- Data Protection and Governance
- Data Subject Rights
- Lawful Basis
- Breach Notification
- Retention and Minimization
- Data Protection Impact Assessments

Privacy is increasingly intertwined with cybersecurity governance.

15.12 Creating a Unified Control Framework

Enterprises must manage overlapping frameworks without duplicating work. A single control may apply to more than a single framework, the ability to map controls across the full body of frameworks to which they apply reduces the number of man-hours associated with assessment evidence gathering and compliance assessments.

Unified Control Framework, UCF, Mappings

- NIST
- ISO
- SOC 2
- CIS
- PCI
- FFIEC
- HIPAA
- Internal Controls

This provides a single source of truth, consistent evidence standards and audits, along with reduced effort and simpler executive level deliverables.

A well-established UCF is essential for large enterprises but can benefit organizations of any size.

15.13 Continuous Compliance and Automation

Standardizing evidence gathering processes helps in repeatability, making continuous compliance verifiable through automation. Automating checks and reporting ensures a standardized deliverable and removes risk of human error.

1. Evidence Collection Automation

- Configuration Checks
- Policy Presence
- Identity Logs
- Cloud Posture

2. Continuous Controls Monitoring

- Real-Time Checks
- Cloud Misconfiguration Alerts
- Identity Drift Detection

3. Automated Reporting

- Audit-Ready Reports
- Evidence Packages
- Dashboard Views

4. CI/CD Compliance Integration

- Scanning at Build Time
- Policy-as-Code
- Infrastructure-as-Code Compliance

Compliance should be continuous, not centered around discrete spot checks.

15.14 Audit Readiness and Engagement

While automation helps with audit processes, they need to be established and ensure controls and audit output align to the appropriate regulations and industry standards. Documentation is foundational and helps standardize every step along the way. Third party assessment organizations have certain expectations for their audit process to go smoothly, an organization's readiness prepares them for that smooth assessment.

Documentation

- Policies and Procedures
- Standards
- Architectural Diagrams

Evidence Collection

- Screenshots
- Exports
- Logs
- Configurations
- Access Review Records

Controls Testing

- Internal Audit
- Red and Purple Team Tests
- Automated Configuration Checks

Pre-Audit Dry Runs

- Internal Audits
- Control Owner Interviews

Organizations must maintain a culture of audit readiness.

15.15 Board and Executive Reporting for Compliance

For executives and boards to lead an organization, they must be kept abreast of current status. This informs short and long term strategy. As key informed parties, they must receive clear and concise information with accurate risk analysis. Any report must be business aligned to allow for strategic guidance.

Key Topics

- Compliance Posture
- Gaps and Remediation
- Audit Results
- Regulatory Exposure
- Upcoming Obligations
- Risk Acceptance Areas
- Strategic Initiatives

Boards need clarity, not technical detail.

15.16 Third-Party and Supply Chain Compliance

Vendor security is a major compliance concern. Validating third parties are compliant with any requirements they align to, and an organization aligns to, helps protect an organization from unforeseen negative situations.

Proper adherence and accountability are contractual stipulations and should not be seen as a simple spot check:

- SOC 2 / ISO Verification
- Contract Clauses
- Security Questionnaires
- Due Diligence Reviews
- Annual Reassessments

Emerging Requirements

- Software Supply Chain Transparency
- SBOM
- Secure Development Practices
- Dependency Scanning

Supply chain compliance is no longer an afterthought; it is now mandatory.

15.17 Compliance Metrics and KPIs

Audits and their outputs have specific purposes tied to the regulatory or industry standards they align to. These are not appropriate business deliverables as they are not meant to provide the clarity and concise information needed by executive leadership, boards of directors or security steering committees. They do not measure compliance program efficacy per se, instead provide a check on compliance coverage. Relevant KPIs must be adopted across governance, operational and risk related tasks. These indicators provide security and compliance leadership the necessary information to assess posture and adjust direction to meet strategy and timeline requirements.

Governance KPIs

- Control Coverage
- Policy Adoption
- Audit Findings

Operational KPIs

- Remediation SLAs
- Evidence Collection Completeness
- Compliance Automation Coverage

Risk KPIs

- Regulatory Violations
- Late Filings
- Exceptions Pending Approval

KPIs convert compliance into measurable compliance maturity.

15.18 Roadmap for Compliance Maturity

Organizations are born every day.

They may not begin with regulatory compliance requirements but find they are covered under one of these umbrellas from one day to the next.

Establishing a plan toward full maturity helps an organization define projects and milestones to reach its goals and requirements. Below is a sample roadmap to that end.

Phase 1: Stabilize

- Define Governance Model
- Create Foundational Controls
- Document Policies

Phase 2: Expand

- Map Frameworks
- Build a Unified Compliance Framework, UCF
- Train Control Owners

Phase 3: Automate

- Continuous Controls Monitoring
- Evidence Automation and CI/CD Compliance Gates

Phase 4: Mature

- Near-Real-Time Compliance and Audit Readiness
- Cross-Framework Reporting

Phase 5: Optimize

- Automation-Driven Continuous Assurance
- Full UCF Integration
- Adaptive Compliance-Based on Business Risk

It is possible to reach compliance maturity through measured progress and dedicated strategy.

15.19 Chapter Summary

Compliance is a strategic asset that strengthens cybersecurity maturity, reduces risk, supports business growth, and enhances trust. It should not be seen as a hindrance to business, but an enabling force.

This chapter provides a regulatory and audit blueprint for governance, bridging compliance requirements with modern security engineering and Zero Trust principles.

Vendor Risk Management and Third-Party Cyber Risk

Vendor Risk Management (VRM) and Third-Party Cyber Risk have become **high-risk areas in cybersecurity**, driven by:

- SaaS Sprawl
- Cloud Supply Chain Dependencies
- Software Component Reuse
- Remote Workforce Reliance on Outsourced Systems
- Supply Chain Compromises

Organizations must implement **third-party risk governance** enforcing:

- Continuous Monitoring
- Zero Trust Architecture
- Contractual Adherence
- Identity Integration
- Software Supply Chain Integrity
- Real-Time Risk Scoring
- Incident Notification Requirements

This chapter provides a complete, executive-grade VRM framework.

16.1 The Modern Third-Party Risk Landscape

Organizations rely on third parties as part of standard business operations. Whether hardware, software, online applications or raw materials, it has become impossible to run nearly any business without relying on third parties.

Third Parties Include

- SaaS Vendors
- Cloud Service Providers
- Contractors and Integrators
- MSPs / MSSPs
- Offshore Teams
- Payroll and Payments Vendors
- Code Libraries (OSS)
- API Partners
- Data Processors and Hosting Providers

Every external dependency becomes an attack pathway.

Third-party risk has become equal to, if not greater than internal risk. There are several risk drivers associated with third parties, including layers of supply chain dependency, lack of visibility, improper identity governance, and regulatory non-compliance.

16.2 Third-Party & Supply Chain Attack Patterns

Over the last decade, there has been an increased incidence of major supply chain attacks, putting thousands of organizations at risk. As it stands, major breaches have impacted aircraft, SaaS vendors, computer manufacturers and public code libraries.

Common Targets

- Vendors with Weaker Security
- Unmanaged SaaS Platforms
- Code Repositories
- CI/CD Pipelines
- Cloud IAM Trust Relationships
- Managed Service Providers

Organizations must treat vendor ecosystems as part of the enterprise attack surface.

16.3 VRM Program Structure

Working with vendors requires not just the start of a business relationship, but a full relationship lifecycle. A mature program takes the full relationship from initial engagement, through collaborative risk reduction toward contract termination and asset return or data deletion.

1. Intake and Classification

- Categorize Vendors by criticality
- Classify data shared with the Vendor
- Assign Risk Tier

2. Due Diligence

- Questionnaires
- Architecture and Compliance Reviews
- Penetration Test Results
- Supply Chain Documentation (SBOM)
- Identity Governance Practices

3. Risk Assessment

- Evaluate Vendor Security Practices
- Rate Risks based on Business Impact
- Review Compensating Controls

4. Governance and Contracting

- Security Clauses
- Breach Notification Timelines
- Data Processing Agreements
- Right-to-Audit Clauses
- Minimum Security Requirements

5. Ongoing Monitoring

- Continuous Monitoring Tools
- Vendor Behavior Analytics

- Identity Drift Detection
- External Attack Surface Scans

6. Incident Response Alignment

- Shared Playbooks
- Communication Expectations
- Escalation Paths

7. Off-boarding

- Revocation of Access
- Deletion Confirmation
- Return of Assets

Third-party security must be lifecycle-driven, not episodic, enforceable through contract stipulations.

16.4 Vendor Classification and Tiering Model

Organizations can classify vendors based on several factors, including business requirements, impact of relationship disruption, and risk levels. While there is no single tiering model that fits all organizations, a sample model is detailed below:

Tier 1: Critical Vendors

- Access to critical business systems
- Handle sensitive data
- Integral to operations
- Compromise impacts revenue or safety

Tier 2: High-Risk Vendors

- Moderate operational impact
- Access to important business systems
- Potential privacy impact

Tier 3: Medium-Risk Vendors

- Limited access
- Low-volume data
- Indirect operational support

Tier 4: Low-Risk Vendors

- No sensitive data
- No privileged access

16.5 Due Diligence Requirements

Document review and validation of security posture are part of due diligence. Following the Zero Trust idea of no implicit trust, these due diligence steps should not be overlooked. There are different components that require due diligence.

Security Documentation Reviews

- Compliance Reports and Certifications
- Regulatory or Industry Attestations
- Penetration Testing Summaries

Technical Evidence

- Architecture Diagrams
- Network Segmentation Detail
- Authentication & Access Controls
- Data Protection, Retention and Deletion Processes

Identity and Access Control

- SSO Integration with MFA Enforcement
- Privileged Account Management
- Least Privilege RBAC

Operational Controls

- Logging and Monitoring
- Backup and Recovery
- Incident Response Maturity
- Vulnerability Management

Software Supply Chain Evidence

- SBOM (Software Bill of Materials)
- VEX (Vulnerability Exploitability Exchange)
- Dependency Management Processes
- Pipeline security

An organization should never rely solely on self-attested answers.

16.6 Contractual and Legal Requirements

Any relationship with a third party needs to be protected. The primary method of protecting that relationship is through contractual obligations and appropriate legal stipulations.

Contracts should require a core set of well defined stipulations and language.

Security Minimums

- MFA
- Encryption Requirements
- Secure SDLC
- Vulnerability Disclosure Policy
- Access Control Standards

Breach Notification

- Aligning with regulatory requirements
- Following industry standards
- Mandatory incident reporting pipeline

Audit Rights

- Right to Request Assessments
- Right to Review Security Artifacts
- Right to Verify Data Deletion

Data Governance Obligations

- Data Residency
- Sub-processors
- Encryption Key Management
- Secure Destruction

Regulatory Requirements and Contractual Obligations

- Regulation-Appropriate Processors
- Agreements Aligned with Legal Requirements
- Interstate or International Data Transfer Rules

Termination Requirements

- Revocation of Access
- Certified Data Deletion
- Return of an Organization's Assets

Contracts are the enforcement arm of vendor risk management.

16.7 Continuous Monitoring

Static annual questionnaires are obsolete.

Environments are increasingly dynamic and monitoring requirements are only becoming more comprehensive over time with increasingly complex real time adjustments leveraging tools like AI.

Modern VRM Components

- External Attack Surface Scanning
- SaaS Security Posture Monitoring (SSPM)
- Identity Drift Detection
- Cloud Configuration Monitoring
- Vendor Breach Intelligence
- Code-Signing Verification
- Observability into Third-Party Integrations

Continuous monitoring replaces point-in-time assurance and increases likelihood of rapid incident response should it be needed.

16.8 SaaS Security and Third-Party SaaS Governance

Shadow IT and SaaS sprawl create security blind spots. An unacceptable level of risk may be introduced by those blind spots. Proper governance and a culture of adherence are fundamental for proper SaaS security, along with due diligence on third party vendor security and history.

SaaS Risks

- Unsafe Sharing Practices
- Unmanaged Admin Roles
- Lack of Logs
- Weak MFA Enforcement
- Data Exfiltration via SaaS
- Excessive Third-Party Integrations

Required Controls

- SSPM (SaaS Security Posture Management)
- SSO Enforcement
- Conditional Access
- Monitoring of External Sharing
- SaaS Entitlement Reviews

SaaS proliferation requires governance as rigorous as cloud.

16.9 Identity Risks in Third-Party Relationships

Third-party identity compromise is a major attack vector that can lead to a complete disruption in business operations. Vendor identity risks necessitate proper control implementation to ensure vendor use is secure.

Identity Risks Include

- Compromised Vendor Accounts
- API Token Misuse
- Improper Identity Governance

Identity Controls Include

- JIT Vendor Access
- SSO Enforcement
- Short-Lived Tokens
- Role Boundary Policies

- IP Allow Lists
- Device Restrictions

Identity is the enforcement layer for vendor trust and proper governance must be prioritized.

16.10 Third-Party Incident Response Integration

Vendor incidents must trigger internal processes that align to defined playbooks.

An organization's incident response processes may have only internal parties involved, but often will include third parties, whether customer or vendor.

Requirements

- Third-Party IR Contact Paths
- Severity Criteria
- Notification SLAs
- Shared Incident Documentation
- Data Exposure Validation
- Containment Coordination

Response is incomplete unless vendors are aligned, along with containment, eradication and recovery efforts are addressed on both sides of the relationship.

16.11 Supply Chain and Software Risk Management

This is one of the most complex areas of VRM. It touches every corner of an organization. It is imperative to implement appropriate controls.

Supply Chain Attacks Target

- Build Systems
- Package Registries

- Signed Artifact Processes
- Upstream Libraries
- Cloud Deployment Scripts

Enterprise Protections

- SLSA Framework Adoption
- Immutable Pipelines
- Automated Dependency Patching
- Developer Training

Supply chain protection is inseparable from VRM. Proper protections involve people, process, technology and proper governance.

16.12 VRM Metrics and KPIs

Assessing vendor risk posture helps to understand organizational risk.

Governance Metrics

- Vendor Risk Tier Distribution
- Number of Overdue Assessments
- VRM Process Completion Rate

Operational Metrics

- Vendor Remediation SLA Adherence
- Continuous Monitoring Alerts
- SaaS Risk Level Changes

Risk Reduction Metrics

- Number of High-Risk Vendors Reduced
- Excessive Privilege Reduction
- Supply Chain Vulnerability Findings

Business Metrics

- Contract Compliance
- Cost of VRM Operations
- Audit Readiness Indicators

These metrics must properly communicate both operational detail and business outcomes.

16.13 Roadmap for VRM Maturity

A mature VRM program enables organizations to have continuous understanding of vendor risk posture.

This enables proper level of risk appetite to be accepted for individual vendors and clear messaging for executive teams, boards of directors and security steering committees in their strategic direction efforts.

Phase 1: Foundations

- Vendor Inventory
- Risk Tiering
- Intake Workflows

Phase 2: Due Diligence

- Questionnaires
- Security Evidence Collection
- Contract Standardization

Phase 3: Continuous Monitoring

- SSPM
- Attack Surface Monitoring
- Identity Drift Detection

Phase 4: Supply Chain Protection

- SBOM
- CI/CD integration
- Dependency Governance

Phase 5: Optimization

- Automated VRM Workflows
- Real-Time Risk Scoring
- Business-Aligned Reporting

A good roadmap and a maturity model for proper vendor risk management is increasingly critical.

16.14 Chapter Summary

Vendor and third-party risk now represent some of the **largest exposures** in the modern enterprise. A mature VRM program integrates:

- Governance
- Identity
- SaaS Security
- Supply Chain Protection
- Continuous Monitoring
- Contractual Controls
- Incident Response Alignment

This chapter equips organizations with the full operational and strategic model needed to manage vendor ecosystems securely and effectively.

Business Continuity, Disaster Recovery and Operational Resilience

Business disruption can cost an immeasurable amount of man hours and have a significant amount of impact to brand reputation, as well as revenue. In order to minimize any business disruption related to cyber incidents, natural disasters or any other unforeseen circumstances impacting normal business operations.

Business Continuity (BC), Disaster Recovery (DR), and Operational Resilience (OR) together form the **enterprise-wide capability** to maintain operation during:

- Cyber Incidents of any nature
- Cloud and other vendor outages
- Data corruption
- Supply Chain failures
- Natural Disasters
- Infrastructure Failures
- Geopolitical Disruption

This chapter provides a fully integrated blueprint for designing, implementing, and governing resilient systems, processes, and business operations.

17.1 The Difference Between BC, DR, and OR

While each element has its own business objective; BC, DR and OR converge with the overall goal of minimizing incidence or impact of disruption.

Business Continuity (BC)

Ensures critical *business processes* continue despite disruption. This focuses on people, process and alternative methods of operating.

Disaster Recovery (DR)

Restores critical *IT systems* and data after disruption. This focuses on use of failover systems and backups, as well as full system restoration.

Operational Resilience (OR)

Ensures the *organization as a whole* can adapt, absorb, and recover from disruptions. The focus is around strategy, governance, architecture, risk appetite and continuous improvement.

Relationship Model

- **OR** = Enterprise big picture
- **BC** = Business operations response
- **DR** = Technical systems response

An organization must integrate all three.

17.2 Business Impact Analysis (BIA)

A BIA is the foundation for resilience planning. Understanding potential impact helps an organization establish its tolerance to it, and thus define it's strategic goals for disaster recovery.

BIA Identifies

- Critical Business Processes, Systems and Applications
- Upstream and Downstream Dependencies
- Maximum Downtime Tolerances
- Financial and Operational Impact of Outages

Key Outputs

- Recovery Time Objective (RTO)
- Recovery Point Objective (RPO)
- Maximum Tolerable Downtime (MTD)
- Criticality Level per System

BIA Categories

- High Impact
- Medium Impact
- Low Impact

The BIA determines DR investment and architectural priorities, rating scenarios and their impact as high, medium or low.

17.3 RTO, RPO and MTD Explained

It is critical to understand the maximum allowable downtime, as well as establishing goals for achieving minimized impact.

Recovery Time Objective (RTO)

How quickly a system must be restored.

Recovery Point Objective (RPO)

The maximum acceptable data loss window.

Maximum Tolerable Downtime (MTD)

The maximum downtime the business can sustain before unacceptable damage.

Examples

- Payment Systems: RTO = minutes, RPO = seconds
- Internal HR Systems: RTO = hours, RPO = hours
- BI and Reporting: RTO = days

It is critical to ensure technical capabilities match business expectations.

17.4 Resilience: Redundancy and High Availability

Resilience objectives are focused on the ability to remain operational in the face of adverse circumstances.

Resilience should be a design consideration from the ground up.

Architectural Controls

- Multi-Region Cloud Deployments
- Appropriate Redundancy

- Multi-Path BGP Routing
- Load Balancing
- Auto-Scaling
- Active/Active, Active/Passive or Hot/Cold Architecture Models

Data Controls

- Real-Time Replication
- Cross-Region Backups
- Snapshot Frequency
- Immutable Backups

Identity Controls

- Redundant IdPs
- Recovery MFA Methods
- Break-Glass Access Workflows

Application Controls

- Active-Active Architectures
- Microservices Segmentation
- Fault isolation

Process can only establish so much operational resilience. To further solidify resilience, architectural investment is required.

17.5 Disaster Recovery Planning (DRP)

Disaster recovery is as successful as the preparation measures taken. Planning for disasters involves accounting for any number of possible factors, and prioritizing recovery efforts based on business impact and operational needs. A full plan must be established:

1. Inventory of Systems and Business Processes

- Prioritized by BIA

2. Recovery Procedures

- Step-by-step Restoration Path
- Responsible Teams
- Verification Steps

3. Backup Strategy

- Frequency
- Retention
- Encryption
- Off-site Storage

4. Failover Procedures

- Automation Triggers
- Manual Failover Processes
- Rollback Strategies

5. Cloud-Specific DR

- Cross-Region Strategies
- Service Failover
- Infrastructure-as-Code Rebuilds

6. Testing and Validation

- Tabletop Tests
- Technical Failover Tests
- Backup/Restore Testing

Regular disaster recovery testing ensures organizational readiness. DR is only as good as the last successful test.

17.6 Business Continuity Planning (BCP)

A business is built on more than just technology. Personnel can continue to run processes with alternative methodologies. Business continuity planning ensures they continue functioning and business operations are minimally impacted.

BC Capabilities

- Alternate Communication Channels
- Remote Work Readiness
- Relocated Staff Capability
- Vendor Continuity
- Manual Workarounds
- Emergency Operations Centers

Business continuity focuses on maintaining active *business operations*, not restoring systems.

17.7 Operational Resilience (OR)

Overlaying both business continuity and disaster recovery is a strategic active model for Operational Resilience. Understanding the organization's risk factors, a focus is placed on ensuring proper controls and responses are in place, and tested regularly.

OR Focus

- Identifying Material Risks
- Stress Testing Enterprise Capabilities
- Aligning Cyber Risk to Business Risk
- Ensuring Regulatory Compliance
- Continuous Improvement
- Customer and Market Resilience

Many regions now have regulatory requirements, such as the Digital Operations Resilience Act encompassing the European Union. In the US, while no single legislation exists, some frameworks are required for specific regulated industries, for example for financial institutions.

17.8 Cloud Resilience and DR Strategies

Cloud environments have specific operational models that must be taken into account when establishing disaster recovery and operational resilience programs.

Conceptually, they align to many of the same principles as traditional on-premise models, but must work within the capabilities of the cloud providers' operating models and feature sets.

Cloud HA + DR Strategy Types

Several approaches exist for cloud resilience and DR.

1. Multi-AZ Active/Passive

Most common setup. Production operations are run out of the active availability zone and failover to the passive zone in case of disruption, limiting costs while providing a viable resilience approach.

2. Multi-AZ Active/Active

Higher cost, near-zero downtime. Both environments are active with production operations running concurrently.

3. Multi-Region Backup + Restore

Lower cost; RTO is longer. Moving beyond availability zones into a more geographically dispersed model for higher resilience, this approach allows for a disaster recovery process that involves provisioning assets in the case of business disruption.

4. Multi-Region Active/Active

Critical systems with global presence. Providing a zero downtime capability, operations are actively serviced from multiple regions, at a higher operational expense than other solutions.

5. Multi-Cloud Failover

Rare, expensive, often unnecessary unless required by regulation. This model involves establishing appropriate level of disaster recovery, across multiple providers.

Cloud DR Characteristics

- Redundant IAM Policies
- Cross-region KMS Replication
- API and Infrastructure Governance
- Container Registry Redundancy
- IaC Templates for Rapid Redeployment

Cloud resilience requires understanding cloud-native failure modes.

17.9 Ransomware Resilience and Recovery

Ransomware is a critical disaster recovery scenario today. Losing access to data can lead to an inability to run day to day operations or service customers; worst case scenario an organization may no longer be viable. Having the data held hostage by attackers adds a layer of difficulty as those attackers, while committing to release the data, may fail to provide the necessary key to decrypt that inaccessible data. Having good data governance and controls, including regular backups, can minimize business disruption.

Ransomware DR requirements

- Immutable Backups
- Offline Backups
- Tested Restore Procedures
- Network Segmentation
- EDR and Behavioral Analytics
- Identity Lockdown Capabilities
- Rapid Containment Architecture

Ransomware-Specific DR Components

- Recovery in Clean Room Environment
- Staged Restoration
- Forensic Review Before Reintegration
- Identity Hygiene Validation

Preparedness determines an organization's survival.

17.10 Communications and Crisis Leadership

In a moment of crisis, communication becomes critical. Clear, concise and strategic messaging is vital to ensuring the right people are a aware of the right information at the right time. The principle of need-to-know is foundational to communication in the midst of active crisis management. Several stakeholders may need to be informed.

Internal Communication

- Security
- IT
- Executives
- Employees
- Board

External Communication

- Customers
- Partners

- Regulators
- Insurers
- Legal Counsel
- Media

Communication Principles

- Accuracy
- Transparency, within legal limits
- Clarity
- No speculation
- Alignment with Legal & PR Teams

Security failures can become business crises: communications must reflect that.

17.11 Backup Strategy and Data Recovery

Beyond the risk of ransomware, data can be inadvertently modified in such a way to invalidate data integrity. Data centers can go dark for any number of reasons, possibly leading to data becoming unavailable. A backup and recovery strategy becomes critical.

Backup Types

- Full
- Differential
- Incremental
- Log Backups
- Snapshot-based Backups

Backup Storage Requirements

- Encryption
- Versioning
- Air-gapped Copies
- Geographically Separate Regions

Backup Validation

- Restore Tests
- Validation of Data Consistency
- Integrity Checking
- Recovery Time Measurement

A data backup strategy without a data recovery capability is insufficient. Backups must be *usable*, not simply *present*.

17.12 Critical Vendors and Dependency Continuity

Organizations rely on vendors and business partners through the course of regular operations. That dependency introduces risk beyond the full control of the organization. Disruption to any of those vendors or business partners can lead to disruption having an unacceptable level of impact to an organization. Proper business continuity planning and disaster recovery procedures should be in place and prioritized based on criticality identified in the BIA.

BC/DR Incorporates

- SaaS Platforms
- Cloud Services

- Telecom Providers
- Payment Processors
- MSP/MSSP Dependencies

Vendor downtime for these components equates to an organization's downtime.

Controls

- Vendor Resilience Assessment
- Contractual Failover Requirements
- Alternative Vendors
- Data Export Capabilities
- Escrow for critical systems

Establishing proper and enforceable controls for dependency continuity is part of an organization's mature operational strategy.

17.13 Human Factors in BC/DR

People are critical to continuity. In moment of crisis, plans must be in place to ensure business continues to run, people may be called to action beyond the scope of their standard operational roles. This ensures business continues, but can also lead to near term burnout. The human factor can be unpredictable, resilience planning must account for as many possible scenarios as possible.

Human Resilience Includes

- Cross-training
- Succession Planning
- Temporary Staffing Plans

- Mental Fatigue Management During Crises
- Health and Safety Plans

If people are not ready, systems won't matter. People *are* the company at its core.

17.14 BC/DR Testing and Exercises

As with any process, BC and DR must be put to the test. This ensures operational readiness in moment of crisis. As such testing must be recurring and realistic.

Test Types

- Tabletop Exercises
- Simulation Exercises
- Partial Failover
- Full Failover
- SaaS Outage Drills
- Ransomware Recovery Tests
- Cloud Region Failover Tests

Evaluation Criteria

- Speed
- Accuracy
- Communication Effectiveness
- System Integrity
- Business Process Functionality

Testing ensures readiness and exposes gaps. The goal is continuous improvement and the ability to minimize RTO.

17.15 Metrics and KPIs for Resilience

To measure efficacy of BC and DR programs, it is critical to collect appropriate metrics. Leveraging these metrics enables proper communication to executive teams and boards of directors, empowering them to strategize and guide an organization toward desired outcomes.

Technical KPIs

- Backup Success Rate
- RTO/RPO Compliance
- Successful DR Test Rate
- Failover Time

Operational KPIs

- Business Continuity Readiness
- Cross-team Communication Metrics
- Staff Preparedness

Strategic KPIs

- Impact Reduction
- Resilience Posture Improvement
- Vendor Dependency Risk

These metrics support board-level resilience oversight.

17.16 Roadmap for Resilience Maturity

A maturity based approach can guide an organization from inception to full maturity, allowing for tracking of progress through use of projects and milestones.

Phase 1: Foundations

- Conduct BIA
- Document BC/DR Plans
- Define RTO/RPO

Phase 2: Architecture

- Implement Resilient Systems
- Deploy Backup Strategy
- Build Cloud DR Foundations

Phase 3: Integration

- Align SOC + IR + BC/DR
- Involve Business Units
- Define Crisis Command Structure

Phase 4: Testing

- Full DR Tests
- Ransomware Simulations
- Cloud Failover Testing

Phase 5: Continuous Resilience

- Automated Monitoring
- Risk-driven Architecture Changes
- Executive-level Reporting

17.17 Chapter Summary

BC/DR & Operational Resilience provide the architecture, processes, and leadership necessary to maintain business operations under stress. A mature resilience program is:

- Cloud-aware
- Identity-aware
- Ransomware-ready
- Vendor Risk-ready
- Risk-based
- Rigorously Tested
- Integrated with IR & SOC

This chapter establishes the enterprise resilience foundation for an organization.

Phase 4: Key Takeaways

Chapter 13: SOC Maturity and Threat Hunting

- **Proactive Identification**: Transitioning from reactive alert triage to actively searching networks for anomalies that evade automated detection.
- **Resource Optimization**: Automating access decisions frees SOC analysts to focus on complex threat hunting.

Chapter 14: Incident Response & Tabletop Exercises

- **Crisis Communications**: Tabletop exercises bridge the gap between technical response playbooks and executive strategies required during a crisis.

Chapter 15: Compliance, Audit, and Regulatory Frameworks

- **Navigating Liability**: Focuses on navigating legal liabilities and proving security efficacy to external regulatory bodies.

Chapter 16: Vendor and Third-Party Risk Management

- **Downstream Vulnerability**: advanced actors frequently exploit weaker downstream partners to compromise primary enterprise targets.
- **Non-Negotiable Skills**: Mathematically assessing and legally mitigating third-party risk is a required executive skill for modern CISOs.

Chapter 17: Business Continuity and Disaster Recovery (BCDR)

- **Operational Survivability**: Ensuring critical business processes survive and recover from catastrophic cyber or physical events.

Phase 5: Advanced Architecture and Executive Synthesis

ADVANCED IAM AND PAM

IDENTITY IS THE *NEW perimeter*, and IAM/PAM are the most strategically important controls in cybersecurity.

This chapter delivers a **full deep dive** into enterprise identity architecture, privileged access security, Zero Trust identity strategy, and protection against identity-born threats (now the dominant vector in modern attacks such as ransomware, supply chain intrusions, and cloud compromises).

This is the most technically detailed IAM/PAM chapter in this material.

18.1 Why Identity Is the Highest-Value Attack Surface

In the modern cloud based world, actions are permitted based on context, the who, what, when and how, enforced by policy. While controls around how can be relatively flexible, giving the who some leeway for executing on their responsibilities. Taking over an identity may grant attackers expansive privileges, putting entire environments at risk.

What Makes Identities Valuable

- Credentials bypass perimeter controls
- Cloud IAM Roles often allow broad privileges
- Identity Federation creates huge trust relationships
- MFA Fatigue Attacks exploit human weaknesses

- OAuth and API tokens are poorly governed
- Service Accounts rarely have lifecycle controls
- Lateral Movement is easier through identity than endpoints
- Privileged Accounts often lack real oversight

What Entices Attackers

- Immediate Access
- Persistence
- Privilege Escalation
- Cloud Access
- Data Exposure
- Ransomware Deployment Channels

Identity is the *center of Zero Trust,* as such, it must be well protected through proper governance and controls.

18.2 IAM Core Components

Identity and access management is not a single technology; it involves as well integrated set of technologies and processes enforcing proper policy. A mature enterprise IAM stack includes:

1. Identity Provider (IdP)

- SSO and MFA
- Federation Protocols
- Lifecycle Management

2. Directory Services

- On-premise and Cloud Directories
- Hybrid Identity Synchronization
- Conditional Sccess

3. Access Governance

- RBAC
- ABAC
- PBAC
- Separation of Duties

4. Privileged Access Management (PAM)

- Vaulting
- Session Management
- Credential Rotation
- Ephemeral Access

5. Identity Threat Detection

- Behavior Analytics
- Impossible Travel
- Session Anomalies
- MFA Abuse and Bypass Detection

Identity now requires continuous monitoring, not one-time authentication.

18.3 Identity Architecture for Zero Trust

Taking continuous monitoring one step further, into continuous validation, elevates Identity governance toward Zero Trust principles.

Enforcing access policy becomes critical and necessitates that validation.

1. Continuous Verification

Identity must be validated **at every access request**, not just login.

2. Least Privilege

Access is granted:

- Minimally
- Temporarily
- Contextually

3. Explicit Trust Boundaries

No implicit trust across:

- Networks
- Devices
- Cloud Accounts
- Tenants
- Applications

4. Risk-Based Access

Authorization Decisions consider:

- Service Health
- Location
- User Behavior
- Session Anomalies

Identity is the first pillar of Zero Trust, is the primary enforcement layer. It should be regarded as such.

18.4 Authentication: Modern Security Controls

Authentication methods have evolved over time. Simple passwords and pass codes, eventually paired with multi-factor practices and now include passkeys. The human element cannot be ignored; it is the first line of defense in guarding identities they are responsible for.

Passwordless Authentication

- FIDO2 / WebAuthn
- Hardware Keys
- Biometrics

MFA Requirements

- Phishing-resistant MFA
- Conditional MFA Escalation
- MFA Burning (limiting repeated MFA pushes)

Adaptive Authentication

Triggered by any unexpected factor during access.

- New Device
- New Location
- TOR Networks
- Untrusted IPs
- High-risk Session Attributes

Attackers target MFA fatigue, not MFA bypass... your program must address that, both with technology and proper cultural awareness.

18.5 Authorization Models

There are many methods of defining access policy. Some AD OUs may have access to certain resources, some attributes that span beyond specific AD OUs may have other access privileges like geographically relevant information. Establishing an overarching granular policy can provide the most comprehensive authorization model.

RBAC: Role-Based Access Control

Good for:

- Repeatable Roles
- Predictable Job Functions

Weakness:

- Role Explosion
- Static Assignments

ABAC: Attribute-Based Access Control

More dynamic:

- Device Posture
- Data Classification
- User Attributes
- Environmental Conditions

PBAC: Policy-Based Access Control

Zero Trust-aligned:

- Dynamic
- Context-aware
- Built on Robust Policies

Authorization must evolve with Zero Trust for true granular control.

18.6 Identity Lifecycle Management (ILM)

This is one of the most overlooked risks. Stale accounts, left over access and excess privileges introduce unnecessary risk. This is about identity governance.

Lifecycle Phases

1. Hire / On-boarding
2. Role Changes
3. Leave / Off-boarding
4. Emergency Access
5. Dormant Accounts

Lifecycle Controls

- Automatic Provisioning
- Automatic Deprovisioning
- HR to IAM Integration
- Access Review Automation
- Service Account Lifecycle Controls
- Privileged Access Lifecycle Enforcement

Identity drift is a leading cause of privilege escalation. Appropriate controls must be in place to limit this risk.

18.7 Service Accounts, API Keys, Machine Identities

Beyond human users, identities exist for machines, services and applications. These can outnumber human identities significantly.

Proper governance is just as required for non-human identities as it is for human identities.

Risks

- Reused API Keys
- Improper Rotation
- Long-lived Credentials
- Embedded Secrets in Code
- CI/CD Pipeline Exposure

Controls

- Secrets Vaulting
- Automatic Key Rotation
- IAM Role-Based Access
- Short-lived Credentials
- Workload Identities
- Signed Tokens

Proper controls must be in place to mitigate risk and machine identities must be governed as strictly as human identities.

18.8 Privileged Access Management

The ability to limit account privileges to a need-to-use approach, only granting appropriate privilege for accounts in appropriate context. PAM is the highest-impact identity control in any enterprise.

PAM Core Capabilities

1. Credential Vaulting
2. Session Brokering
3. Session Recording
4. Just-In-Time (JIT) Access
5. Privileged Account Discovery
6. Password Rotation
7. Break-Glass Access

Privileged Identities Include

- Domain Admins
- Cloud Admins
- Root Accounts
- Database Admins
- Application Admins
- Network/Firewall Admins
- CI/CD and DevOps Service Accounts

PAM reduces blast radius, exposure, and misuse risk. It is central to a mature access privilege program.

18.9 Just-in-Time (JIT) and Just-Enough-Privilege (JEP)

Identity privilege must be ephemeral. Impermanent privilege posture is critical to reducing risk of privilege misuse or abuse. Two approaches help with privilege control:

Just-In-Time (JIT)

- Privileges granted only when requested
- Access removed after use
- Session monitored
- Token-based ephemeral elevation

Just Enough Privilege (JEP)

- Fine-grained permissions

- Segmentation of roles
- Limited administrative scopes

Together these eliminate persistent admin accounts and help mitigate the risk of inappropriate privilege use.

18.10 Cloud Identity and Access Management

Cloud identities and on-premise identities are not created equal. Both in how they are created and managed as well as how they are used, cloud identities introduce their own risks and necessitate their own controls.

Cloud Identity Risks

- Excessive IAM Permissions
- Wildcard Privileges
- Retention of Unused Roles
- Trust Relationships between Accounts
- Overly Permissive Service Accounts

Cloud IAM Controls

- IAM Access Analyzer
- Least Privilege Policies
- Role Assumption
- Cloud-native JIT
- CSPM Platforms
- Cloud Identity Behavior Analytics

Cloud identity misconfigurations are common compromise vectors. Cloud identities must be well protected and well configured.

18.11 Federation, SSO and Trust Relationships

Single Sign-On (SSO) centralizes identity control. Providing access across multiple applications, it eases identity management as well as identity use.

Benefits

- Fewer Credentials
- Unified Auditability
- Centralized MFA Enforcement
- Better User Experience

Federation Security Requirements

- SAML/OIDC Contract Review
- Mandatory MFA for Federation
- Token Signing Key Protection
- Short Session Lifetimes
- Monitoring of Token Issuance Anomalies

Federation is a high-value target for attackers. Proper controls must be implemented to safeguard appropriate identity use.

18.12 Identity Threat Detection and Response

With the ability to monitor for policy bypass, excess privilege use and other anomalies, ITDR technologies integrate with identity providers, flow analysis and event correlation to get a continuous understanding of appropriate and inappropriate identity use, allowing SOC teams to investigate and address issues when identified.

Key Detection Areas

- Impossible Travel
- Unusual Session Lengths
- MFA Fatigue
- Token Replay
- OAuth Token Abuse
- Suppressed Logs
- Disabled Alerts
- Dormant User Access
- Anomalous Cloud IAM Actions
- Unusual Session Times

ITDR Tools

- EDR Identity Sensors
- XDR with Identity Analytics
- Identity Behavior Analytics (IBA)
- Cloud-native Anomaly Detection
- SSO-integrated Risk Scoring
- Dedicated ITDR Technologies

Identity Detection Correlation

- Endpoint Signals
- Cloud Signals
- Authentication Signals
- User Behavior
- Network Flow

Proper detection and response around identity anomalies is a part of a mature modern cybersecurity program.

18.13 Segmentation Across Components

Segmentation across the various components of an authorized action provides a granular model for access, limiting paths for attackers to compromise. Identity segmentation limits the possible blast radius.

Types of Segmentation

- Role Segmentation
- Admin Segmentation
- Environment Segmentation
- Cloud Account Segmentation
- Service Segmentation

Segmentation reduces lateral movement opportunities.

18.14 Break-Glass Access

In the case of compromised administrative identities, or lost access to identity use, the risk of losing access to an application or environment completely can be high.

Practices akin to on-premise out of band network management access must be in place for identities as well.

The break-glass access identities are the last line of access and should be the most secure identities.

Emergency Access Characteristics

- Tightly Controlled
- Short-Lived
- Logged
- Reviewed Post-Event

Break-Glass Account Characteristics

- Isolated
- Unique Credentials
- Monitored 24/7
- Hardware MFA Only
- Outside of Normal IAM Flow

These accounts protect the business but also carry risk. They must be highly protected.

18.15 Identity Governance and Administration

IGA extends IAM into governance and certification: clear lifecycle enforcement.

IGA Elements

- Access Requests and Reviews
- Birthright Provisioning

- Entitlement Analysis
- Separation of Duty Policies
- Certification Campaigns

IGA Maturity Indicators

- Automated Access Reviews
- Risk-scored Entitlements
- Delegated Workflow Approvals
- Integration with HR Systems

IGA enforces ongoing access correctness.

18.16 Identity Metrics and KPIs

To measure the efficacy of any comprehensive identity and access management program, several metrics can be used. This can ensure clear and concise communication to key strategic stakeholders, including executive teams, boards of directors and other key stakeholders.

Operational Metrics

- Dormant Accounts
- Total Privileged Accounts
- Excessive Privilege Incidents
- MFA Exceptions

Security Metrics

- Identity Drift

- Identity Risk Scores
- Number of Identities with Admin Privileges
- JIT Elevation Frequency

Governance Metrics

- Access Review Completion Rate
- Separation of Duty Violations
- Provisioning and Deprovisioning SLA Adherence

KPIs articulate the maturity of identity controls.

18.17 Roadmap for IAM and PAM Maturity

No matter where organizations are along their IAM and PAM maturity journey, they are on a path to the same destination: automated workflow, continuous monitoring and enforcing dynamic risk-based access.

Phase 1: Stabilization

- SSO/MFA Rollout
- Passwordless Evaluation and Basic Access Reviews

Phase 2: Hardening

- PAM Introduction
- Service Account Inventory
- Least Privilege Enforcement
- Cloud IAM Governance

Phase 3: Integration

- IGA Implementation
- Identity Analytics
- ITDR Deployment

Phase 4: Zero Trust Identity

- Continuous Authentication and Identity Segmentation
- Policy-based Access Control
- JIT Access

Phase 5: Optimization

- Automated Identity Workflows
- Dynamic Risk-based Access
- Adaptive Zero Trust Enforcement

Identity is a multi-year transformation. Project timelines and milestones can ensure a steady journey towards a fully mature IAM and PAM posture.

18.18 Chapter Summary

Identity security and privilege management are the foundation of Zero Trust and the highest business-impact control domain.

This chapter provides a complete architecture for:

- Modern Identity Systems
- Advanced Authentication
- Cloud IAM Governance

- PAM & JIT
- Identity Threat Detection
- IGA
- Privileged Access Lifecycle Management

This is the identity operating system of a modern organization.

Network Security and Zero-Trust Architecture

Network security has transformed from **perimeter-centric firewalls** to **identity-driven, context-aware, software-defined Zero Trust architecture (ZTA)**.

This chapter provides an end-to-end blueprint for designing, implementing, and governing modern network security within an enterprise or cloud environment.

19.1 Why Traditional Security No Longer Works

The expansion of the internet and its use for business purposes and beyond over the last 20+ years has fundamentally changed the way organizations use technology. In a world where most people have smart devices and are connected nearly 24/7, the expectation to be able to perform almost any task, at any time, from anywhere has become common place.

An 'online presence' is now a requirement for any major organization, especially those looking to grow and provide their customers and employees with flexibility.

Inevitably, a 'presence' accessible to AI agents will become a secondary requirement as adoption grows over the next several years.

Legacy Assumptions

- Trusted Internal Networks
- Untrusted External Networks
- Strong Perimeter Firewalls
- VPNs for Remote Access

Modern Realities

- Cloud-first Infrastructure
- Remote/Work-from-Anywhere Workforce
- SaaS Adoption
- Microservices and APIs
- Hybrid Identity Models
- Mobile and Unmanaged Devices
- IoT and OT Networks

Attackers no longer "break in," they **log in**, move laterally, escalate privileges, and exfiltrate data using trusted pathways.

Zero Trust solves this by eliminating implicit trust.

19.2 Principles of Zero Trust Network Architecture

Network design built around enforcing Zero Trust principles through integrated technologies is the heart of Zero Trust Network Architecture:

1. Never Trust, Always Verify

It is important to understand what is happening in the environment in as close to real time as possible.

Every packet, identity, device, and session must be validated continuously.

2. Assume Breach

Architect the network so that:

- Compromise is contained
- Lateral movement is limited
- Blast radius is minimized

3. Identity Is the New Perimeter

Network access must tie back to:

- User Identity
- Device Identity
- Risk Posture
- Privilege Level
- Data Classification

4. Microsegmentation

Workloads, users, and applications are isolated at the smallest possible boundary.

5. Continuous Authorization

Authorization decisions must be dynamic based on:

- Device Posture
- User Behavior
- Network Context
- Real-time Risk Scoring

6. Strong Policy Enforcement

Policies must follow:

- User
- Device
- Application
- Data

ZTA is not a "network project," nor is it a specific "network design" ... it is a **business, architecture, and identity initiative**.

19.3 Security Architecture in a Zero Trust World

In alignment to ZTNA principles, technologies integrate to provide controls ensuring enforcement capabilities. Secure configuration for each technology involved is critical.

Identity-Based Access

- SSO, MFA, Federation
- Per-request Authorization
- Just-in-Time Access

Microsegmented Networks

- User-to-App Segmentation
- Workload-to-Workload Segmentation
- Segmentation across VPCs, VNets, VNET Peering, etc.

Software-Defined Networking (SDN)

- Policy-driven
- API-driven
- Decoupled from physical appliances

Secure Access Service Edge (SASE)

- Secure Web Gateway, SWG
- Cloud Access Security Broker, CASB
- Firewall as a Service, FWaaS
- Software Defined WAN, SD-WAN

Secure Service Edge (SSE) for SaaS/Cloud

- Identity-aware Proxies
- DLP
- TLS Interception
- SaaS Access Governance

Cloud-Native Security Controls

- Security Groups
- IaaS Firewall Rules
- Microsegmented Containerization

Network security is now a **logical control plane**, not a physical perimeter.

19.4 Microsegmentation

Microsegmentation is foundational to Zero Trust Architecture. It is a design principle founded on the concept of granular access control.

Segmentation Types

User-to-App Segmentation

Users see only the applications they are authorized to access.

App-to-App Segmentation

Restrict services by:

- Identity
- Workload type
- Environment (prod/dev/test)
- Function

Device Segmentation

Network access based on device posture:

- Managed vs Unmanaged
- EDR Presence
- OS Version
- Patch Compliance

Network Microperimeters

Logical barriers around:

- Critical Assets
- Critical Business Data
- OT Environments
- Regulated Systems

Segmentation is the backbone of Zero Trust, providing controls that can stop lateral movement, reduce blast radius and enforce least privilege.

19.5 Network Detection and Response (NDR)

Network Detection and Response processes and technologies monitor traffic to identify anomalous patterns, assess their risk and respond to them. NDR is a key pillar of a comprehensive detection strategy.

Common Modern NDR Detections

- Lateral Movement
- Encrypted Malicious Traffic
- Beaconing Patterns

- Anomalous Commands
- Insider Threat Movements
- Data exfiltration

NDR Capabilities

- Deep Packet Inspection (DPI)
- Behavior-based Analytics
- Encrypted Traffic Metadata Analysis
- ML-driven Anomaly Detection

NDR is the complement to EDR and SIEM, forming a strong trifecta of detection capabilities.

19.6 Firewall Modernization

Legacy firewalls have capabilities designed around legacy perimeter focused security and cannot address modern threats and enforce Zero Trust alone.

Enhanced capabilities are necessary as part of a modern Zero Trust ready security architecture.

Next-Generation Firewalls (NGFW) Features

- Application-layer Filtering
- Behavior Analytics
- TLS proxy
- User Identity Enforcement
- Automated Policy Orchestration

Firewall Policy Modernization

- Tighten outbound internet access
- Enforce identity-based rules
- Create microperimeters around critical resources

Firewalls remain a necessary component of network security, but they must be part of a broader ZTA design.

19.7 Secure Access and ZTNA vs VPN

Remote access approaches have changed over time.

VPN once provided users access to network resources and protective measures, also introducing risk to the target network from the accessing endpoint. VPN is legacy technology.

Problems with VPN

- Full network exposure
- High lateral movement risk
- Inconsistent MFA requirements
- No continuous authorization
- Poor device posture checks

ZTNA is the modern replacement for VPN. As an access model that enforces Zero Trust principles, ZTNA eliminates risks introduced by traditional VPN access.

ZTNA Advantages

- App-level Access
- Identity and Device-based Access

- Real-time Risk Scoring
- No Network-level Exposure
- Integrates with SASE/SSE

By adopting a ZTNA access model and transitioning away from traditional VPN remote access technologies, organizations reduce risk while allowing for continuous access privilege validation.

19.8 Cloud Network Security

Cloud networks require different controls than on-premise environments. Requiring configuration, alternative design and identity considerations, appropriate control design helps reduce risk to cloud specific threats.

Cloud Control Layers

- IAM-based Network Access
- VPC Segmentation
- Security Groups and NACLs
- Service Endpoints
- Private Links
- Firewall as a Service, FWaaS
- Cloud-native WAF

Cloud-Specific Threats

- Overly permissive security groups
- Misconfigured VPC Peering
- Exposed Management APIs

- Serverless Functions exposed publicly
- API Gateway misconfiguration

Cloud networks require **identity-first** access and minimal exposure.

19.9 API and Application Network Security

Modern application design has evolved from use of various application layer protocols to a set of common ones, reducing the risk introduced through excessive firewall allow rules through required transport layer ports.

APIs are now the dominant communication layer.

Required Controls

- API Gateway Enforcement
- Rate Limiting
- OAuth/OIDC Token Validation
- JWT Signing
- mTLS between Services

API Threats

- Token Replay
- Data Exfiltration
- Injection
- Privilege Escalation
- Insecure Direct Object References (IDOR)

As the API pathways now serve most communication, they must be treated as high-value network pathways, with controls implemented as such.

19.10 OT / ICS and Critical Infrastructure Network Security

Operational Technology and Industrial Control Systems are technologies used within critical infrastructure for manufacturing and industrial environments. These blend the digital and physical worlds, necessitating their own security considerations.

Risks

- Unpatchable Systems
- Proprietary Protocols
- Flat Networks
- Vendor-managed Equipment

Controls

- Segmentation from IT Systems
- Unidirectional Gateways (data diodes)
- Strict Vendor Access Controls
- Anomaly Detection on OT protocols

OT should follow Zero Trust applied through isolation, monitoring and other controls, while also needing proper segmentation from traditional IT environments.

19.11 DNS Security

Domain Name Service is the phone book for accessing networked resources. Like many technologies, it can be used for unintended purposes such as tunneling other data or redirecting traffic to unintended destinations. It is important to implement proper controls around DNS in order to limit the risk of unauthorized modification or unintended communications:

- Domain Categorization
- Blocking High-risk TLDs
- DNSSEC
- DNS Query Logging
- Detection of DNS Exfiltration or Malicious Zone transfer

DNS safeguards are important for limiting risk and DNS telemetry is invaluable for threat hunting.

19.12 DDoS Protection and Resilience

One of the core principles of the CIA triad is availability. Any disruption to availability of resources can have significant business impact and cause reputation damage. Denial of Service attacks can focus around exhausting resources to a point of making them unavailable, while distributed approaches use distributed sources so as to increase scale and make detection and mitigation more difficult. Comprehensive DDoS prevention may not be guaranteed, but with proper defensive measures, the risk may be significantly reduced:

- Cloud-based DDoS Mitigation
- Rate-limiting
- CDN-based Absorption
- WAF Integration

DDoS is not only a network threat; it impacts availability KPIs and business reputation.

19.13 Network Threat Hunting

Threat hunting thrives on scenario driven models with likelihood and impact ratings for prioritization. While some methodologies focus on endpoint-based signals, it is important to also monitor network traffic for signs of traffic indicating successful compromise:

- Lateral Movement
- Command and Control (C2)
- Encrypted Traffic Anomalies
- Unusual Port/Protocol Combinations
- Unauthorized Internal Scanning

NDR and SIEM integration along with strong threat intelligence data enrichment power threat informed hunting.

19.14 Network Security Metrics and KPIs

To properly assess the efficacy of a Zero Trust enforcing network security program, it is critical to collect metrics that enable clear and concise understanding of security posture with the ability to communicate that posture to executive teams, boards of directors and security steering committees.

These metrics also provide SOC leadership with the information it needs to adjust and improve posture over time.

Operational KPIs

- Blocked Malicious Traffic
- Segmentation Coverage
- Firewall Rule Review Cycles
- ZTNA Adoption Rates

Risk KPIs

- Number of Critical Exposed Services
- Unauthorized Lateral Movement Attempts
- Cloud Misconfiguration Findings

Zero Trust KPIs

- Percentage of Applications behind ZTNA
- Percentage of Users with Identity-based Network Access
- Segmentation Completeness

These KPIs track measurable security posture improvement and can help provide clear messaging to key leadership stakeholders.

19.15 Roadmap for Network and ZTA Maturity

Regardless of where an organization sits on their ZTA journey, it is beneficial to define goals, projects, timelines and milestones to be successful.

Phase 1: Assessment

- Map Network Assets
- Identify Crown Jewels
- Evaluate Segmentation Gaps

Phase 2: Quick Wins

- ZTNA Replacing VPN
- Identity-based Firewall Rules
- Secure internet Access Rollout

Phase 3: Segmentation

- Microsegmentation of Critical Assets
- Prod and Dev Environment Isolation
- SaaS Access via SSE

Phase 4: Network Modernization

- SD-WAN
- SASE/SSE rollout
- NDR integration

Phase 5: Full Zero Trust Architecture

- Per-request Authorization
- Continuous Evaluation
- Dynamic Risk Enforcement

Network evolves into an *identity*-driven service.

19.16 Chapter Summary

Network security is no longer defined by borders or perimeters. Modern environments necessitate more context and more granular controls.

Network security is defined by:

- Identity
- Context
- Software-defined Policies
- Microsegmentation
- Continuous Verification
- Zero Trust Principles
- Cloud-native Controls
- Traffic Behavior Analytics

This chapter provides a blueprint for network modernization and Zero Trust adoption in the enterprise.

Governance, Risk Management and Executive Leadership

Governance, Risk Management, and Executive Security Leadership (GRC + ESL) form the **operating system** for building, scaling, and leading a cybersecurity program.

This chapter covers the **strategic, organizational, and executive-level** responsibilities of the CISO, including:

- Governance Architecture and Risk Frameworks
- Policy Development
- Organizational Roles
- Executive Communication
- Board-level Reporting
- Strategic Planning
- Culture Building
- Security Financial Management

This chapter prepares CISOs to operate at the executive table.

20.1 The CISO's Role in Governance

The CISO role has been in place since the mid 1990s and initially focused on technical elements: software and hardware. Since that time, the role has evolved and responsibilities have grown, incorporating organization-wide governance, risk management and business objectives.

CISO Responsibilities

1. Clear decision-making authority
2. Formal processes for evaluating cybersecurity risk
3. Policies and standards
4. Cross-functional alignment
5. Board transparency and accountability

Governance is not documentation... it is the *decision-making framework* of the security program.

Governance Responsibilities

- Establish the security charter
- Define roles and responsibilities
- Approve policies and standards
- Oversee third-party risk
- Lead the cyber risk committee
- Report cyber posture to the board

A CISO must build governance that is **repeatable, defensible, and scalable,** while leading an organization's security through strategy and key stakeholder buy in.

20.2 Cyber Governance Operating Model

A full governance model incorporates several teams, each with their own responsibilities, all aligning to an organization's north star.

The stakeholders involved have varying roles within the organization and all contribute to its overall operational success.

1. Executive Steering Committee

A CISO bridges the gap between the Executive Steering Committee and IT.

Membership

- CEO
- CIO
- CISO
- GC (Legal)
- CFO
- COO

Responsibilities

- Approve investment decisions
- Resolve cross-functional blockers
- Prioritize enterprise risk reduction

2. Cyber Risk Committee

A CISO understands the business direction, the risk the business accepts, and the strategies in play to protect the organization.

Membership

- IT Leadership
- GRC
- IR/SOC
- Architecture
- Data Governance and Privacy

Responsibilities

- Manage Cyber Risks
- Oversee Controls
- Evaluate Metrics
- Approve Exceptions

3. Working Groups

- IAM
- Cloud, Application and Network Security
- Application Security
- BC/DR
- Compliance and Governance

Governance is an ecosystem of coordinated teams defining strategy, allocating budget, implementing technology and process, and monitoring and responding to risk while working to meet business objectives.

20.3 Policy Framework and Standards

Policies define rules of business operations, strategic approaches to running and maintaining an organization; the 'what' and 'why.' Standards specify minimum requirements to align toward those policies. Procedures define step by step methods for meeting the standards. Guidelines provide recommended guardrails within which to operate.

Policy Hierarchy

1. **Policy:** Senior-level Requirements
2. **Standard:** Technical Requirements
3. **Procedure:** Step-by-step Processes
4. **Guidelines:** Best Practices

Key Policies

- Information Security
- Acceptable Use
- Identity and Access Management
- Incident Response
- Change Management
- Vendor Risk

- Data Governance
- Cloud Security
- Application Security
- Logging and Monitoring

Policies Characteristics

- Business-friendly
- Outcomes-oriented
- Technology-neutral
- Enforceable

A well-documented body of policy and supporting components ensure strategic alignment and desired business outcomes.

20.4 Enterprise Risk Management

Cybersecurity is only one element of a comprehensive Enterprise Risk Management program and must be well integrated into that ERM.

Cyber Risk Categories

- Operational Risk
- Compliance Risk
- Reputational Risk
- Financial Risk
- Strategic Risk

Risk Components

- Threat
- Vulnerability
- Impact
- Likelihood
- Control maturity

Risk Register Assets

- Risk description
- Owner
- Controls
- Business Impact
- Likelihood
- Residual Risk
- Mitigation Plan

Technical controls are implemented to address cyber risk. Cyber risk is assessed and communicated in *business* context.

20.5 Risk Quantification: FAIR and Beyond

Transitioning from qualitative to quantitative risk analysis enables a repeatable and objective rating based on a common set of variables. Enterprises increasingly use risk quantification to prioritize investments. The Factor Analysis of Information Risk, FAIR framework[1] from the FAIR Institute provides a well-rounded framework for assessing risk with a quantitative approach.

Open FAIR is the open and vendor neutral standard based on the original FAIR framework.

Open FAIR Framework: Risk Taxonomy and Risk Analysis

- Model risk in financial terms
- Calculate probable loss
- Support investment decisions
- Enable cost-benefit analysis

Benefits of Quantification

- Improves communication with CFO
- Supports budget requests
- Aligns risk language with business leaders

Quantification turns cybersecurity into a **finance-aligned** function in support of overall business objectives.

20.6 Security Strategy and Roadmap Development

An organization's security strategy must align to overall business objectives.

Security Strategy Components

- Business Strategy
- Digital Transformation
- Regulatory Requirements
- Risk Tolerance
- Technology Evolution

A roadmap evolves over time and must be **value-driven**, not just "project-driven."

Roadmap Components

- Foundational and Zero-Trust Initiatives
- Cloud Transformation
- Data Governance
- SOC Modernization
- Automation and AI Integration
- Staffing and Headcount Planning

20.7 Organizational Design for Security Leadership

Core Functions

1. **Governance, Risk and Compliance (GRC)**: Policy, compliance, audit, VRM.
2. **Security Engineering and Architecture**: Identity, cloud, network, application, data.
3. **Security Operations**: SOC, IR, threat intel, threat hunting.
4. **Product Security (AppSec)**: SSDLC, bug triage, supply chain, DevSecOps.
5. **Privacy and Data Protection**: DPO, privacy, data classification.
6. **Business Security Officers (BSOs)**: Embedded liaisons within business units.
7. **Program Management**: PMO support for security transformation.

Security functions may originate as additions to traditional roles, as the organization grows, those functions become roles in and of themselves. Organizational design must reflect maturity and business needs.

20.8 Executive Communication and Storytelling

CISOs bridge the gap between technical and non-technical communication of security and risk, translating issues into business impact narratives.

Best Practices

- Lead with risk, not technology
- Frame issues in revenue, operations, reputation
- Use metrics appropriate for executives
- Avoid acronyms unless necessary
- Provide concise, outcome-driven recommendations

Executives want concise clarity, not detail.

20.9 Board Reporting and Oversight

Often the highest level of strategic direction for organizations, boards are increasingly accountable for cyber oversight. This oversight is a core governance priority.

Board Reporting Inclusions

- Enterprise Risk Posture
- Major Initiatives
- Incident Trends
- SOC Maturity
- Compliance and Audit Results

- Vendor Risk
- Zero Trust Progress
- Staffing and Retention
- Budget Status
- Upcoming Regulatory Changes

Do Not Include

- Alert Counts
- Raw Technical Data
- Tool-specific Explanations

The right information in the right format enables boards to make strategic decisions. Boards care about **risk, exposure, and readiness**.

20.10 Crisis Leadership and Executive Decisions

Central to crisis management is a calm posture, an ability to communicate and coordinate, and when needed, the authority to make critical decisions.

CISO Required Traits

- A Clear Communicator
- A Calm Decision-maker
- A Trusted Advisor
- An Interpreter of Technical risk
- A Tactical and Strategic Leader

Crisis Leadership Responsibilities

- Guide the CEO
- Coordinate with Legal
- Support communications
- Drive containment strategy
- Manage internal teams
- Advise on disclosure decisions

Often serving as an advisory role in normal operations in conjunction with other responsibilities, CISOs take on more advisory responsibilities in moments of crisis. They must clearly communicate options, risks and possible outcomes to executive teams while making decisions that impact crisis timelines and business outcomes.

Leadership under pressure is a core CISO competency.

20.11 Regulatory and Legal Engagement

As the primary risk and governance stakeholder, the CISO maintains relationships with various functions across an organization and third parties:

- Regulators
- Auditors
- Legal Counsel
- Privacy Officers
- Insurance Investigators

Responsibilities

- Accurate and Timely Reporting
- Regulatory Alignment

- Audit Response Governance
- Legal Defensibility

Cybersecurity is increasingly governed by law, with new legislation proposed and coming into effect every year across the globe.

20.12 Metrics and KPIs for Executive Leadership

Operational Metrics

- Detection and Response Times
- Vulnerability Remediation SLAs
- IAM Coverage
- Logging and Monitoring Completeness

Risk Metrics

- Enterprise Risk Heatmap
- Changes in Residual Risk
- Exceptions Inventory

Strategic Metrics

- Zero Trust Maturity
- Security Roadmap Progress
- Staffing and Skill Coverage
- Compliance Posture

Metrics measure program efficacy and power executive trust.

20.13 Financial Management for CISOs

The role of a CISO goes beyond technical acumen. It incorporates standard business operations requirements and enterprise risk management background into a unified practice.

CISOs must master:

- Budgeting and Forecasting
- Capital vs Operational Spend
- Contract Negotiation
- Licensing Strategies
- Optimization of Vendor Overlap
- Cost-benefit Analysis

Cybersecurity is a **capital-intensive business function** with focus on limiting risk to business operations.

20.14 Culture, Behavior and Change Management

Security is everyone's responsibility. Security culture is the multiplier that determines program success. Leadership sets the example and the rest of the organization follows. Culture cannot be delegated... it must be led.

Culture Levers

- Leadership Modeling
- Incentives and Accountability
- Awareness Programs
- Embedded Security Champions
- Positive Reinforcement

20.15 Roadmap for GRC + Executive Leadership

Often enterprise and business skills are acquired over time as new roles are taken and new responsibilities are assigned.

Phase 1: Foundation

- Policies and Risk Register
- Governance Structure

Phase 2: Maturity

- Enterprise Risk Integration
- Board Reporting
- Data-driven Metrics

Phase 3: Leadership

- Strategic Security Roadmap
- Executive Communication Cadence
- Cross-functional Alignment

Phase 4: Optimization

- Risk Quantification
- Cyber-financial Modeling
- Continuous Governance Automation

This roadmap transforms a technical leader into an executive.

20.16 CISO Roadmap for Executive Leadership Functional Transition

Executive career trajectories may be specialized, but as an organization evolves, executives may find themselves jumping into security roles, for a quick level set:

Phase 1: Foundation

- Security Literacy and Risk Basics
- Governance Foundations

Phase 2: Maturity

- IAM and Cloud Basics
- IR Leadership and Compliance Literacy

Phase 3: Leadership

- Road-mapping
- Cross-functional Leadership
- Board Communications

Phase 4: Optimization

- Cyber-financial Modeling
- Strategic Decision Making
- Governance Automation

This roadmap transforms an executive into a security ready executive.

20.17 Chapter Summary

Governance and risk management are the backbone of a modern cybersecurity program. Executive leadership transforms technical controls into **business outcomes**.

This chapter equips CISOs with the frameworks, communication models, risk processes, and leadership practices needed to operate effectively at the highest levels of the organization.

Security Metrics Reporting and Executive Dashboards

Security metrics and reporting are the *communication engine* of a cybersecurity program. Security leadership's ability to influence executives, secure budget, demonstrate progress, and justify strategic investments depends entirely on:

- Clarity of the metrics
- Narrative behind those metrics
- Alignment with business outcomes
- Mapping to risk and resilience

This chapter provides the full framework for building **security leadership ready, board-ready, and engineering-ready** security metrics and dashboards.

21.1 What Makes a Good Security Metric?

Not all metrics are created equal. The wrong data, incomplete data, or the right data with the wrong story can lead to sub-optimal decision making at all levels.

Metrics are tracked over time to assess the impact of past decisions, and thus influence decisions moving forward, ensuring they align with the strategic vision for the overarching organization.

Metric Qualifiers

1. **Accuracy**: Based on high-confidence data, not estimates.
2. **Repeatability**: Same calculation, every time.
3. **Understandability**: Executives quickly grasp the meaning.
4. **Business-Alignment**: Connects to revenue, operations, risk, or resilience.
5. **Actionability**: Leads to decision-making or prioritization.
6. **Behavior-Driving**: Encourages the right organizational actions.
7. **Comparative**: Shows trends over time, not snapshots.

Bad security metrics create confusion and can lead to poor decisions. Good metrics create *credibility*.

21.2 Categories of Security Metrics

Metrics are gathered from all elements of an enterprise cybersecurity and risk management program. Your reporting framework should cover the following categories:

Operational Metrics (SOC, IR, Vulnerability, IAM)

Measuring the efficacy of security operations is important and helps understand defensive posture.

Examples

- Mean Time to Detect (MTTD)
- Mean Time to Respond (MTTR)
- Number of Critical Vulnerabilities Overdue
- Patching Compliance Rate
- Phishing Failure Rate

- Number of Identity Anomalies Detected

- Percentage of Logs ingested into SIEM

Operational metrics show **how well security is functioning**.

Risk Metrics (Enterprise Risk, Attack Surface)

With an established risk appetite, it is important to collect appropriate metrics to understand an organization's posture as compared to the acceptable risk.

Examples

- Risk Heatmap and Trends

- Business-critical Asset Exposure

- Number of High-risk Exceptions

- External Attack Surface Risk Score

- Supply Chain Risk Index

- Crown Jewel Protection Score

Risk metrics show **enterprise exposure** and **risk reduction trends.**

Strategic Metrics (Roadmap, Transformation, ZT)

As transformation programs progress over time, the capability to assess their trend toward completion is critical. These measurements allow for strategic re-alignment, prioritization and budget allocation.

Examples

- Zero Trust Maturity Score

- Security Roadmap Progress

- Identity Modernization Progress

- SOC Modernization Completion

- Cloud Security Guardrail Adoption

Strategic metrics show the **direction and momentum** of programs.

Compliance and Audit Metrics

With accountability to external certifying parties, compliance and audit metrics measure alignment with industry, contractual or regulatory requirements. The risk of not meeting these requirements can be financial and legal.

Examples

- Audit Findings by Severity
- SOC 2 / ISO Control Coverage
- Evidence Collection Completeness
- Vendor Risk Assessment Completion Rate
- Access Review Completion Rate

Compliance metrics show **adherence to external standards**.

Business Impact Metrics

In order for executive teams and boards to make strategic decisions, they must understand the impact of their security programs through metrics.

Examples:

- Reduction in Downtime
- Avoided Losses from prevented incidents
- Quantified Financial Risk Reduction
- Cost per Incident

Business impact metrics show **true enterprise value**.

21.3 Role-Based Reporting

The need to understand current standpoint and trends over time is not limited to executive leadership and boards of directors.

Metrics help other stakeholders identify areas for improvement and where efforts are trending in the right direction; and implement strategic adjustments in effort.

Metrics must be tailored for each audience.

Board of Directors

Taking a look at the *big picture* requires the greatest understanding with concise and clear information.

Board Priorities

- Risk
- Exposure
- Resilience
- Compliance
- Material Incident Trends
- Strategic Investment Needs

Board Metrics

- Enterprise Risk Heatmap
- Zero Trust Progress
- Incident Trends (high-level)
- Cyber Insurance Coverage
- Critical Vendor Risk
- BC/DR Readiness

Boards want concise clarity, no noise.

Executive Leadership (CEO, CFO, COO)

The ability to guide an organization's operations in a cost-efficient way while strategically adjusting business objectives with security in mind necessitates appropriate risk context.

Executives Priorities

- Business Disruption
- Risk to Revenue
- Cost Optimization
- Customer Trust
- Regulatory Risk

Executive Metrics

- Quantified Financial Exposure
- High-risk Vulnerabilities on Critical Systems
- Regulatory Compliance Status
- Staffing and Skill Gaps
- Security Transformation Progress

Executives need metrics that connect to business value.

IT Leadership

The efficacy of an IT department's efforts, at a high level, is measured by quantifying IT based disruption to business operations.

IT leadership focuses on limiting the likelihood of IT related outages and unauthorized access.

IT Leadership Priorities

- Operational Performance
- System Stability
- Remediation Workloads

IT Metrics

- Patching SLAs
- System Hardening Trends
- Audit Findings by IT Owner
- CI/CD Security Gate Failures

These metrics drive operational improvement.

Security Leadership

Security leadership must understand the defensive posture they provide an organization.

The ability to assess the delta between what is considered *normal* behavior and what is *active* behavior is critical. Security priorities are fairly narrowly defined, but span a vast landscape of responsibilities.

Security Leadership Priorities

- Rich Operational Data
- Detection Engineering Metrics
- IR Performance
- Threat Intel Alignment

Security Metrics

- Detection Coverage by ATT&CK
- SOC Efficiency
- Identity Anomalies
- Cloud Misconfiguration Trends

Security leaders need deep visibility.

Engineering and DevOps

Security by design. Integrating secure practices in application development helps limit risk. Metrics allow an understanding of these secure practices and trending over time.

Engineering Priorities

- Code Security Metrics
- Pipeline Failures
- Dependency Vulnerabilities

AppSec Metrics

- SAST/DAST Pass Rates
- Dependency Vulnerability Age
- Code Review Security Defects
- Insecure Library Removal Rate

AppSec metrics must integrate with DevOps workflows.

21.4 CISO Dashboard Design Principles

A paragraph of text can provide detail and context. A paragraph of text takes time and effort to digest. The same detail and context can be expressed through visual figures, enabling rapid understanding, which can be extremely useful when needing to digest several bodies of data in a short time frame.

Dashboard Characteristics

1. **Simple**: No more than 12 to 18 primary KPIs.
2. **Visual**: Graphs, charts, heatmaps. No walls of text.
3. **Trend-Focused**: Executives care about direction, not details.
4. **Risk-Aligned**: Each KPI mapped to one of the following.
    a. Strategic Risk
    b. Operational Risk
    c. Compliance Risk
    d. Financial Risk
5. **Outcome-Focused**: Metrics must track results, not activities.
6. **Automated**: Manual dashboards fail within weeks.

21.5 KPIs by Domain

The right data is critical for properly communicating security posture:

SOC and Detection KPIs

- MTTD
- MTTR
- Percent of Alerts Auto-Triaged

- ATT&CK Detection Coverage
- False Positive Rate
- Automation Utilization

Identity KPIs

- MFA Adoption Rate
- Passwordless Rollout Progress
- Privileged Account Reduction
- Service Account Governance Score
- Identity Anomaly Detection Rate
- JIT Adoption

Cloud Security KPIs

- Number of Critical Misconfigurations
- CSPM Risk Score
- Unused High-risk Permissions
- Multi-region Resilience Validation

Vulnerability Management KPIs

- Critical Vulnerability SLA Compliance
- Vulnerability Age on Crown Jewels
- Patch Completeness and Exception Rates
- Attack Surface Reduction Score

AppSec KPIs

- SAST/DAST Coverage
- Number of Critical Findings per Release
- Supply Chain Vulnerability Exposure
- API Security Pass Rate

Data Security KPIs

- DLP Events per Category
- Sensitive Data Store Inventory Accuracy
- Encryption Coverage
- Anomalous Data Access

Third-Party/Vendor Risk KPIs

- Vendor Assessment Completion Rate
- High-risk Vendor Count
- SSPM Risk Score
- Supply Chain Exposure Index

Compliance KPIs

- Audit Findings and Policy Alignment Score
- Evidence Collection SLA
- Control Completeness Score

21.6 Security Scorecards

Regular review of security posture trends is important. Frequency of these reviews can vary based on the audience role and function. The use of security scorecards provides an easy to digest visual representation that enables their audience to get the necessary context for their role so as to align activities toward desired outcomes.

Scorecards Purposes

- Monthly IT Leadership Reviews
- Quarterly Board Updates
- Annual Audit Cycles
- Vendor Performance Management

Scorecard Structure

- KPI
- Measurement
- Trend
- Owner
- Risk Rating
- Action Plan

Scorecards convert complex security posture into actionable insights.

21.7 Cyber Risk Heatmaps

Heat maps are an efficient visual representation of data allowing for rapid understanding of context.

Mature Risk Heatmap Components

- Impact (financial/regulatory/operational)
- Likelihood
- Control Maturity
- Velocity of Impact
- Mitigation Plan

Heatmaps are essential for executive and board reporting.

21.8 Reporting Cadence

Reporting frequency varies based on audience. The closer to operational activities the audience is, the more frequent the cadence of reporting. Below is a sample cadence structure.

Daily

- SOC Metrics
- Incident Updates
- Detection Anomalies

Weekly

- Engineering Leadership Updates
- Cloud and Identity Posture Review

Monthly

- Executive Steering Committee Scorecard

Quarterly

- Board Reporting
- Risk Heatmaps
- Roadmap Updates

Annually

- Budget Planning
- Strategy Review
- Multi-year Roadmap Refresh

Cadence drives security alignment with the business.

21.9 Risk Narrative and Storytelling

Metrics alone are just data. Placing these numbers into context through proper narrative ensures they empower strategic decision making and next steps. Metrics must be paired with narrative.

The Goals of a Good Narrative

- Explains Context
- Identifies Trends
- Recommends Action
- Outlines ROI
- Anticipates Questions

Executives invest when they understand *why* something matters.

21.10 Common Metric Pitfalls

While there are data to be collected, they may not be data of value. As the saying goes "just because you can, doesn't mean you should." Inclusion of superfluous metrics creates noise and can introduce confusion.

Avoid:

- Vanity Metrics (alert counts)
- Meaningless Metrics (blocked attacks)
- Data Overload and Technical Jargon
- Manual Metric Collection
- Inconsistent Reporting

Metrics must enhance clarity, not create confusion.

21.11 Roadmap for Metrics Maturity

A mature security metrics program is well defined, risk oriented and automated where possible. A sample roadmap toward maturity is detailed below.

Phase 1: Establish

- Define KPIs
- Automate Data Sources
- Build Dashboards

Phase 2: Mature

- Integrate Risk Scoring
- Connect KPIs to Business Outcomes
- Improve Data Quality

Phase 3: Advance

- Predictive Analytics
- AI-driven Insights
- Automated Board Reporting

Metrics maturity accelerates security maturity.

21.12 Chapter Summary

Security metrics and reporting are not about numbers; they are about **influence, clarity, and trust**.

A mature organization uses metrics to:

- Communicate Risk
- Justify Investment
- Track Progress
- Maintain Executive Alignment
- Strengthen Governance
- Inform Strategy

This chapter provides a blueprint for building a data-driven, executive-ready security reporting engine.

Architecture, Engineering, and Platform Security

Security Architecture and Platform Security define *how* technology environments are built, integrated, secured, and operated.

This is the discipline that ensures security is:

- Embedded in infrastructure
- Standardized across platforms
- Enforceable through policy-as-code
- Aligned with Zero Trust principles
- Validated through continuous engineering

This chapter delivers a blueprint for designing and governing secure systems across on-premise, cloud, hybrid, SaaS, and distributed architectures.

22.1 The Role of Security Architecture

Taking security strategy and converting that into practical implementation is the backbone of security architecture.

It's translating the direction into technical design engineers can work with:

- Technical Controls
- Implementation Patterns
- Cloud-native Guardrails
- Platform Standards
- Engineering Requirements
- Secure-by-Default Configurations

The ability to take these considerations in context of business operations and outcomes is a security specialization underlying the role of a Security Architect:

- Designing secure network and cloud architectures
- Evaluating new technologies
- Defining guardrails and patterns
- Resolving design conflicts
- Ensuring scalability and resilience
- Advising on trade-offs between risk and usability

Architecture is where theory becomes implementation.

22.2 Architecture Domains - Enterprise-Scope

Security architecture is expansive in scope and considers elements of infrastructure implementation, application design, data protection and incident response:

- Identity Architecture
- Cloud Architecture
- Network and Zero Trust Architecture
- Application Architecture
- Data Protection and Governance Architecture

- Container and Kubernetes Architecture
- Endpoint and Mobile Architecture
- API and Integration Architecture
- Logging and Observability Architecture
- Resilience and HA Architecture

Security architecture must be cross-disciplinary and integrated.

22.3 Zero Trust Architecture Patterns

Zero Trust principles inform enforcement capable architectures, as such, Zero Trust is an embedded design principle, not an afterthought.

Key Architectural Patterns

Identity-Centric Access

- Least Privilege
- Continuous Validation
- Device Posture Enforcement

Microsegmentation

- App-to-App
- User-to-App
- Workload Isolation

Cloud-Native Gateways

- API Gateways
- Identity-aware Proxies
- Service Mesh Enforcement

Policy-as-Code

- Automated Guardrails
- IaC Scanning
- Compliance-as-Code

Data-Centric Security

- Tokenization
- DLP Policy Engines
- Encryption Key Management

Zero Trust Architecture defines the target state for modern environments.

22.4 Cloud Architecture & Platform Security

In a modern architecture world, secure architectural challenges introduced by cloud use must be outweighed by the business outcome opportunities, lest excessive risk be tolerated. Compounding risk are the latest premier models from leading AI providers that are accelerating the rate of recon, reverse engineering, and automated compromise attempts.

Core Cloud Security Architecture Principles

Shared Responsibility

Cloud providers secure infrastructure; customers secure configurations and data.

Secure Landing Zones

- Network Guardrails
- Identity Guardrails
- Logging Baselines
- Security Tooling Integration

Multi-Account or Multi-Subscription Structure

- Isolation of Environments
- Blast Radius Reduction
- Clearer Governance

Infrastructure as Code (IaC)

- Immutable Infrastructure
- Version Control
- Standardized Security

Cloud-Native Security Controls

- Policies
- Monitoring Tools

Cloud architecture must embed security into provisioning and operations.

22.5 Platform Security Fundamentals

The underlying set of common systems and services form the platforms upon which applications are built and communication occurs. Securing these systems is the function of platform security.

Components to Consider

- Operating Systems
- Cloud VMs and Serverless Functions
- Container Runtimes
- Databases
- CI/CD Systems
- Messaging Queues

Platform Security Controls

- OS & Kernel Hardening
- Secure Configurations
- Managed Identities
- Patch Automation
- Network Restrictions
- Encryption Enforcement
- Monitoring Baseline

Platforms must be **secure by default, difficult to misuse, and sufficiently monitored**.

22.6 Hardening and Secure Configuration

Much like traditional OS hardening processes have enabled successful use of endpoints by corporate personnel, infrastructure hardening enables successful and secure use of resources. Several hardening strategies and guidelines can be used in the course of full infrastructure hardening.

Secure Baseline Components

- CIS Benchmarks
- Security Technical Implementation Guides
- Vendor Templates
- Hardened Images
- Secure Docker Base Images

Baseline Controls

- Disable unnecessary services
- Enforce logging and auditing
- Restrict outbound internet access
- Disable legacy protocols
- Enforce least privilege on system-level accounts

Hardening reduces attack surface across all environments.

22.7 Kubernetes and Container Security Architecture

Modern workloads rely on containers. Securing those containers is foundational to limiting risk of unauthorized use and compromise.

Container Security

- Minimal Base Images
- Vulnerability Scanning
- Secrets Management
- Non-root Execution
- Signing Images

Kubernetes Security

- RBAC Enforcement
- Network Policies
- Pod Security Standards
- Admission Controllers
- Service Mesh Enforcement (mTLS)
- Cluster Segmentation

Kubernetes is powerful, but insecure by default. Secure implementation and design practices should always be used.

22.8 API, Integration and Service Mesh Security

APIs have become one of the main data retrieval and modification approaches in modern application design, making them a high value attack vector. Securing API implementations is important to limit risk of compromising data confidentiality and integrity.

API Security Requirements

- Authentication (OAuth/OIDC)
- Authorization Enforcement
- Rate Limiting
- Injection Prevention
- mTLS
- Schema Validation

Service Mesh Enhancements

- Per-service Identity
- Encrypted Traffic, internal to clusters
- Zero Trust Workload Communication
- Centralized Policy Enforcement

APIs and service meshes must align with Zero Trust.

22.9 Data Architecture and Security

Data is an organization's most valuable asset. It must remain secure at rest, in transit and throughout the entire data lifecycle.

Data Security Architecture Considerations

- Discovery and Classification
- Data Lineage
- Encryption at-rest and in-transit

- Tokenization and Masking
- Key Management (KMS/HSM)
- Least Privilege Data Access
- Data Retention Governance
- Secure Analytics Environments

Data must be protected *in storage, in motion, and in use.*

22.10 Application and Platform Integration Architecture

Applications rely on common dependencies, integrate data access and modification, and leverage APIs while running on top of platforms. Security architects must consider several moving parts in secure application and platform integration:

- Dependencies
- Integration Patterns
- Trust Relationships
- API Exposure
- Cross-platform Authentication
- Event-driven Architectures

Integration brings modernization, and levels of risk.

22.11 DevSecOps Architecture

A secure SDLC goes beyond the practice of not hard coding secrets.

It relies on additional validating controls to ensure the least amount of risk is introduced by any involved components.

Build Pipeline Security

- SAST
- Dependency Scanning
- Secrets Scanning
- Container Scanning
- Artifact Signing

Deploy Pipeline Security

- IaC Scanning
- Policy-as-Code
- Automated Configuration Drift Detection

Runtime Security

- Workload Identity Monitoring
- Behavioral Analytics
- Cloud-native Threat Detection

DevSecOps brings security into **every stage of development**, not just runtime.

22.12 Observability, Logging and Telemetry

While secure implementation involves technologies that enforce secure configurations and policies are maintained, it is important to consider continuous validation methodologies, including appropriate levels of logging and monitoring.

Logging Requirements

- Cloud Audit Logs
- Endpoint Logs
- Identity Logs
- Application Logs
- Network Logs
- API Telemetry

Telemetry Controls

- Centralized Log Aggregation
- Tamper-resistant Storage
- Retention Policies
- Privacy Filtering
- Schema Normalization

Observability is the "nervous system" of the organization and enables appropriate anomaly identification and incident response.

22.13 Architecture Review Boards (ARB)

Key stakeholders with appropriate levels of approval authority come together to review proposed architecture design. The design must align to business goals, technology requirements and standards, and risk tolerance. ARB governance ensures consistency and quality.

ARB Responsibilities

- Approve new architecture
- Evaluate risks
- Enforce standards
- Resolve cross-team conflicts
- Ensure alignment to security strategy

ARB ensures architecture is aligned to business and security goals.

22.14 Control Frameworks for Architecture

Organizations have the opportunity to align with several security focused frameworks. Secure architecture considers which framework, or frameworks, are most appropriate and ensures the design appropriately maps to control requirements. Organizations with compliance requirements elevate the level of adherence from *ideally follows* to *must follow*.

Architecture Alignment

- NIST CSF 2.0
- NIST SP 800-53
- ISO 27001
- CIS Controls
- MITRE ATT&CK
- Zero Trust Architecture
- Cloud-specific Standards

Mapping ensures designs meet regulatory and risk requirements.

22.15 Platform Risk and Threat Modeling

Continuous comprehensive platform threat modeling involves all components that the platform interacts with as well as the platform itself: system, application, infrastructure and network.

Threat Modeling Consideration Stages

1. System Design:
    a. Identify threats before deployment.
2. Application Level:
    a. Attack Paths
    b. APIs and Data Flows
    c. Identity
    d. Privilege boundaries
3. Cloud Level:
    a. IAM misconfigurations
    b. Public exposure
    c. Cross-account trust
    d. Data exfiltration paths
4. Network Level:
    a. Modeling
    b. Lateral movement
    c. Segmentation
    d. Protocol abuse

22.16 Architecture Metrics and KPIs

Measuring the success of a security architecture program involves measuring adoption rates and exceptions to standards, along with risk tolerance alignment. Some useful KPIs are listed below.

Security Architecture KPIs

- Number of Approved Patterns
- Pattern Adoption Rate
- Number of Architectural Exceptions
- Exception Aging
- Design Review SLA

Cloud and Platform KPIs

- Misconfigurations Detected
- CSPM Risk Score
- IaC Compliance Rate
- Image Vulnerability Age

DevSecOps KPIs

- Dependency Vulnerability Age
- Pipeline Security Failures
- Secrets Found in Code

Metrics guide architectural maturity.

22.17 Roadmap for Architecture and Platform Security

Achieving architecture and platform security maturity involves design, implementation and operational enforcement components.

Phase 1: Foundations

- Secure Baselines
- Landing Zones
- Standard Architecture Patterns

Phase 2: Expansion

- Segmentation Models
- PAM Integration
- DevSecOps Enforcement

Phase 3: Automation

- Policy-as-Code
- IaC Guardrails
- Auto-scaling Enforcement

Phase 4: Zero Trust Architecture

- Full Identity-based Access
- Microsegmentation
- Service Mesh Enforcement

Phase 5: Optimization

- Architectural Drift Reduction
- Proactive Threat Modeling

Architecture is a living system, not a static document.

22.18 Chapter Summary

Security Architecture and Platform Security are the enablers of every other cybersecurity function. This chapter provides a modern blueprint for:

- Secure Cloud Architectures
- Zero Trust Enforcement
- Platform Hardening
- DevSecOps
- API and Service Mesh Protection
- Data Architecture
- Observability Design
- Architectural Governance

This is the full technical operating model behind an enterprise-grade security program.

Phase 5: Key Takeaways

Chapter 18: Advanced IAM and PAM

- **Scalable Implementation**: Implements complex federated identities, just-in-time access, and zero-standing privileges.

Chapter 19: Network Security and ZTA Deployment

- **Session-Based Decisions**: Deploying technical infrastructure to enforce dynamic, per-session policy decisions.

Chapter 20: Governance and Executive Leadership

- **Corporate Consolidation**: Consolidating discrete technical controls into overarching corporate governance structures.

Chapter 21: Security Metrics and Executive Dashboards

- **Stripping Technical Jargon**: Dashboards must articulate financial risk reduction and operational readiness in terms financial officers understand.

Chapter 22: Platform Security Engineering

- **Self-Defending Platforms**: Designing platforms that natively resist exploitation through secure engineering principles.

Phase 6: Future Planning

AI Security, Governance, And Responsible AI

AI is having its 'horse drawn carriage to Model T' moment. From "experiment" to "core business tool," common use within organizations is introducing risk that didn't exist until recently

AI has begun generating code, building marketing materials, running analytics... often with little thought to AI Governance and Security.

As one of the main cross-functional executives within an organization, a CISO leverages functional authority and technical depth to craft an AI Security and Governance strategy. The CISO bridges the technology and governance gap while leading the implementation of security controls around that technology.

This chapter provides a practical blueprint for governing AI risk without becoming the "department of no" that blocks every AI initiative.

It is critical to find shadow AI, prevent data leakage, build governance that works, and position security as an enabler rather than a blocker. This will foster a culture of compliance instead of bypassing unenforceable limitations.

23.1 The AI Threats That Actually Matter

As of this writing, the primary threats that a CISO needs to address are covered under a few categories. These are likely to expand over time.

Sensitive Data to Public AI: Company sensitive data fed into public AI tools and under accounts not owned by the company. Users upload and prompt outside the scope of SOC visibility, and DLP is unlikely to catch this.

AI-Aided Adversaries: From prompt injection, to rapidly developed spearphishing campaigns, custom malcode and vulnerability recon. Adversaries are using bleeding edge AI tools to craft bleeding edge threats.

Company AI Systems Leaking Data: Training an LLM is one of the first stages in its lifecycle within an organization. The internal data that is used to train the model is still in there somewhere, and careful prompt crafting may inadvertently expose that data... a process that can be automated and executed from outside of the environment.

Shadow AI: Employees under constant productivity pressure begin to adopt tools that make their lives easier. These tools are often new and have not been assessed by corporate security and supply chain stakeholders. Tools outside of an organization's control end up with company data.

Deepfakes are good enough to work: Deep fakes of internal executives, or other key organization representatives can lead to normally unauthorized actions being approved, leading to possible losses in the millions.

The common thread:

- AI amplifies speed and scale
- Attacks happen faster
- Data leaks bigger
- The blast radius is wider

23.2 Build Governance That Doesn't Block Everything

AI governance can struggle if it moves at the pace of traditional Risk Committee assessment. The goal is to facilitate the 'yes' to using with the 'secure' to implementation.

Create a fast-path approval process: Repeatable and actionable, clear steps and requirements... these elements help facilitate clarity and can lead to an improved and more rapid approval process.

Define clear risk tiers: A browser extension that performs one action, like checking grammar, and a chatbot that processes customer data are two very different use cases, and two very different risk profiles.

An Approved AI Tool Catalog: Begin by assessing the most common tools and establish acceptable use standards and appropriate monitoring architecture. Provide a catalog of approved tools for users before they ask or go rogue.

Culture of AI Security: Back to 'Security is Everyone's Responsibility," each department should have well informed security champions well versed in AI security. Governance scales through delegation, not centralization.

Assume AI Use: Shadow AI is a reality. Don't block, monitor instead. Make the authorized tools and uses easy enough to use so that users don't default to unapproved tools.

The goal isn't perfect control; it's informed risk-taking with reasonable guardrails.

23.3 Find and Fix Shadow AI Before It Bites You

You can't secure what you can't see.

- **Network Telemetry:**
    - API Calls to Known Services
    - DNS Queries
    - Cloud Proxy Logs
- **Check IdP Platorms:**
    - OAuth Grants for Known Services
    - SSO Logins
- **Endpoint Telemetry:**
    - Browser Extensions
    - Desktop AI Apps
    - EDR Telemetry
- **Ask the Users:**
    - What tools are being used already?
    - What do those tools do?
    - Are there tools that can be approved that perform these actions?

Once you've found Shadow AI, don't immediately shut it all down. That creates resentment and drives usage further underground.

- **Assess Tool Risk:**
    - Is it processing sensitive data?
    - Where does the data go?
    - What are the terms of service?
    - Who owns the training rights?

Some tools are low-risk and can be approved as-is. Others need to be replaced with enterprise alternatives.

- **Offer better alternatives:** Enterprise grade tooling can make people's lives easier.
- **Block Truly Dangerous Tools**
    - Vague data retention policies
    - Offshore hosting with no contractual protections
    - Services explicitly harvesting user data for model training.

Block those at the DNS or proxy level.

Shadow AI discovery is ongoing, not a one-time project. Set up continuous monitoring.

23.4 Prevent AI Data Leakage

Data going into AI systems is data leaving your control. Treat every AI interaction as potential data exfiltration.

- **Extend DLP Policies to AI services:**
    - Sensitive data in prompts sent to external AI APIs
        - PII
        - Source code
        - API keys
        - Internal project names

Block or alert depending on risk tolerance.

- **Inspect AI API Traffic:**
    - TLS inspection at the proxy layer
        - Large data transfers
        - Repeated uploads of structured data
        - Prompts containing sensitive keywords
- **Classify Data before it reaches AI:**
    - Confidential / Restricted / Public
    - Source Code / Customer DB / Financial Systems
- **User Awareness Training:**
    - Don't paste customer data into public AI tools.
    - Don't upload proprietary code for debugging.
    - Don't use AI to analyze confidential documents unless the tool is approved for that use case
- **Data Retention and Training Opt-Outs:** Enterprise AI vendors will often agree not to use your data for model training if you ask.
    - Get it in writing
    - Verify through technical controls where possible
- **Monitor for Training Data Memorization:**
    - Red team the models
    - Watch for internal data leaks

The hard truth: Not all AI data leakage can be stopped. Focus on preventing the catastrophic cases like regulated data, trade secrets, and credentials, accepting residual risk on everything else.

23.5 Secure the AI You're Building Internally

If your organization is developing AI models, not just using third-party tools, you need a secure development lifecycle.

Phase 1: Data Collection and Preparation

Where did this training data come from, and more importantly, can you prove it?

Poisoned data leads to poisoned models: public sources can include bias, inaccuracy and malicious elements.

Identify sensitive data in training sets. If it's there mask it, tokenize it, or use synthetic data. Don't bake real customer data into model weights.

Phase 2: Model Development

- Treat models like risky applications
- Peer review process for changes
- Segmented and secure development environments
- Test for adversarial robustness
- Red team the model before production

If you can break it in your lab, adversaries will break it in production.

Phase 3: Deployment

API security matters more for AI than traditional apps because AI APIs process untrusted natural language input. Every prompt is user-controlled input that could be malicious:

- Implement:
    - Rate Limiting
    - Input validation

    - Output filtering

- Monitor for Model Drift

Performance degradation over time isn't just a quality issue, it can also be a security signal.

Drift might indicate:

- Data poisoning
- Adversarial manipulation
- Unanticipated Environmental Changes

Phase 4: Monitoring and Response

Log everything:

- Inputs
- Outputs
- Model Decisions

You'll need this for incident response, compliance audits, and debugging failures.

But also monitor for abuse:

- Unusual Query Patterns
- Extraction Attempts
- Prompts Designed to Leak Training Data

Build incident response procedures for AI-specific issues:

- What do you do when your model makes a catastrophically bad decision?
- How do you roll back a poisoned model?
- Who has authority to kill a production AI system?

This isn't theoretical. AI systems fail in production. Plan for it.

23.6 Red Team Your AI

AI red teaming is different from traditional penetration testing. You're not just looking for CVEs and misconfigurations: you're testing how the AI behaves under adversarial conditions.

- **Prompt injection testing:**
  - Can you trick the AI into ignoring its instructions?
  - Commands that override system prompts, leak internal instructions, or bypass safety filters.
- **Data extraction:**
  - Can you get the model to regurgitate training data?
  - Try asking for verbatim reproductions of documents, personal information, or proprietary content.
- **Jailbreaking:**
  - Can you make the AI do things it's not supposed to?
  - Many "safety-aligned" models can be tricked into generating harmful content through creative prompting.
- **Model evasion:**
  - Can you craft inputs that fool the AI's decision-making?
  - Exploit *how* models process input to produce incorrect outputs.
- **Supply chain testing:**
  - Are you using pre-trained models from third parties?
  - Backdoors, bias, or unexpected behaviors.
  - Open-source does not mean 'safe.'

Run AI red team exercises continuously, not just during initial deployment. Models change. Adversarial techniques evolve. What was secure six months ago might be vulnerable today.

If you don't have internal AI red team expertise, bring in specialists. This is a distinct skill set from traditional offensive security.

23.7 Use AI to Defend, *Not* to Decide

AI isn't just an attack surface... it's also a defensive tool. Use it intelligently.

- **AI-powered threat detection:** can correlate signals faster than human analysts. SIEM with AI can surface patterns that rule-based detection misses.

- **Automated triage:** reduces alert fatigue. Let AI sort high-confidence true positives from probable false positives. But don't let AI close alerts automatically without human review.

- **Natural language query for security data:** makes SOC analysts more effective. Analysts can ask questions in plain English and get answers from AI-assisted search. Keep in mind the nature of the underlying data: garbage in, garbage out.

- **The catch:** Don't let AI make high-stakes security decisions autonomously. AI should assist, not replace, human judgment.

AI makes mistakes. You need human oversight to catch errors, challenge assumptions, and apply context the AI doesn't have.

23.8 Navigate the Regulatory Chaos

- **Track what applies to you:**

    - EU AI Act if you operate in Europe.

    - NIST AI RMF for federal contractor or voluntary alignment.

    - State-level laws if you're in Colorado or other states with AI-specific legislation.

    - Sector rules if you're in healthcare, finance, or critical infrastructure.

- **Inventory every AI system:**
    - What it does
    - What data it uses
    - Who owns it
    - What risk tier it falls into under relevant regulations
    - How it reasoned
- **Focus on high-risk systems first:**
    - Employment decision systems
    - Customer data
    - Legal
    - Intellectual Property
- **Document everything.** Build documentation into your AI lifecycle from the start. Retrofitting documentation during an audit is painful.
- **Don't wait for perfect clarity:** If you wait until everything is finalized, you'll be years behind. Start building good practices now based on emerging frameworks. Compliance follows good engineering.

Regulatory readiness is a competitive advantage. Organizations that get ahead of AI regulations will move faster when compliance becomes mandatory.

23.9 Make AI Security Someone's Job

AI security doesn't happen automatically. Someone needs to own it.

Option 1: CISO Ownership

This works if AI is a top-tier strategic priority and you have bandwidth.

You set policy, chair the governance committee, and drive the roadmap.

Option 2: Hire an AI Security Lead

This person reports to you and focuses full-time on AI risk, governance, and technical security. They're the bridge between your security team and the AI engineering teams.

Option 3: Federate It

Embed AI security champions in each business unit and engineering team. They apply your policies locally and escalate risks to central security. This scales better but requires coordination.

Whichever model you choose, make the accountability explicit. If AI security is "everyone's job," it's no one's job.

Build a cross-functional AI working group:

- Security
- Legal
- Compliance
- Data Governance
- Engineering
- Business Stakeholders

Regular review of use cases, policy, metrics and risk will help ensure the organization stays up to date with the latest threats across the AI landscape.

23.10 Measure What Matters

You need metrics to demonstrate progress and hold teams accountable.

Governance Metrics

- Percentage of AI Systems with Completed Risk Assessments
- Time to Approve new AI Tool Requests
- AI Governance Committee Meeting Frequency

Security Metrics

- Number of Shadow AI Tools Detected and Assessed
- AI-related Incidents by Severity
- Mean Time to Remediate AI Vulnerabilities
- DLP Policy Triggers for AI Services
- Chain-of-Thought Monitoring

Operational Metrics

- AI Security Training Completion Rate
- Third-party AI Vendor Assessments Completed
- Drift Monitoring
- Percentage of Sanctioned vs. Unsanctioned AI Usage

Pick a few metrics that matter to your business and track them consistently. Don't build a metrics program so complex that no one looks at it.

23.11 Begin Planning

AI security feels overwhelming. Here's a 90-day plan:

Week 1-2: Discovery

- Run shadow AI discovery across network, SaaS, and endpoints
- Survey teams about what AI tools they're using
- Inventory known AI systems and categorize by risk
- Identify approved agentic harnesses

Week 3-4: Quick Wins

- Publish acceptable use policy and approved tool catalog for AI
- Extend DLP rules to cover top AI services
- Block obviously dangerous AI tools

Week 5-8: Governance

- Form AI governance working group
- Define risk tiers and approval processes
- Build fast-path approval for low-risk AI tools
- Start vendor AI security assessments

Week 9-12: Enablement

- Launch AI security training for developers and business users
- Deploy sanctioned AI tools with proper data controls and continuous monitoring
- Pilot AI red teaming on highest-risk internal models

This isn't a complete program. It's a foundation you can build on.

23.12 The Bottom Line

This is new technology as use-cases will expand. AI security is now a part of the CISO body of responsibility given the role's cross functional responsibilities and, likely soon if not already, an element of the defined CISO charter for an organization. It is beneficial to begin the AI Security and Governance planning sooner rather than later.

The organizations that get this right will move faster, take smarter risks, and build AI systems that don't explode in production. The ones that don't may discover their vulnerabilities through incidents, regulatory actions, and public failures.

The goal is to enable AI adoption with informed risk management:

- Governance that works
- Identified and reduced Shadow AI
- Prevent catastrophic data leakage
- Red team your models
- Use AI to defend, with human oversight.

Position security as a *strategic enabler* around AI use instead of the team that says "no" to innovation.

Quantum Computing Staying Ahead of the Threats

Quantum computing will break most of the encryption you rely on. Not "might break" .... will break. And the timeline is likely shorter than expected.

Every TLS connection. Every VPN tunnel. Every digital signature. Every certificate. The cryptographic foundation of modern security depends on math problems that quantum computers can solve trivially.

This isn't science fiction, quantum chips are already in development who are on trajectory toward Cryptographically Relevant Quantum Computers, CRQC. Nation-states are investing billions. The question isn't whether quantum computers will break your encryption, it's when.

Adversaries are likely already harvesting encrypted data today to decrypt later when quantum computers arrive. They're patient. They can wait ten years if the data is valuable enough.

This chapter provides a practical roadmap for quantum readiness: understanding the threat, inventorying your cryptographic landscape, planning your migration to post-quantum cryptography, and building organizational readiness for a multi-year transformation effort.

This is this generation's Y2K. Start preparing now or face a crisis later.

24.1 What Quantum Computers Actually Threaten

Quantum computing exploits quantum mechanics, superposition, entanglement, and interference, to perform calculations that are impossible for classical computers. A sufficiently powerful quantum computer can run Shor's algorithm, which breaks the public-key cryptography that protects nearly everything.

What Breaks

- **RSA encryption:** Used everywhere (TLS, VPNs, email encryption, code signing)
- **Elliptic Curve Cryptography (ECC):** Increasingly common, just as vulnerable
- **Diffie-Hellman key exchange:** How we establish secure connections
- **Digital signatures (DSA, ECDSA):** How we verify software, documents, and identities

What Survives

- **Symmetric encryption (AES-256):** Quantum computers reduce effective key strength by half, but AES-256 remains secure
- **Hash functions (SHA-256, SHA-384):** Weakened but not broken with larger key sizes

The immediate impact isn't just confidentiality, it's integrity.

When digital signatures break, you lose the ability to verify software updates, validate certificates, or trust firmware. The entire chain of digital trust collapses.

This affects every part of your infrastructure: web servers, VPN gateways, PKI, email security, code signing, blockchain, IoT devices, secure boot, and anything that relies on public-key cryptography.

24.2 Harvest Now, Decrypt Later Is Already Happening

The most urgent quantum threat isn't a future attack; it's happening right now.

The Threat Model

Nation-state adversaries are intercepting and storing encrypted traffic today. They can't decrypt it with current technology. But they're betting that quantum computers will be available within approximately 10 years, or less. When that happens, they'll decrypt everything they've collected.

Those at Risk

Any organization with data that remains sensitive for longer than the time-to-quantum timeline:

- Government Classified Information (decades of sensitivity)
- Healthcare Records (lifetime sensitivity)
- Financial Data (multi-year sensitivity)
- Intellectual Property (product lifecycle sensitivity)
- M&A Negotiations, Legal Communications, Trade Secrets

What Drives the Urgency

Your encrypted VPN traffic from today could be decrypted in 2035. If the data inside is still sensitive then, you have a problem now. You can't retroactively protect data that's already been harvested.

What To Do

Prioritize Post-Quantum Cryptography, PQC, for data with long confidentiality requirements. If you're transmitting data today that must remain confidential for 10+ years, you need quantum-resistant encryption now, not later.

Reduce your exposure:

- Minimize data retention and shorten encryption key lifetimes
- Limit what you transmit over potentially monitored channels

Monitor for large-scale data exfiltration that might indicate harvest-now-decrypt-later activity, for example massive volume transfers out.

The harvest is already underway. You're deciding now what adversaries will be able to read in ten years.

24.3 NIST Standards

NIST finalized post-quantum cryptography standards in 2024. You now have approved algorithms to replace the ones quantum computers will break.

ML-KEM (FIPS 203): Module Lattice-Based KEM

- Replaces RSA and ECC for key exchange
- Formerly called CRYSTALS-Kyber
- Use this for encrypting data in transit and at rest

ML-DSA (FIPS 204): Module Lattice-Based DSA

- Replaces RSA and ECDSA for digital signatures
- Formerly called CRYSTALS-Dilithium
- Use this for code signing, certificate signing, and authentication

SLH-DSA (FIPS 205): Stateless Hash-Based DSA

- Alternative signature scheme
- Formerly called SPHINCS+
- Conservative fallback if lattice-based crypto is broken

Additional standards in progress:

- FN-DSA (FALCON) for constrained environments
- More signature schemes under evaluation

What This Means

You finally have production-ready, standards-based algorithms. No more waiting for "eventual" standards. The standards exist. Now you have to deploy them.

Implementation Considerations

These algorithms have different performance characteristics than RSA/ECC:

- Larger Key Sizes
- Different Computational Costs
- New Implementation Risks

Test thoroughly before production deployment. Performance impacts vary by use case.

24.4 Inventory Your Cryptography

You cannot migrate to post-quantum cryptography if you don't know what cryptography you're currently using. Most organizations may not have comprehensive cryptographic inventory.

Network Layer

- TLS certificates and configurations across all web servers, APIs, and load balancers
- VPN implementations and their cipher suites
- Internal certificate authorities and PKI infrastructure

Application Layer

- Encryption at Rest
- Application-level Encryption
- Key Management Systems
- Code Signing Certificates and Processes

Infrastructure

- Firmware Signing for Network Devices, Servers, and Endpoints
- Secure Boot Implementations
- IoT and Embedded Device Cryptography
- Cloud Provider Encryption Services

Supply Chain

- Third-party Software Dependencies using cryptography
- Vendor-provided Encryption
- Open-source Libraries with cryptographic functions

How to discover it

- **Automated scanning:**
  - Network Traffic Analysis
  - Certificate Management Platforms
  - Application Scanning Tool

- **Manual review:**
  - Code Reviews for cryptographic function calls
  - Architecture Documentation Review
  - Vendor Questionnaires for third-party cryptography
- **Classification:**
  - Algorithm Type (RSA, ECC, AES)
  - Key Size
  - Quantum Vulnerability (yes/no)
  - Migration Priority (critical/high/medium/low).

This inventory effort is comparable to Y2K code remediation. It's tedious, time-consuming, and absolutely necessary.

Start now.

24.5 Build a Migration Plan

Post-quantum cryptography migration is a multi-year enterprise transformation. Treat it accordingly.

Phase 1: Assessment and Planning (Months 1-6)

1. Complete cryptographic inventory.
2. Assess quantum risk exposure by data sensitivity and timeline.
3. Develop migration roadmap with clear milestones.
4. Secure executive sponsorship and multi-year budget.

Phase 2: Pilot and Validation (Months 6-12)

1. Test PQC algorithms in lab environments.
2. Measure performance impact on representative workloads.
3. Validate interoperability with existing systems.
4. Assess vendor readiness for PQC support.

This phase prevents catastrophic mistakes in production. Do not skip it.

Phase 3: Hybrid Deployment (Year 2-3)

1. Deploy hybrid encryption: classical algorithms + PQC running in parallel.
2. Start with highest-risk systems (long-lived data, high-value targets, regulatory requirements).
3. Update PKI infrastructure to support PQC certificates.
4. Implement PQC-capable TLS configurations on critical services.
5. Migrate key management systems to support PQC keys.

Hybrid mode provides quantum resistance while maintaining backward compatibility. Organizations will likely be in hybrid mode for years while waiting for vendors, legacy systems, and third parties to catch up.

Phase 4: Full Migration (Year 3-5)

1. Transition to PQC-only configurations where feasible.
2. Retire quantum-vulnerable algorithms on systems that support PQC.
3. Update policies and standards to mandate PQC for new deployments.

Some systems will never migrate (end-of-life products, vendor-abandoned hardware). These exceptions should be documented and compensating controls implemented.

Phase 5: Continuous Operations

1. Monitor for cryptographic drift back to legacy algorithms
2. Track NIST and industry standard evolution
3. Maintain cryptographic agility

24.6 Don't Break Digital Signatures

Everyone focuses on encryption, but breaking digital signatures is worse.

Why Signatures Matter

Broken encryption means some data is exposed, broken digital signature, *all* data is at risk:

- **Software updates become untrustworthy.** If adversaries can forge signatures, they can push malicious updates that systems will accept as legitimate. Every software update becomes a potential supply chain attack.

- **Certificates become meaningless.** Forged TLS certificates let adversaries impersonate any website. Forged code signing certificates let malware appear legitimate. The entire PKI collapses.

- **Secure boot fails.** Firmware signature verification breaks. Adversaries can implant persistent malware at the firmware level that survives OS reinstalls.

- **Contracts and documents lose legal validity.** Digitally signed contracts, medical records, and financial transactions can be forged. Legal non-repudiation disappears.

Impact Areas

- PKI and Certificate Authorities
- Code Signing for Software Releases
- Firmware Signing for Devices
- Document Signing for Legal Records
- Blockchain Transaction Validation
- Device Attestation and Identity

Migration Priority

Migrate digital signatures to PQC before you migrate encryption. The integrity risk is existential; the confidentiality risk is data-specific.

Focus PQC signature migration on:

- Certificate Authorities and PKI Infrastructure
- Software Update Signing Processes
- Firmware Signing for Critical Systems
- High-value Document Signing

Do not delay signature migration while you wait for perfect encryption migration plans.

24.7 Vendors Will Make or Break Migration Timelines

Organizations depend on third parties whose quantum readiness directly impacts their migration timeline.

Vendor Dependency Categories

An organization may leverage myriad vendors, each with their own PQC plans.

Infrastructure Vendors

- Cloud Providers
- Network Equipment Vendors
- Endpoint Vendors

Vendor PQC timelines constrain deployment options.

Software Vendors

- Enterprise Applications
- Security Tools (SIEM, EDR)
- Collaboration Platforms.

If they don't support PQC, organizations will be forced to remain in hybrid mode.

IoT and Embedded Devices

- Medical Devices
- Industrial Control Systems
- Building Management Systems.

Many will never receive PQC updates. They are security debt.

What to Ask

- What is the vendor's PQC migration roadmap and timeline, and which standards will they implement?
- Will they support hybrid encryption during transition?
- What is their plan for legacy products that can't be updated?
- Can they provide cryptographic agility (easy algorithm switching)?

Contractual Requirements

Add PQC migration commitments to vendor contracts. Require vendors to notify you of cryptographic vulnerabilities. Demand regular quantum readiness reporting. Include PQC support timelines in SLAs.

Reality check: Many vendors don't have PQC plans yet. Some won't prioritize it until customer demand forces them to. CISOs should be willing to be part of that customer demand. Vendor engagement should begin sooner rather than later, it may take a while to get answers... then it's off to the implementations.

24.8 Build Organizational Readiness

Quantum readiness requires sustained executive commitment, cross-functional coordination, and multi-year budget allocation.

Governance Structure

- **Executive sponsor:** CISO, CIO, or CTO. Someone with budget authority and strategic influence. This is a board-level risk.

- **Quantum readiness working group:** Cross-functional team with security, IT, engineering, legal, procurement, and business representation. Meets regularly to track progress and make decisions.

- **Technical leads:** Cryptography experts, infrastructure architects, and application security engineers who execute the migration.

Workforce development

Teams may need training on cryptography fundamentals. Many security professionals may not understand public-key crypto deeply enough to execute a PQC migration.

External expertise may be beneficial for specialized areas: PQC algorithm selection, performance optimization, cryptographic agility architecture.

The board and senior leadership should receive executive briefings with established cadence. They need to understand and track quantum risk, timeline, and investment requirements, over time.

Budget Planning

Multi-year budget allocation for:

- Cryptographic Inventory Tools and Services
- PQC Testing and Validation Infrastructure
- Vendor Migrations and Upgrade Costs
- Consulting and Specialized Expertise
- Workforce Training and Certification
- Ongoing Monitoring and Compliance

This is not a one-time project cost; it's sustained operational investment.

Role Definition

A Quantum Readiness Program Manager should be designated. This person owns the roadmap, tracks milestones, coordinates across teams, and reports to executives.

24.9 Measure Progress

Metrics are critical for the ability to track progress and hold teams accountable.

Inventory Metrics

- Percentage of Cryptographic Assets Inventoried
- Number of Quantum-vulnerable Systems Identified
- Cryptographic Asset Classification Completion Rate

Migration Metrics

- Percentage of Systems Migrated to PQC or Hybrid Encryption
- Number of PQC Pilot Deployments Completed
- Vendor PQC Readiness Assessment Completion Rate

Risk Metrics

- Quantum Risk Exposure Score by Business Unit
- Harvest-Now-Decrypt-Later Risk Assessment Completion
- Time-to-Migrate for Critical Systems

Operational Metrics

- Cryptographic Drift Detection and Remediation Rate
- Certificate Rotation Compliance: shorter lifetimes for quantum era
- PQC Interoperability Test Pass Rate

The Board should receive metrics at least quarterly. Make quantum readiness visible at the executive level.

24.10 Begin Planning

Quantum readiness feels overwhelming. Start with a 90-day plan:

Week 1-4: Executive Alignment

- Brief the board on quantum risk and timeline
- Secure executive sponsorship (CISO, CIO, or CTO)

- Form quantum readiness working group
- Allocate initial budget for assessment phase

Week 5-8: Initial Assessment

- Strating with critical systems, launch cryptographic inventory effort
- Conduct harvest-now-decrypt-later, HNDL, risk assessment
- Identify highest-priority systems for migration
- Engage top-tier vendors on their PQC roadmaps

Week 9-12: Planning and Piloting

- Develop multi-year PQC migration roadmap
- Set up PQC testing lab environment
- Pilot NIST PQC algorithms on non-critical systems
- Train security and engineering teams on PQC basics

This isn't a complete program. It's the foundation.

24.11 The Bottom Line

Quantum computing will break the cryptographic foundation of modern security. The timeline is measured in years, not decades. There are effectively three choices:

Option 1: Start Preparing Now

- Inventory cryptography
- Build a migration plan

- Pilot PQC implementations
- Engage vendors
- Train teams
- Allocate budget

This is hard, expensive, and time-consuming, but organizations that prepare now will be ready for 'Q-Day.'

Option 2: Wait and See

- Hope the timeline slips
- Hope someone else solves the problem
- Hope your vendors move faster than they historically have
- Hope quantum computers are harder to build than experts predict

This puts the organization at risk, both in data exposure and in reputation, should data be decrypted in the future.

Option 3: Ignore it Entirely

- Assume quantum computers won't impact the organization.
- Only act when it becomes urgent.

This is how organizations end up in crisis mode, throwing money at emergency migrations while adversaries are already exploiting the vulnerability.

Many organizations will choose Option 2 by default. They'll "monitor the situation" without committing resources. This can be a significant, business impacting misstep down the line.

The organizations that prepare now will navigate the transition smoothly. The ones that wait will face a painful, expensive, crisis-driven migration under time pressure.

Make it someone's job: Start now. Build the inventory. Develop the roadmap. Secure the budget.

Encrypted data from today will either be secure in 2035 or it won't. Those decisions are being made right now.

Phase 6: Key Takeaways

Chapter 23: AI Security and Governance

- **Dual-Use Nature**: AI acts both as a complex new attack surface (data poisoning) and an accelerant for defensive detection.

- **Responsible Policy**: Establishing policies to ensure automated systems do not violate privacy regulations or introduce bias.

Chapter 24: Quantum Computing and Crypto Agility

- **"Harvest Now, Decrypt Later"**: Adversaries exfiltrate encrypted data today, assuming future quantum power will shatter current algorithms.

- **Crypto Agility**: The engineered capability to rapidly replace cryptographic primitives without disrupting underlying network infrastructure.

- **Long-Term Forecasting**: A CISO must possess rigorous technological forecasting to mitigate risks that may not weaponize for a decade.

Appendices

Appendix A

NIST Cybersecurity Framework (CSF) 2.0

Six Core Functions

1. GOVERN (GV) - NEW in 2.0

- GV.OC: Organizational Context
- GV.RM: Risk Management
- GV.RR: Roles, Responsibilities and Authorities
- GV.PO: Policy
- GV.SC: Supply Chain
- GV.OV: Oversight

1. IDENTIFY (ID)

- ID.AM: Asset Management
- ID.RA: Risk Assessment
- ID.IM: Improvement

1. PROTECT (PR)

- PR.AA: Identity Management, Authentication and Access Control
- PR.DS: Data Security
- PR.PS: Platform Security
- PR.IR: Technology Infrastructure Resilience
- PR.AT: Awareness and Training

1. DETECT (DE)

- DE.CM: Continuous Monitoring
- DE.AE: Anomaly and Event Detection

1. RESPOND (RS)

- RS.MI: Incident Mitigation
- RS.CO: Incident Response Reporting and Communications
- RS.AN: Incident Analysis
- RS.MA: Incident Management

1. RECOVER (RC)

- RC.RP: Incident Recovery Plan Execution
- RC.CO: Incident Recovery Communications

Maturity Levels

- Level 1: Ad Hoc
- Level 2: Basic
- Level 3: Intermediate

- Level 4: Advanced
- Level 5: Optimized

NIST SP 800-53 Rev. 5 Control Families

1. AC - Access Control
2. AT - Awareness & Training
3. AU - Audit & Accountability
4. CA - Assessment, Authorization & Monitoring
5. CM - Configuration Management
6. CP - Contingency Planning
7. IA - Identification & Authentication
8. IR - Incident Response
9. MA - Maintenance
10. MP - Media Protection
11. PE - Physical and Environmental Security
12. PL - Planning
13. PM - Program Management
14. PT - Personally Identifiable Information Processing and Transparency
15. PS - Personnel Security
16. RA - Risk Assessment
17. SA - System & Services Acquisition
18. SC - System & Communications Protection

19. SI - System & Information Integrity
20. SR - Supply Chain Risk Management (New in Rev 5)

NIST SP 800-207 Zero Trust Architecture

Core Principles

1. All data sources and computing services are considered resources
2. All communication is secured regardless of location
3. Access is granted on a per-session basis
4. Access is determined by dynamic policy
5. The enterprise monitors and measures the integrity and security posture of all assets
6. All resource authentication and authorization is dynamic and strictly enforced
7. The enterprise collects as much information as possible to improve posture

Zero Trust Architecture Components

- Policy Enforcement Point (PEP): Where decisions are enforced
- Policy Decision Point (PDP): Where policy decisions are computed
  - Policy Engine (PE)
  - Policy Administrator (PA)
- Resource Systems: Services being accessed

Five Zero Trust Pillars

1. Identity: Users and Workload Identities
2. Device/Endpoint: Posture, Attestation and Compliance
3. Network/Workload: ZTNA, Microsegmentation, Service Mesh
4. Application/APIs: AuthN/AuthZ, API governance
5. Data: Classification, Access, Lineage, Risk

NIST SP 800-37 Risk Management Framework (RMF)

1. PREPARE: Governance structures, roles, risk tolerance
2. CATEGORIZE: Impact level determination (Low, Moderate, High)
3. SELECT: Control selection from NIST SP 800-53
4. IMPLEMENT: Technical control deployment
5. ASSESS: Validate control effectiveness
6. AUTHORIZE: Risk acceptance decision
7. MONITOR: Continuous monitoring and assessment

CIS Controls v8.1

18 CIS Controls across three implementation groups.

Implementation Groups (IG)

1. IG 1: Basic Cyber Hygiene
2. IG 2: Foundational Security Practices
3. IG 3: Advanced Security Practices

Controls

1. Inventory and Control of Enterprise Assets
2. Inventory and Control of Software Assets
3. Data Protection
4. Secure Configuration of Enterprise Assets and Software
5. Account Management
6. Access Control Management
7. Continuous Vulnerability Management
8. Audit Log Management
9. Email and Web Browser Protections
10. Malware Defenses
11. Data Recovery
12. Network Infrastructure Management
13. Network Monitoring and Defense
14. Security Awareness and Skills Training
15. Service Provider Management
16. Application Software Security
17. Incident Response Management
18. Penetration Testing

MITRE ATT&CK Framework Structure

14 Tactics on the Enterprise Matrix

1. Reconnaissance: Gathering information
2. Resource Development: Establishing resources
3. Initial Access: Getting into the network
4. Execution: Running malicious code
5. Persistence: Maintaining foothold
6. Privilege Escalation: Gaining higher-level permissions
7. Defense Evasion: Avoiding detection
8. Credential Access: Stealing credentials
9. Discovery: Understanding the environment
10. Lateral Movement: Moving through the network
11. Collection: Gathering data of interest
12. Command and Control: Communicating with compromised systems
13. Exfiltration: Stealing data
14. Impact: Disrupting availability or integrity

Key ATT&CK Matrices

- Enterprise: Windows, macOS, Linux, Cloud, Network, Containers
- Mobile: iOS, Android
- ICS: Industrial Control Systems

Cloud Security Frameworks

1. Cloud Security Alliance (CSA) Cloud Controls Matrix (CCM)

17 Control Domains:

- Application and Interface Security
- Audit Assurance and Compliance
- Business Continuity Management and Operational Resilience
- Change Control and Configuration Management
- Data Security and Information Lifecycle Management
- Datacenter Security
- Encryption and Key Management
- Governance and Risk Management
- Human Resources Security
- Identity and Access Management
- Infrastructure and Virtualization Security
- Interoperability and Portability
- Mobile Security
- Security Incident Management, E-Discovery, and Cloud Forensics
- Supply Chain Management, Transparency and Accountability
- Threat and Vulnerability Management
- Universal Endpoint Management

2. CIS Benchmarks

- Cloud-specific hardening guides for AWS, Azure, GCP, Kubernetes

3. FedRAMP

- Federal Risk and Authorization Management Program
- Based on NIST 800-53
- Required for cloud services working with US government

4. ISO 27017 and 27018

- ISO 27017: Cloud security controls
- ISO 27018: Cloud privacy controls

5. CISA Zero Trust Maturity Model

- Pillars
  - Identity
  - Devices
  - Networks
  - Applications and Workloads
  - Data
- Maturity Stages
  - Traditional
  - Initial
  - Advanced
  - Optimal

    - Endpoint

Compliance and Regulatory Frameworks

SOC 2 Trust Services Criteria

Common Criteria (CC1-CC9):

- CC1: Control Environment
- CC2: Communications and Information
- CC3: Risk Assessment
- CC4: Monitoring of Controls
- CC5: Control Activities
- CC6: Logical and Physical Access Controls
- CC7: System Operations
- CC8: Change Management
- CC9: Risk Mitigation

Trust Service Categories:

- Security (Required)
- Availability
- Processing Integrity
- Confidentiality
- Privacy

PCI DSS v4.0

12 Requirements across 6 Domains:

1. Install and Maintain Network Security Controls
2. Apply Secure Configurations
3. Protect Stored Account Data
4. Protect Cardholder Data with Strong Cryptography
5. Protect All Systems and Networks from Malicious Software
6. Develop and Maintain Secure Systems and Software
7. Restrict Access by Business Need to Know
8. Identify Users and Authenticate Access
9. Restrict Physical Access
10. Log and Monitor All Access
11. Test Security of Systems and Networks Regularly
12. Support Information Security with Organizational Policies

HIPAA Security Rule

Three Safeguard Categories:

1. Administrative Safeguards: Security management, workforce security, training
2. Physical Safeguards: Facility access, workstation use, device controls
3. Technical Safeguards: Access control, audit controls, integrity, transmission security

GDPR (General Data Protection Regulation)

Seven Principles:

1. Lawfulness, fairness and transparency
2. Purpose limitation
3. Data minimization
4. Accuracy
5. Storage limitation
6. Integrity and confidentiality
7. Accountability

CMMC 2.0 (Cybersecurity Maturity Model Certification)

Three Levels:

- Level 1: Basic Cyber Hygiene (17 practices)
- Level 2: Advanced Cyber Hygiene (110 practices from NIST 800-171)
- Level 3: Expert (110+ practices from NIST 800-172)

Post-Quantum Cryptography (NIST Standards)

NIST-Approved PQC Algorithms (2024)

Key Encapsulation Mechanisms:

- ML-KEM (CRYSTALS-Kyber): Primary algorithm for general encryption

Digital Signatures:

- ML-DSA (CRYSTALS-Dilithium): Primary algorithm for digital signatures
- SLH-DSA (SPHINCS+): Backup stateless hash-based signature
- FN-DSA (FALCON): For applications needing smaller signatures

Migration Plan Timeline:

- Phase 1 (2024-2025): Assessment & Planning
- Phase 2 (2025-2027): Pilot & Validation
- Phase 3 (2027-2030): Hybrid Deployment
- Phase 4 (2030-2033): Full Migration
- Phase 5 (2033+): Continuous Operations

Appendix B

Template 1: Security Policy Framework Structure

Information Security Policy

Policy Number: ISP-001
Effective Date: [Date]
Review Cycle: Annual
Owner: CISO
Approver: Board of Directors

1. Purpose

[Define the purpose of securing organizational information assets]

2. Scope

- Applicable To: All employees, contractors, vendors, business partners
- Systems Covered: All information systems, data, networks, applications
- Geographic Coverage: Global operations

3. Policy Statements

1. Information must be classified based on sensitivity
2. Access granted on least privilege principle
3. All systems must be maintained with current security patches
4. Incident response procedures must be followed

5. Security awareness training is mandatory

4. Roles and Responsibilities

- CISO: Overall accountability
- IT Security Team: Implementation
- Business Unit Leaders: Compliance within units
- All Employees: Adherence to policy

5. Compliance

- Non-compliance may result in disciplinary action
- Exceptions require written approval from CISO

6. Related Documents

- Acceptable Use Policy
- Incident Response Plan
- Data Classification Standard

Template 2: Risk Assessment Template

Asset Risk Assessment

Asset Name: [System/Application Name]
Asset Owner: [Name/Department]
Assessment Date: [Date]
Assessor: [Name]

Asset Details

- Description: [Brief description]
- Classification: [Confidential/Internal/Public]
- Business Criticality: [High/Medium/Low]
- Data Sensitivity: [PII/PHI/Financial/IP/General]

Threat Assessment

Risk Scoring: Risk Score = Likelihood × Impact*Risk Levels*:

- *1-4*: Low Risk (Green)
- *5-12*: Medium Risk (Yellow)
- *13-25*: High Risk (Red)

Control Assessment
Risk Treatment Decision

- [ ] Accept
- [ ] Mitigate
- [ ] Transfer
- [ ] Avoid

Justification: [Explanation of decision]
Risk Owner: [Name]
Target Remediation Date: [Date]

Template 3: Incident Response Plan Structure

Incident Response Plan

1. Incident Response Team

2. Incident Severity Classification

Severity 1 (Critical):

- Active breach with data exfiltration
- Ransomware encryption of critical systems
- Complete system outage affecting revenue
- Response Time: Immediate
- Escalation: CISO, CEO, Board

Severity 2 (High):

- Suspected breach under investigation
- Malware on critical systems contained

- Partial system outage
- Response Time: Within 1 hour
- Escalation: CISO, CIO

Severity 3 (Medium):

- Failed attack attempts
- Malware on non-critical systems
- Policy violations
- Response Time: Within 4 hours
- Escalation: Security Manager

Severity 4 (Low):

- Security alerts requiring investigation
- Minor policy violations
- Response Time: Within 24 hours
- Escalation: SOC Team

3. Incident Response Phases

Phase 1: Detection & Analysis

- [ ] Alert received and validated
- [ ] Severity determined
- [ ] IR team notified
- [ ] Initial scope assessment
- [ ] Evidence preservation started

Phase 2: Containment

- [ ] Short-term containment (isolate affected systems)
- [ ] Long-term containment (network segmentation)

- [ ] Evidence collected
- [ ] Stakeholders notified

Phase 3: Eradication

- [ ] Root cause identified
- [ ] Malware/threat removed
- [ ] Vulnerabilities patched
- [ ] Systems validated clean

Phase 4: Recovery

- [ ] Systems restored from clean backup/rebuild
- [ ] Services gradually brought online
- [ ] Enhanced monitoring implemented
- [ ] Business operations validated

Phase 5: Post-Incident

- [ ] Incident documentation completed
- [ ] Lessons learned meeting held
- [ ] Improvements identified and implemented
- [ ] Executive report delivered

Template 4: Communications

Internal Alert Template

TO: [Distribution List]
FROM: Security Operations Center
SUBJECT: Security Incident - [Severity Level]
TIME: [Timestamp]

INCIDENT SUMMARY:
- Type: [Malware/Breach/DDoS/etc.]
- Affected Systems: [List]
- Current Status: [Under Investigation/Contained/Resolved]
- Impact: [Business impact description]
ACTIONS REQUIRED:
- [Specific actions for recipients]
NEXT UPDATE: [Timeframe]

Executive Briefing Template

INCIDENT BRIEF - [Date/Time]
SITUATION:
- What happened
- When it was detected
- Current status
IMPACT:
- Systems affected
- Data at risk
- Business operations impact
- Customer/regulatory implications
RESPONSE:
- Immediate actions taken
- Containment status
- Expected resolution time
RECOMMENDATIONS:
- Short-term actions
- Long-term improvements

Template 4: Vendor Security Assessment Questionnaire

Vendor Risk Assessment

Vendor Name: [Company]
Service Provided: [Description]
Assessment Date: [Date]
Vendor Tier: [Critical/High/Medium/Low]
Vendor Classification Criteria
Tier 1 (Critical):

- Access to sensitive data (PII, PHI, financial)
- Critical business function dependency
- Integration with core systems
- Assessment: Full security review + audit rights

Tier 2 (High):

- Access to internal data
- Important business function
- Limited system integration
- Assessment: Detailed questionnaire + SOC 2 review

Tier 3 (Medium):

- Minimal data access
- Non-critical function
- No system integration
- Assessment: Standard questionnaire

Tier 4 (Low):

- No data access
- Easily replaceable
- Assessment: Basic due diligence

Security Questionnaire

1. Governance & Risk Management

- [ ] Do you have a dedicated CISO or equivalent?
- [ ] Is there a formal risk management program?
- [ ] How often are risk assessments conducted?
- [ ] Do you maintain a risk register?

2. Compliance and Certifications

- [ ] SOC 2 Type II (provide report)
- [ ] ISO 27001 (provide certificate)
- [ ] PCI DSS (if applicable)
- [ ] HIPAA (if applicable)
- [ ] FedRAMP (if applicable)
- [ ] GDPR compliance (if EU data)

3. Data Security

- [ ] How is data encrypted at rest?
- [ ] How is data encrypted in transit?
- [ ] Where is data stored geographically?
- [ ] What is the data retention policy?
- [ ] How is data securely destroyed?
- [ ] Is multi-tenancy implemented securely?

4. Access Control

- [ ] Is MFA required for all access?
- [ ] How is privileged access managed?
- [ ] What is the access review frequency?
- [ ] How are accounts deprovisioned?

5. Security Operations

- [ ] Is there 24/7 security monitoring?
- [ ] What SIEM solution is used?
- [ ] How are security incidents handled?
- [ ] What is the average response time?

- [ ] Are penetration tests conducted? (provide results)
- [ ] What vulnerability management process exists?

6. Business Continuity

- [ ] What is the RTO/RPO?
- [ ] How often are backups tested?
- [ ] Is there a documented DR plan?
- [ ] When was the last DR test?

7. Incident Response

- [ ] Is there a documented IR plan?
- [ ] What is the notification SLA for security incidents?
- [ ] Have there been any breaches in the last 3 years?
- [ ] If yes, provide details

8. Supply Chain Security

- [ ] How are subcontractors vetted?
- [ ] Is there a vendor risk management program?
- [ ] What secure development practices are followed?

Assessment Results

Risk Score: [1-10]
Risk Level: [Low/Medium/High/Critical]
Key Findings:

1. [Finding]
2. [Finding]
3. [Finding]

Required Actions:

1. [Action with due date]

2. [Action with due date]

Approval Decision:

- [ ] Approved
- [ ] Approved with Conditions
- [ ] Rejected

Conditions/Requirements: [List any requirements]
Next Review Date: [Date]

Template 5: Security Metrics Dashboard Structure

Executive Security Dashboard

Reporting Period: [Month/Quarter]
Report Date: [Date]

1. Security Posture Summary

Overall Security Score: [0-100]

2. Risk Metrics

Open Critical/High Risks: [Number]

- Critical: [#] (Target: 0)
- High: [#] (Target: <5)

Risk Reduction:

- Risks Mitigated This Period: [#]
- Risks Accepted: [#]
- New Risks Identified: [#]

Top 3 Risks:

1. [Risk description] - [Owner] - [Due date]
2. [Risk description] - [Owner] - [Due date]
3. [Risk description] - [Owner] - [Due date]

3. Incident Metrics

Incidents by Severity:

- Severity 1: [#]
- Severity 2: [#]
- Severity 3: [#]
- Severity 4: [#]

Mean Time To Detect (MTTD): [Hours]
Mean Time To Respond (MTTR): [Hours]
Mean Time To Contain (MTTC): [Hours]
Notable Incidents:

1. [Brief description - status]

4. Vulnerability Management
Total Vulnerabilities: [#]

- Critical: [#] (SLA: 7 days)
- High: [#] (SLA: 30 days)
- Medium: [#] (SLA: 90 days)

Patch Compliance: [%]
Systems Scanned: [#/total] ([%])
Overdue Remediation:

- Critical: [#]
- High: [#]

5. Identity & Access
Total Identities: [#]

- Active Users: [#]
- Privileged Accounts: [#]
- Service Accounts: [#]

MFA Adoption: [%] (Target: 100%)
Passwordless Adoption: [%]
Access Reviews Completed: [#/total] ([%])
Dormant Accounts Removed: [#]
6. Security Training & Awareness

Training Completion Rate: [%]
Phishing Simulation Click Rate: [%] (Target: <5%)
Reported Phishing Attempts: [#]

7. Compliance Status

Audit Findings:

- Open: [#]
- Overdue: [#]

8. Key Initiatives Progress

9. Budget & Staffing

Budget Utilization: [%] of annual budget
Open Security Positions: [#]
Average Time to Fill: [Days]

10. Executive Summary

Key Achievements:

- [Achievement]
- [Achievement]

Areas of Concern:

- [Concern and mitigation plan]
- [Concern and mitigation plan]

Actions Required:

- [Action item for executive team]

Template 6: Tabletop Exercise Scenario

Ransomware Attack Tabletop Exercise

Exercise Date: [Date]*Duration*: 2 hours*Facilitator*: [Name]

Scenario Inject 1 (T+0 minutes)

TIME: Monday, 6:00 AM

SITUATION: The SOC has received multiple EDR alerts indicating suspicious file encryption activity on 15 workstations across the Finance department. Users are reporting they cannot access files, and ransom notes have appeared on screens.

DISCUSSION POINTS:

1. Who needs to be notified immediately?

2. What immediate containment actions should be taken?

3. How do we determine the scope?

4. What evidence should be preserved?

EXPECTED ACTIONS:

- [ ] Activate IR team
- [ ] Isolate affected systems
- [ ] Disable user accounts if compromised
- [ ] Snapshot systems for forensics
- [ ] Assess backup integrity

Scenario Inject 2 (T+30 minutes)

UPDATED SITUATION: Investigation reveals 150+ systems are affected across multiple departments. The ransomware appears to have spread via compromised privileged account. Backups from the last 3 days are also encrypted. Attackers are demanding $5M in Bitcoin for decryption keys.

DISCUSSION POINTS:

1. How do we communicate this to executives?

2. Do we pay the ransom?

3. How do we rebuild operations?

4. When do we notify customers/regulators?

5. What communication do we provide to employees?

EXPECTED ACTIONS:

- [ ] Executive briefing
- [ ] Legal counsel engaged
- [ ] Cyber insurance activated

- [ ] Assessment of recovery options
- [ ] External forensics engaged

Scenario Inject 3 (T+60 minutes)

UPDATED SITUATION: Media outlet has contacted PR department stating they received a tip about a "major breach" at the company. Attackers have posted on dark web claiming to have exfiltrated 500GB of sensitive data.

DISCUSSION POINTS:

1. What is our public statement?
2. Do we notify law enforcement?
3. What are our regulatory notification requirements?
4. How do we handle customer inquiries?

Debrief Questions (T+90 minutes)

1. What went well?
2. What gaps were identified?
3. What should be improved in our IR plan?
4. What additional tools/capabilities are needed?
5. Are roles and responsibilities clear?
6. Are communication templates adequate?
7. Is decision-making authority clear?

Action Items

Template 7: CISO Charter

[Organization Name] Information Security Charter1. Mission Statement The mission of the Information Security Program is to protect [Organization Name]'s information assets, ensure business continuity, and mitigate risks to an acceptable level, enabling the secure achievement of strategic business objectives.

2. Purpose and Scope This Charter establishes the authority and responsibility of the Chief Information Security Officer (CISO) to direct, monitor, and report on the information security status of [Organization Name]. The scope includes all employees, contractors, third-party vendors, information systems, networks, and data owned or processed by [Organization Name].

3. Authority The CISO is appointed by the and is granted the authority to:

- Draft, approve, and enforce information security policies and standards.
- Halt any system deployment or business activity that presents an unacceptable risk to the organization until mitigating controls are implemented.
- Conduct audits and assessments of internal departments and third-party vendors.
- Declare a cybersecurity incident and initiate the Incident Response Plan (IRP).

4. Roles and Responsibilities

- **CISO:** Responsible for the strategy, execution, and oversight of the Information Security Program. Reports quarterly to the on the state of security.
- **Executive Management:** Responsible for approving the risk appetite and providing resources (budget/staffing) to meet security objectives.
- **Data Owners:** Responsible for classifying data and approving access rights based on business need.
- **All Employees:** Responsible for adhering to security policies and reporting suspicious activity.

5. Oversight and Reporting The CISO shall chair the **Information Security Steering Committee (ISSC)**, which meets [Monthly/Quarterly] to review risk metrics, policy exceptions, and major initiatives.

Approved By: ____________________

Date: ______________

Appendix C

#

3PAO (Third-Party Assessment Organization): An accredited organization that performs independent security assessments for FedRAMP authorization.

A

ABAC (Attribute-Based Access Control): Access control method that evaluates attributes (user, resource, environment) to make authorization decisions.

Access Control: Security measures that regulate who or what can view or use resources in a computing environment.

Adaptive Trust: Security approach that continuously evaluates trust levels based on contextual factors and adjusts access accordingly.

AI Security: Practice of protecting AI systems from attacks and preventing AI from being weaponized, including prompt injection prevention and model security.

API (Application Programming Interface): Set of protocols and tools for building application software and enabling system integration.

API Gateway: Management tool that sits between clients and backend services, handling authentication, rate limiting, and monitoring.

AppSec (Application Security): Practice of making applications more secure through the software development lifecycle.

ATT&CK (Adversarial Tactics, Techniques, and Common Knowledge): MITRE framework documenting adversary behaviors and tactics.

Attack Surface: Sum total of points where an unauthorized user can try to enter or extract data from an environment.

Audit Trail: Chronological record of system activities that enables reconstruction and examination of events.

B

Backup Strategy: Systematic approach to data backup including frequency, storage location, retention, and testing procedures.

BCP (Business Continuity Planning): Framework for continuing business operations during and after disruption.

BeyondCorp: Google's Zero Trust security model emphasizing perimeter-less design and context-aware access.

BIA (Business Impact Analysis): Process assessing potential disruption effects on business operations.

Blast Radius: Extent of potential damage from a security breach or system failure.

Blue Team: Defensive security team responsible for protecting the organization against attacks.

Break-Glass Access: Emergency access mechanism that provides privileged access during critical situations.

C

CA (Certificate Authority): Trusted entity that issues digital certificates for identity verification.

CCM (Cloud Controls Matrix): CSA framework mapping cloud security controls across compliance frameworks.

CCPA (California Consumer Privacy Act): California law providing consumers rights regarding personal information.

CIEM (Cloud Infrastructure Entitlement Management): Tools managing identities and access permissions across cloud environments.

CIA Triad: Confidentiality, Integrity, and Availability - core principles of information security.

CIS Controls: Prioritized set of actions for cyber defense developed by Center for Internet Security.

CISO (Chief Information Security Officer): Executive responsible for an organization's information and cybersecurity strategy.

CMMC (Cybersecurity Maturity Model Certification): Framework for defense contractors protecting Controlled Unclassified Information.

Compensating Control: Alternative security measure implemented when primary control isn't feasible.

Configuration Drift: Gradual deviation of system configurations from approved baselines.

Continuous Monitoring: Ongoing observation and analysis of security posture and compliance.

Credential Stuffing: Attack using stolen username/password pairs from data breaches to gain unauthorized access.

CSPM (Cloud Security Posture Management): Tools identifying misconfigurations and compliance risks in cloud infrastructure.

CUI (Controlled Unclassified Information): Government information requiring safeguarding but not classified.

CWPP (Cloud Workload Protection Platform): Security solutions protecting cloud workloads across VMs, containers, and serverless.

D

Data Classification: Process of organizing data by sensitivity level to determine appropriate protection measures.

Data Exfiltration: Unauthorized transfer of data from a computer or network.

Data Lineage: Documentation of data's origin, movements, and transformations throughout its lifecycle.

Data Minimization: Practice of limiting data collection to only what's necessary for specific purposes.

DDoS (Distributed Denial of Service): Attack overwhelming systems with traffic from multiple sources.

Deepfake: AI-generated synthetic media that appears authentic, often used for social engineering.

Defense in Depth: Layered security approach using multiple defensive mechanisms.

Detection Engineering: Discipline of designing, implementing, and maintaining detection capabilities for security threats.

DevSecOps: Integration of security practices into DevOps workflows from the beginning.

DNSSEC (Domain Name System Security Extensions): Security protocols adding authentication to DNS responses.

DR (Disaster Recovery): Process of regaining access to systems and data after a disaster.

DRP (Disaster Recovery Planning): Documented procedures for responding to disaster scenarios.

DREAD: Microsoft threat modeling framework assessing Damage, Reproducibility, Exploitability, Affected users, and Discoverability.

DSPM (Data Security Posture Management): Tools providing visibility into sensitive data location, access, and risk.

Dwell Time: Duration an attacker remains undetected in a network after initial compromise.

E

East-West Traffic: Network traffic between servers/workloads within a data center, as opposed to north-south (client-server).

EDR (Endpoint Detection and Response): Security solution monitoring endpoints for suspicious activities and enabling rapid response.

Egress Control: Monitoring and restricting outbound network traffic.

Encryption at Rest: Data protection when stored on physical media.

Encryption in Transit: Data protection during transmission across networks.

Entitlement: Permission or right granted to an identity to access a resource.

F

FAIR (Factor Analysis of Information Risk): Framework for quantifying information risk in financial terms.

False Positive: Legitimate activity incorrectly identified as malicious.

FedRAMP (Federal Risk and Authorization Management Program): US government program for cloud service security assessment.

FIDO2: Authentication standard enabling passwordless authentication using public key cryptography.

Firewall: Network security device monitoring and controlling traffic based on security rules.

Firmware: Permanent software programmed into hardware devices.

G

GDPR (General Data Protection Regulation): EU regulation on data protection and privacy.

GitOps: Operational framework using Git as single source of truth for declarative infrastructure.

GRC (Governance, Risk, and Compliance): Integrated approach to managing governance, risk management, and regulatory compliance.

Guardrails: Automated policy enforcement preventing configuration drift and non-compliant deployments.

H

Harvest Now, Decrypt Later: Threat where adversaries collect encrypted data now to decrypt with future quantum computers.

Heatmap: Visual representation of data using color-coding to show severity or frequency.

HIPAA (Health Insurance Portability and Accountability Act): US law protecting sensitive patient health information.

HITECH (Health Information Technology for Economic and Clinical Health Act): Expands HIPAA to address electronic health records.

HSM (Hardware Security Module): Physical device managing digital keys and performing cryptographic operations.

Hybrid Cryptography: Approach using both classical and post-quantum algorithms during transition period.

Hygiene (Cyber): Basic security practices maintaining minimum security standards.

I

IaaS (Infrastructure as a Service): Cloud computing model providing virtualized computing resources.

IAM (Identity and Access Management): Framework ensuring right individuals access right resources at right times.

IaC (Infrastructure as Code): Managing infrastructure through machine-readable definition files.

IdP (Identity Provider): System creating, maintaining, and managing identity information.

IGA (Identity Governance and Administration): Policies and technologies ensuring appropriate identity and access management.

ILM (Identity Lifecycle Management): Process managing user identities from creation to deletion.

Immutable Logs: Audit logs that cannot be altered or deleted after creation.

Impossible Travel: Security alert triggered when account access occurs from geographically distant locations in impossible timeframe.

Incident Response: Organized approach to addressing and managing security incidents.

IoC (Indicators of Compromise): Forensic data indicating potential security breach.

IR (Incident Response): See Incident Response.

ISMS (Information Security Management System): Systematic approach to managing sensitive information.

ISO 27001: International standard for information security management systems.

ISO 27017: ISO standard for cloud security controls.

ISO 27018: ISO standard for cloud privacy controls.

ITDR (Identity Threat Detection and Response): Security approach focused on identity-based threats.

J

JEA (Just Enough Administration): PowerShell security technology limiting administrator access to specific tasks.

JIT (Just-In-Time): Providing access privileges only when needed and for limited duration.

Jump Server: Intermediary system used to access and manage devices in separate security zones.

K

Key Management: Administration of cryptographic keys including generation, exchange, storage, and destruction.

KMS (Key Management Service): Cloud service for creating and managing cryptographic keys.

KPI (Key Performance Indicator): Measurable value demonstrating effectiveness of achieving objectives.

KRI (Key Risk Indicator): Metric providing early warning of increasing risk exposure.

Kubernetes: Open-source container orchestration platform.

L

Lateral Movement: Post-compromise tactic where attackers move through a network to reach target assets.

Least Privilege: Security principle of providing minimum access necessary to perform job functions.

Logging: Recording of events occurring in systems and networks for monitoring and analysis.

M

Machine Identity: Digital identity assigned to non-human entities like applications, services, devices.

Malware: Malicious software designed to harm, exploit, or compromise systems.

MDR (Managed Detection and Response): Outsourced service providing threat detection and response.

Mean Time To Detect (MTTD): Average time to discover security incident after occurrence.

Mean Time To Respond (MTTR): Average time to respond to and remediate security incident.

MFA (Multi-Factor Authentication): Authentication requiring two or more verification factors.

Microsegmentation: Network security technique creating secure zones to isolate workloads and secure them individually.

MITRE ATT&CK: See ATT&CK.

mTLS (Mutual TLS): Authentication method where both client and server verify each other's identity.

MTD (Maximum Tolerable Downtime): Maximum time a business can be without a resource before unacceptable impact.

N

NDR (Network Detection and Response): Security solution monitoring network traffic for threats.

NIST (National Institute of Standards and Technology): US agency developing technology standards.

NIST CSF (Cybersecurity Framework): Voluntary framework for managing cybersecurity risk.

NIST SP 800-53: Catalog of security and privacy controls for federal information systems.

NIST SP 800-207: Zero Trust Architecture publication.

NIST SP 800-37: Risk Management Framework publication.

Non-Repudiation: Assurance that someone cannot deny the validity of action or communication.

North-South Traffic: Network traffic between client and server, typically crossing security boundaries.

O

OPA (Open Policy Agent): Policy engine for cloud-native environments.

OT (Operational Technology): Hardware and software controlling industrial operations.

OWASP (Open Web Application Security Project): Nonprofit focused on software security.

OWASP Top 10: List of most critical web application security risks.

P

PaaS (Platform as a Service): Cloud computing model providing platform for application development.

PAC (Policy as Code): Managing security policies through code.

PAM (Privileged Access Management): Tools and processes controlling and monitoring privileged access.

Passwordless Authentication: Authentication without traditional passwords, using biometrics, tokens, or keys.

Patch Management: Process of acquiring, testing, and deploying software updates.

PBAC (Policy-Based Access Control): Access control using policies to make authorization decisions.

PCI DSS (Payment Card Industry Data Security Standard): Security standards for organizations handling credit cards.

PDP (Policy Decision Point): Component evaluating access requests against policies in Zero Trust.

Penetration Testing: Simulated cyberattack to evaluate security.

PEP (Policy Enforcement Point): Component enforcing access decisions in Zero Trust.

Perimeter Security: Traditional security model focused on network boundaries (now considered legacy).

Persistence: Adversary technique maintaining access to compromised systems.

PHI (Protected Health Information): Health information protected under HIPAA.

Phishing: Social engineering attack using fraudulent communications to trick recipients.

PII (Personally Identifiable Information): Data identifying specific individuals.

PKI (Public Key Infrastructure): Framework managing digital certificates and public-key encryption.

Playbook: Documented procedures for responding to specific security scenarios.

Policy Engine: Component in Zero Trust that computes access decisions.

Post-Quantum Cryptography (PQC): Cryptographic algorithms resistant to quantum computer attacks.

Principle of Least Privilege: See Least Privilege.

Privacy Engineering: Systematic approach to embedding privacy into systems design.

Privileged Account: Account with elevated access permissions.

Prompt Injection: AI security attack manipulating AI system behavior through crafted inputs.

Purple Team: Collaborative security team combining red (offensive) and blue (defensive) activities.

Q

QSA (Qualified Security Assessor): Organization certified to perform PCI DSS compliance audits.

Quantum Computing: Computing using quantum mechanics principles, threatening current cryptography.

Quantum Resistance: Cryptographic systems resistant to quantum computer attacks.

R

Ransomware: Malware encrypting data and demanding payment for decryption.

RBAC (Role-Based Access Control): Access control based on user roles.

Red Team: Offensive security team simulating adversary attacks.

Resilience: Ability to maintain operations during disruption and recover quickly.

Risk Acceptance: Formal decision acknowledging and accepting specific risk without mitigation.

Risk Appetite: Amount and type of risk an organization is willing to take.

Risk Assessment: Process identifying and evaluating risks.

Risk Register: Document cataloging identified risks and their details.

RMF (Risk Management Framework): NIST framework for managing organizational risk.

RPO (Recovery Point Objective): Maximum acceptable amount of data loss measured in time.

RTO (Recovery Time Objective): Target time for restoring systems after disruption.

Runtime Protection: Security monitoring and protecting applications while executing.

S

SaaS (Software as a Service): Cloud computing model delivering applications over the internet.

SAML (Security Assertion Markup Language): Standard for exchanging authentication and authorization data.

SANS (SysAdmin, Audit, Network, and Security): Organization providing cybersecurity training and certification.

SASE (Secure Access Service Edge): Cloud-based security model combining networking and security functions.

SBOM (Software Bill of Materials): Inventory of software components and dependencies.

Schema Validation: Verifying data structure and format meet defined schema.

SD-WAN (Software-Defined Wide Area Network): Technology simplifying WAN management using software control.

Secrets Management: Controlling access to API keys, passwords, certificates, and tokens.

Security Architecture: Design of security controls supporting business objectives.

Security Orchestration: Coordinating security tools and processes for automated workflows.

Security Posture: Organization's overall cybersecurity strength.

Segmentation: Dividing network into isolated segments to contain breaches.

Service Mesh: Infrastructure layer controlling service-to-service communication.

Shadow AI: Unauthorized AI tools and services used by employees without IT approval.

Shadow IT: IT systems deployed and used without organizational approval.

Shared Responsibility Model: Cloud security model defining provider vs. customer security obligations.

SIEM (Security Information and Event Management): Platform collecting and analyzing security data.

SOAR (Security Orchestration, Automation and Response): Platform automating security operations.

SOC (Security Operations Center): Centralized unit monitoring and responding to security incidents.

SOC 2: Audit framework for service organizations' security controls.

SoD (Separation of Duties): Security principle dividing critical functions among different people.

SSDLC (Secure Software Development Lifecycle): Integrating security into all phases of software development.

SSE (Security Service Edge): Cloud-based security services including SWG, CASB, and ZTNA.

SSO (Single Sign-On): Authentication allowing access to multiple systems with one login.

SSPM (SaaS Security Posture Management): Tools assessing and managing SaaS application security.

STRIDE: Microsoft threat modeling framework: Spoofing, Tampering, Repudiation, Information Disclosure, Denial of Service, Elevation of Privilege.

Supply Chain Attack: Compromising organization through vulnerabilities in supply chain.

Supply Chain Security: Protecting against risks in supply chain and third-party relationships.

T

Tabletop Exercise: Discussion-based simulation testing incident response procedures.

Tactics, Techniques, and Procedures (TTPs): Patterns of activities used by threat actors.

Telemetry: Automated data collection from systems for monitoring and analysis.

Threat Actor: Individual or group conducting malicious cyber activities.

Threat Hunting: Proactive search for threats that evade automated detection.

Threat Intelligence: Information about threats used to prepare and prevent attacks.

Threat Modeling: Identifying and prioritizing potential threats to applications or systems.

TLS (Transport Layer Security): Cryptographic protocol providing secure communication.

Token: Digital object representing user authentication or authorization.

TSC (Trust Services Criteria): AICPA criteria for SOC 2 engagements.

TTP: See Tactics, Techniques, and Procedures.

U

UEBA (User and Entity Behavior Analytics): Detecting threats through behavioral analysis.

UCF (Unified Control Framework): Mapping multiple compliance frameworks to single control library.

Unique ID: Property providing distinctive identifier for database records.

V

Vault: Secure storage system for secrets and sensitive data.

Vendor Risk Management (VRM): Process assessing and mitigating risks from third-party vendors.

VPN (Virtual Private Network): Encrypted connection over internet (legacy approach being replaced by ZTNA).

Vulnerability: Weakness that can be exploited by threats.

Vulnerability Management: Identifying, assessing, and remediating security vulnerabilities.

W

WAF (Web Application Firewall): Filtering HTTP traffic between web application and internet.

Workload: Unit of work performed by computing resources.

Workload Identity: Digital identity assigned to applications, services, or workloads.

WORM (Write Once Read Many): Storage preventing data modification after initial write.

X

XDR (Extended Detection and Response): Platform integrating multiple security products for unified detection and response.

Z

Zero Day: Previously unknown vulnerability being exploited before patch available.

Zero Trust: Security model eliminating implicit trust and requiring continuous verification.

Zero Trust Architecture (ZTA): Implementation of Zero Trust principles across enterprise.

ZTNA (Zero Trust Network Access): Technology providing secure application access based on identity and context, replacing VPN.

Appendix D

Chapter 1: Executive Summary

COSO Enterprise Risk Management Framework | Author/Organization: Committee of Sponsoring Organizations of the Treadway Commission (COSO) | URL: https://www.coso.org/guidance-on-erm | Description: Official framework for enterprise risk management, emphasizing governance, culture, strategy, performance, review, and reporting; foundational for translating cyber risk into business risk as referenced in CISO leadership books.

Microsoft Digital Defense Report 2025 CISO Executive Summary | Author/Organization: Microsoft | URL: https://cdn-dynmedia-1.microsoft.com/is/content/microsoftcorp/microsoft/bade/documents/products-and-services/en-us/security/CISO-Executive-Summary-MDDR-2025.pdf | Description: Provides actionable cybersecurity priorities for CISOs, including identity protection, workforce upskilling, perimeter defense, vulnerability management, and intelligence sharing amid AI-driven threats.

NIST Cybersecurity Framework (CSF) 2.0 | Author/Organization: National Institute of Standards and Technology (NIST) | URL: https://www.nist.gov/cyberframework | Description: U.S. government standard for managing cybersecurity risk, offering profiles for governance, identify, protect, detect, respond, and recover functions essential for executive-level CISO strategies.

ISO/IEC 27001:2022 Information Security Management | Author/Organization: International Organization for Standardization (ISO) | URL: https://www.iso.org/standard/27001 | Description: Global standard for establishing, implementing, and maintaining an information security management system (ISMS), critical for CISOs aligning security with business objectives.

The CISO Evolution: Business Knowledge for Cybersecurity Executives | Author/Organization: Matthew K. Sharp and Kyriakos (Rock) Lambros | URL: https://www.cisoevolution.com/book | Description: Book detailing business acumen for CISOs, including chapters on business decisions, translating cyber risk to enterprise risk using COSO, and board communication.

A Day in the Life of a CISO | Author/Organization: Multiple global CISOs (O'Reilly Media) | URL: https://learning.oreilly.com/library/view/-/9781806110698/ | Description: Insights from 29 CISOs on cyber strategy, risk management, AI threats, team building, breach recovery, and leadership skills for executive summaries and decision-making.

CISO Desk Reference Guide Executive Primer | Author/Organization: Bill Bonney, Gary Hayslip, Matt Stamper | Description: Executive guide outlining CEO/CFO expectations for CISOs, security program support, and organizational resilience building.

You CAN Stop Stupid: Stopping Losses from Accidental and Malicious Actions | Author/Organization: Ira Winkler | Description: Framework for quantitative risk analysis, measuring information risk, and strengthening risk management programs for CISO executive reporting.

Start with Why | Author/Organization: Simon Sinek | Description: Leadership book on the "Golden Circle" framework for inspiring teams and communicating cybersecurity strategy to executives and boards.

Writing for Impact: Executive Summaries | Author/Organization: Markerbench | URL: https://www.markerbench.com/posts/writing-for-impact-exec-summaries/ | Description: Guide to crafting persuasive executive summaries with key findings, recommendations, and action-oriented language for cybersecurity assessments.

Chapter 2: NIST Cybersecurity Framework (CSF) 2.0

NIST Cybersecurity Framework 2.0 | Author/Organization: NIST | URL: https://nvlpubs.nist.gov/nistpubs/CSWP/NIST.CSWP.29.pdf| Description: Official PDF document detailing CSF 2.0 components, including the Core (Functions, Categories, Subcategories), Profiles, Tiers, and the new Govern Function for risk management strategy.

Cybersecurity Framework | Author/Organization: NIST | URL: https://www.nist.gov/cyberframework | Description: Official NIST resource center for CSF 2.0, offering downloads, Quick Start Guides, Profiles, Informative References, FAQs, and videos to implement the framework.

NIST Cybersecurity Framework 2.0 Reference Tool | Author/Organization: NIST (via CSF Tools) | URL: https://csf.tools/reference/nist-cybersecurity-framework/v2-0/ | Description: Searchable online tool for browsing, searching, and exporting CSF 2.0 Core guidance in human- and machine-readable formats, aiding implementation.

SP 1303: NIST Cybersecurity Framework 2.0: Enterprise Risk | Author/Organization: NIST | URL: https://csrc.nist.gov/pubs/sp/1303/final | Description: Official guide introducing CSF 2.0 for enterprise-wide risk planning and integration processes.

SP 1308: NIST Cybersecurity Framework 2.0 (Integration with NICE Framework) | Author/Organization: NIST | URL: https://csrc.nist.gov/pubs/sp/1308/ipd | Description: Quick Start Guide (dated March 2025) showing how to align CSF 2.0 with the NICE Workforce Framework for addressing cybersecurity risks.

NIST Cybersecurity Framework 2.0 Factsheet | Author/Organization: NIST | URL: https://www.nist.gov/document/nistcsfupdatefactsheet | Description: Official factsheet on CSF 2.0 update process, based on standards and practices to manage risks, with calls for public input and workshops.

NIST CSF 2.0: Everything You Need to Know About the Update | Author/Organization: Hyperproof | URL: https://hyperproof.io/resource/nistcsf2-0-update/ | Description: Comprehensive overview of CSF 2.0 changes, including the new Govern Function, six core functions, Tiers as an appendix, and NIST's suite of implementation tools.

Unpacking the NIST Cybersecurity Framework 2.0 | Author/Organization: IBM | URL: https://www.ibm.com/think/insights/nist-cybersecurity-framework-2 | Description: Analysis of CSF 2.0 evolution from 1.1, emphasizing Govern function, Organizational and Community Profiles, and shift from best to common practices for all organizations.

NIST CSF 2.0: Understanding and Implementing the Govern Function | Author/Organization: Arctic Wolf | URL: https://arcticwolf.com/resources/blog/nist-csf-2-0-understanding-and-implementing-the-govern-function/ | Description: Detailed guide on CSF 2.0's six core functions, with focus on Govern subcategories like Organizational Context for cybersecurity risk management.

Chapter 3: NIST SP 800-53 (Revision 5)

NIST SP 800-53 Rev. 5: Security and Privacy Controls for Information Systems and Organizations | Author/Organization: National Institute of Standards and Technology (NIST) | URL: https://csrc.nist.gov/publications/detail/sp/800-53/rev-5/final | Description: The definitive catalog of security and privacy controls for federal information systems, organized into 20 control families. Rev. 5 integrates privacy controls and expands supply chain risk management guidance.

NIST SP 800-53B: Control Baselines for Information Systems and Organizations | Author/Organization: National Institute of Standards and Technology (NIST) | URL: https://csrc.nist.gov/publications/detail/sp/800-53b/final |

Description: Companion document providing low, moderate, and high baseline control selections to simplify implementation for organizations of varying risk profiles.

NIST SP 800-53A Rev. 5: Assessing Security and Privacy Controls | Author/Organization: National Institute of Standards and Technology (NIST) | URL: https://csrc.nist.gov/publications/detail/sp/800-53a/rev-5/final | Description: Procedures for assessing the effectiveness of security and privacy controls, aligned with the Risk Management Framework (RMF).

NIST SP 800-53 Release 5.2.0 — CPRT Browser | Author/Organization: NIST Computer Security Resource Center | URL: https://csrc.nist.gov/projects/cprt/catalog#/cprt/framework/version/SP_800_53_5_1_0/home | Description: Latest incremental update to SP 800-53 Rev. 5, available via the Cybersecurity and Privacy Reference Tool with machine-readable exports and cross-framework mappings.

NIST Online Informative References (OLIR): SP 800-53 Mappings | Author/Organization: NIST | URL: https://csrc.nist.gov/projects/olir/informative-reference-catalog | Description: Official cross-framework mappings enabling organizations to leverage SP 800-53 compliance work toward ISO/IEC 27001 and other international standards.

AWS Security Hub: NIST SP 800-53 Rev. 5 Standard | Author/Organization: Amazon Web Services | URL: https://docs.aws.amazon.com/securityhub/latest/userguide/nist-standard.html | Description: Cloud-native implementation of SP 800-53 Rev. 5 controls within AWS, providing automated compliance checks and continuous monitoring.

Microsoft Azure Policy: NIST SP 800-53 Rev 5 Regulatory Compliance | Author/Organization: Microsoft | URL: https://learn.microsoft.com/en-us/azure/governance/policy/samples/nist-sp-800-53-r5 | Description: Azure built-in policy initiatives mapping Azure services to NIST SP 800-53 Rev. 5 controls for hybrid and cloud-native compliance programs.

CIS Controls v8 Mapping to NIST SP 800-53 Rev. 5 | Author/Organization: Center for Internet Security (CIS) | URL: https://www.cisecurity.org/wp-content/uploads/2021/11/CIS-Controls-v8-Mapping-to-NIST-SP800-53-Rev-5.xlsx | Description: Authoritative cross-reference mapping CIS Controls v8 safeguards to NIST SP 800-53 Rev. 5 controls for unified framework management.

FedRAMP Authorization Framework and SP 800-53 Rev. 5 | Author/Organization: General Services Administration / FedRAMP PMO | URL: https://www.fedramp.gov/documents-templates/ | Description: Federal Risk and

Authorization Management Program documentation leveraging SP 800-53 Rev. 5 as its foundational control baseline for cloud service authorization.

NIST SP 800-53 Rev. 5 — A Practical Guide for Security Executives | Author/Organization: ISACA | URL: https://www.isaca.org/resources/isaca-journal | Description: Executive-level guidance on operationalizing SP 800-53 Rev. 5, including prioritization strategies, control tailoring, and integration with existing GRC programs.

Chapter 4: Zero Trust Architecture (NIST 800-207)

Zero Trust Architecture (NIST SP 800-207) | Author/Organization: National Institute of Standards and Technology (NIST) | URL: https://nvlpubs.nist.gov/nistpubs/specialpublications/NIST.SP.800-207.pdf | Description: Official NIST standard defining Zero Trust Architecture as an end-to-end cybersecurity plan with principles like no implicit trust, continuous verification, and risk-based access to resources, serving as the core framework for ZTA implementations.

CISA Zero Trust Maturity Model V2.0 | Author/Organization: Cybersecurity and Infrastructure Security Agency (CISA) | URL: https://www.cisco.com/c/en/us/solutions/collateral/enterprise/design-zone-security/zt-frameworks.html | Description: U.S. government roadmap for agencies transitioning to Zero Trust, outlining maturity stages (Traditional, Initial, Advanced) across technology pillars like identity, devices, and networks to build implementation plans.

Zero Trust Architecture Technology Book | Author/Organization: General Services Administration (GSA) | URL: https://buy.gsa.gov/api/system/files/documents/zero-trust-architecture-tech-book-508c.pdf | Description: Data-centric ZTA guide structured around five pillars (Identity, Devices, Networks, Applications & Workloads, Data), providing steps for preparation, categorization, control selection, implementation, assessment, authorization, and monitoring.

Zero Trust Frameworks Architecture Guide | Author/Organization: Cisco | URL: https://www.cisco.com/c/en/us/solutions/collateral/enterprise/design-zone-security/zt-frameworks.html | Description: Comprehensive guide mapping various Zero Trust frameworks (including CISA and NIST) to Cisco's model, detailing maturity criteria and cross-pillar integration for enterprise deployments.

Federal Zero Trust Data Security Guide | Author/Organization: CIO.gov (U.S. Federal Government) | URL: https://resources.data.gov/assets/documents/Zero-Trust-DataSecurityGuide_RevisedMay2025_CIO.govVersion.pdf | Description: Focuses on data security in Zero Trust, covering encryption, monitoring, controls, and risk management to secure data assets within federal ZTA strategies.

A CISO's Guide: Avoid the Common Pitfalls of Zero Trust Deployments | Author/Organization: Cato Networks | URL: https://www.catonetworks.co

m/blog/cisos-guide-avoiding-common-pitfalls-of-zero-trust-deployments/ | Description: Practical advice for CISOs on Zero Trust pitfalls, emphasizing key tenets like implicit deny, user-centric deployment, and mapping journeys without harming business operations.

Community Webinar on Zero Trust: Architecture Principles, Threats | Author/Organization: CISO Platform | URL: https://www.cisoplatform.com/profiles/blogs/community-webinar-on-zero-trust-architecture-principles-threats | Description: Webinar overview of ZTA principles (assume breach, continuous verification), logical components (devices, networks, apps, data), benefits like lateral movement prevention, and implementation steps starting with identity.

Zero Trust Architecture (Sample Chapter from Book) | Author/Organization: Pearson (PTG Media, likely from "Zero Trust Architecture" book) | URL: https://ptgmedia.pearsoncmg.com/images/9780137899739/samplepages/9780137899739_Sample.pdf | Description: Book excerpt on Zero Trust organizational dynamics, addressing challenges like competing teams, cloud misconceptions, and Cisco capabilities in policy, governance, and identity.

NSA Zero Trust Recommendations | Author/Organization: National Security Agency (NSA), referenced in CISO Platform webinar | URL: https://www.cisoplatform.com/profiles/blogs/community-webinar-on-zero-trust-architecture-principles-threats | Description: Guidance documents from NSA on Zero Trust threats, components, and architecture, integrated with NIST and CISA for comprehensive principles like real-time verification and anomaly detection.

Chapter 5: Risk Management Framework (RMF)

NIST SP 800-37 Revision 2: Risk Management Framework for Information Systems and Organizations | Author/Organization: National Institute of Standards and Technology (NIST) | URL: https://nvlpubs.nist.gov/nistpubs/SpecialPublications/NIST.SP.800-37r2.pdf

NIST SP 800-37 Rev. 2, Risk Management Framework for Information Systems and Organizations | Author/Organization: National Institute of Standards and Technology (NIST) | URL: https://csrc.nist.gov/pubs/sp/800/37/r2/final

NIST Risk Management Framework (RMF) Overview | Author/Organization: National Institute of Standards and Technology (NIST) - Computer Security Resource Center (CSRC) | URL: https://csrc.nist.gov/projects/risk-management

NIST Risk Management Framework RMF Resources | Author/Organization: National Institute of Standards and Technology (NIST) - Computer Security Resource Center (CSRC) | URL: https://csrc.nist.rip/Projects/risk-management

Introduction to the Risk Management Framework (RMF) Student Guide | Author/Organization: Center for Development of Security Excellence (CDSE) | URL: https://www.cdse.edu/Portals/124/Documents/student-guides/CS124-guide.pdf

NIST Risk Management Framework (RMF) | Author/Organization: SailPoint Technologies | URL: https://www.sailpoint.com/identity-library/nist-risk-management-framework

A Complete Guide to the NIST Risk Management Framework | Author/Organization: EC-Council | URL: https://www.eccouncil.org/cybersecurity-exchange/incident-handling/nist-risk-management-framework-rmf-guide/

Understanding the NIST Risk Management Framework | Author/Organization: Secureframe | URL: https://secureframe.com/blog/nist-rmf

What is NIST RMF? Risk Management Framework Guide | Author/Organization: Onspring | URL: https://onspring.com/resources/guide/guide-what-is-nist-rmf/

A Guide to the NIST Risk Management Framework - NIST SP 800-37 | Author/Organization: Security Scientist | URL: https://www.securityscientist.net/blog/a-guide-to-the-nist-risk-management-framework-nist-sp-800-37/

Chapter 6: CIS Controls v8.1

CIS Critical Security Controls Version 8.1 | Author/Organization: Center for Internet Security (CIS) | URL: https://www.cisecurity.org/controls/v8-1

CIS Critical Security Controls v8.1 White Paper | Author/Organization: Center for Internet Security (CIS) | URL: https://www.cisecurity.org/insights/white-papers/cis-critical-security-controls-v8-1

CIS Controls v8.1 Guide (PDF) | Author/Organization: Center for Internet Security (CIS) / ETIR – STI/UnB | URL: https://etir.unb.br/wp-content/uploads/2024/10/CIS_Controls__v8.1_Guide__2024_06.pdf

CIS Critical Security Controls v8.1 Industrial Control Systems (ICS) Guide | Author/Organization: Center for Internet Security (CIS) | URL: https://www.cisecurity.org/insights/white-papers/cis-critical-security-controls-v8-1-industrial-control-systems-ics-guide

CIS Controls Navigator v8.1 | Author/Organization: Center for Internet Security (CIS) | URL: https://www.cisecurity.org/controls/cis-controls-navigator

CIS Controls v8.1 Framework Overview | Author/Organization: Drata | URL: https://help.drata.com/en/articles/11145651-cis-v8-1-framework-overview

CIS Controls v8 Released (v8 Context Applicable to v8.1) | Author/Organization: SANS Institute | URL: https://www.sans.org/blog/cis-controls-v8

CIS Controls v8.1 Guide (PDF) | Author/Organization: Arkansas Legislative Audit | URL: https://arklegaudit.gov/docs/cis_controls_guide.pdf

Center for Internet Security Controls v8.1 (XLS Mapping Tool) | Author/Organization: New York State Executive Chamber (EFC) | URL: https://efc.ny.gov/center-internet-security-controls-v81

CIS V8.1 Framework | Author/Organization: Compliance Manager GRC | URL: https://www.compliancemanagergrc.com/standards/cis-v8-1/

Chapter 7: MITRE ATT&CK Framework

MITRE ATT&CK® | Author/Organization: MITRE Corporation | URL: https://attack.mitre.org

MITRE ATT&CK®: Design and Philosophy (March 2020) | Author/Organization: MITRE Corporation | URL: https://attack.mitre.org/docs/ATTACK_Design_and_Philosophy_March_2020.pdf

Getting Started with ATT&CK (October 2019) | Author/Organization: MITRE Corporation | URL: https://www.mitre.org/sites/default/files/2021-11/getting-started-with-attack-october-2019.pdf

Updates | MITRE ATT&CK® (v18, October 2025) | Author/Organization: MITRE Corporation | URL: https://attack.mitre.org/resources/updates/

Get Started - MITRE ATT&CK® | Author/Organization: MITRE Corporation | URL: https://attack.mitre.org/resources/

ATT&CK Navigator | Author/Organization: MITRE Corporation | URL: https://attack.mitre.org/resources/attack-navigator/

ATT&CK Evaluations | Author/Organization: MITRE Corporation | URL: https://attack.mitre.org/resources/attack-evaluations/

MITRE ATT&CK Matrix for Enterprise | Author/Organization: MITRE Corporation | URL: https://attack.mitre.org/matrices/enterprise/

MITRE ATT&CK for ICS | Author/Organization: MITRE Corporation | URL: https://attack.mitre.org/matrices/ics/

MITRE ATT&CK for Mobile | Author/Organization: MITRE Corporation | URL: https://attack.mitre.org/matrices/mobile/

Chapter 8: Detection Engineering & SIEM Modernization

Detection-as-Code: The New Standard for Cloud SIEM | Author/Organization: DEMICON | URL: https://demicon.com/en/insights/detection-as-code-the-new-standard-for-cloud-siem

What is Detection Engineering? | Author/Organization: SentinelOne | URL: https://www.sentinelone.com/cybersecurity-101/threat-intelligence/detection-engineering/

The Art and Science of Threat Detection: SIEM and Detection Engineering Essentials | Author/Organization: Annoyed Engineer |

URL: https://annoyed.engineer/2024/11/12/the-art-and-science-of-threat-detection-siem-and-detection-engineering-essentials/

Implementing SIEM and SOAR platforms: Practitioner Guidance | Author/Organization: (Official Standard Document | URL: https://media.defense.gov/2025/May/27/2003722066/-1/-1/0/Implementing-SIEM-and-SOAR-platforms-Practitioner-guidance.PDF | Description: PDF) U.S. Department of Defense

Build Smarter Threat Detection with Next-Gen SIEM | Author/Organization: (CrowdStrike Falcon Next-Gen SIEM Framework) CrowdStrike | URL: https://www.crowdstrike.com/en-us/blog/build-smarter-threat-detection-with-next-gen-siem/

State of SIEM Detection Risk | Author/Organization: (Key Report | URL: https://cardinalops.com/wp-content/uploads/2025/06/25-CardinalOps-2025-State-of-SIEM-Report.pdf | Description: PDF) CardinalOps

NIST SIEM Requirements and Standards | Author/Organization: (Official NIST Standards Framework) Sumo Logic | URL: https://www.sumologic.com/glossary/nist-siem-requirements-and-standards

MITRE ATT&CK Framework | Author/Organization: (Key Framework for Threat Detection Mapping) MITRE | URL: https://attack.mitre.org/

Detection Engineering Framework | Author/Organization: (Open-Source Tools and Best Practices) olafhartong/sysmon-modular | URL: https://github.com/olafhartong/sysmon-modular

Sigma Detection Rules | Author/Organization: (Open Detection Rules Standard for SIEM) SigmaHQ | URL: https://github.com/SigmaHQ/sigma

Chapter 9: Cloud Security Frameworks & Architectures

CIS Benchmarks | Author/Organization: Center for Internet Security (CIS) | URL: https://www.cisecurity.org/benchmark/

NIST SP 800-53 | Author/Organization: National Institute of Standards and Technology (NIST) | URL: https://csrc.nist.gov/publications/detail/sp/800-53/rev-5/final

Cloud Controls Matrix (CCM) | Author/Organization: Cloud Security Alliance (CSA) | URL: https://cloudsecurityalliance.org/artifacts/cloud-controls-matrix-v4/

NIST Cybersecurity Framework (CSF) | Author/Organization: National Institute of Standards and Technology (NIST) | URL: https://www.nist.gov/cyberframework

ISO/IEC 27001 | Author/Organization: International Organization for Standardization (ISO) | URL: https://www.iso.org/standard/27001

ISO/IEC 27017 | Author/Organization: International Organization for Standardization (ISO) | URL: https://www.iso.org/standard/43757.html

FedRAMP | Author/Organization: Federal Risk and Authorization Management Program | URL: https://www.fedramp.gov/

CSA STAR | Author/Organization: Cloud Security Alliance (CSA) | URL: https://cloudsecurityalliance.org/star/

PCI DSS | Author/Organization: PCI Security Standards Council | URL: https://www.pcisecuritystandards.org/

SOC 2 | Author/Organization: American Institute of CPAs (AICPA) | URL: https://www.aicpa.org/interestareas/frc/assuranceadvisoryservices/socforserviceorganizations.html

Chapter 10: Identity & Access Management

Public Identity and Access Management (PIAM) Framework Guide | Author/Organization: IDManagement.gov | URL: https://www.idmanagement.gov/experiments/pid/framework/

Identity and Access Management Standard | Author/Organization: Wharton School (University of Pennsylvania) | URL: https://support.wharton.upenn.edu/help/iam-standard

Identity and Access Management Framework: A Guide | Author/Organization: Legit Security | URL: https://www.legitsecurity.com/aspm-knowledge-base/identity-access-management-framework

Understanding Privileged Access Management Standards: ISO, NIST and More | Author/Organization: SSH Communications Security | URL: https://www.ssh.com/academy/compliance/understanding-privileged-access-management-standards-iso-nist-and-more

Identity and Access Compliance Roadmap | Author/Organization: Identity Management Institute | URL: https://identitymanagementinstitute.org/identity-and-access-compliance-roadmap/

IAM's 4 Core Pillars: IGA, AM, PAM, AD Management | Author/Organization: One Identity | URL: https://www.oneidentity.com/the-four-pillars-of-iam/

Identity & Access Management Standards and Frameworks | Author/Organization: NIST | URL: https://www.nist.gov/identity-access-management

NIST SP 800-53 (Security and Privacy Controls for Information Systems) | Author/Organization: NIST (referenced in PAM standards) | URL: https://csrc.nist.gov/publications/detail/sp/800-53/rev-5/final

ISO/IEC 27001:2022 (Information Security Management) | Author/Organization: International Organization for Standardization (ISO) (PAM and access control focus) | URL: https://www.iso.org/standard/27001

ISO/IEC 27002:2022 (Information Security Controls) | Author/Organization: ISO (access policies and PAM guidance) | URL: https://www.iso.org/standard/27002

Chapter 11: Data Governance & Data Security

DAMA-DMBOK Framework | Author/Organization: DAMA International | URL: https://www.alation.com/blog/data-governance-framework/

COBIT Framework | Author/Organization: ISACA | URL: https://www.alation.com/blog/data-governance-framework/

DCAM (Data Management Capability Assessment Model) | Author/Organization: EDM Council | URL: https://www.alation.com/blog/data-governance-framework/

NIST Cybersecurity Framework | Author/Organization: National Institute of Standards and Technology (NIST) | URL: https://www.nist.gov/cyberframework

ISO/IEC 27001 & 27002 | Author/Organization: International Organization for Standardization (ISO) | URL: https://www.connectwise.com/blog/11-best-cybersecurity-frameworks

Data Governance Standards (Quality, Security, Privacy, Lifecycle) | Author/Organization: Atlan | URL: https://atlan.com/data-governance-standards/

HITRUST Common Security Framework (CSF) | Author/Organization: Health Information Trust Alliance (HITRUST) | URL: https://www.connectwise.com/blog/11-best-cybersecurity-frameworks

SOC Standards (for Cybersecurity, Availability, Confidentiality) | Author/Organization: American Institute of CPAs (AICPA) | URL: https://www.connectwise.com/blog/11-best-cybersecurity-frameworks

Risk IT Framework & ITAF (IT Audit Framework) | Author/Organization: ISACA | URL: https://www.isaca.org/resources/frameworks-standards-and-models

10 Core Elements of Data Governance Framework (Strategy, Policy, Security, Quality) | Author/Organization: Claravine | URL: https://www.claravine.com/resources/data-governance-framework/

Chapter 12: Secure Development & DevSecOps

NIST SP 800-218 Secure Software Development Framework (SSDF) Version 1.1 | Author/Organization: NIST | URL: https://csrc.nist.gov/projects/ssdf

BSA Framework for Secure Software | Author/Organization: BSA | The Software Alliance, (2019)

Supply-chain Levels for Software Artifacts (SLSA) Framework | Author/Organization: SLSA Project, (via JFrog)

OWASP Software Assurance Maturity Model (SAMM) | Author/Organization: OWASP Foundation, (via SEI report)

Microsoft Security Development Lifecycle (SDL) Practices | Author/Organization: Microsoft | URL: https://www.microsoft.com/en-us/securityengineering/sdl/practices

Team Software Process for Secure Software Development (TSP-Secure) | Author/Organization: Carnegie Mellon University SEI | URL: https://www.sei.cmu.edu/library/file_redirect/2013_019_001_297287.pdf/

Systems Security Engineering Capability Maturity Model (SSE-CMM) | Author/Organization: International Systems Security Engineering Association (ISSEA) | URL: https://www.sei.cmu.edu/library/file_redirect/2013_019_001_297287.pdf/

Secure Software Development Lifecycle (SSDLC) Overview | Author/Organization: JFrog | URL: https://jfrog.com/learn/devsecops/ssdlc-secure-software-development-lifecycle/

Secure SDLC (SSDLC) Guide | Author/Organization: Wiz | URL: https://www.wiz.io/academy/application-security/secure-sdlc

Secure Software Development Lifecycle (SSDLC) | Author/Organization: Snyk | URL: https://snyk.io/articles/secure-sdlc/

Chapter 13: Security Operations Center (SOC) Maturity & Threat Hunting

The SOC Hierarchy of Needs: A Maturity Model for Modern Operations | Author/Organization: Prophet Security | URL: https://www.prophetsecurity.ai/blog/the-soc-hierarchy-of-needs-a-maturity-model-for-modern-operations | Description: This article outlines a five-layer maturity model for SOCs, from alert management to proactive hunting and posture improvements, emphasizing AI-driven automation for operational excellence. https://www.prophetsecurity.ai/blog/the-soc-hierarchy-of-needs-a-maturity-model-for-modern-operations

SOC Maturity Models Explained | Author/Organization: Q-Sec | URL: https://q-sec.com/soc-knowledge-base/soc-maturity-models-explained | Description: This resource details a five-level SOC maturity progression from reactive to strategic/adaptive, incorporating threat hunting, automation, metrics like MTTD/MTTR, and integration with enterprise risk management. https://q-sec.com/soc-knowledge-base/soc-maturity-models-explained

What is Threat Hunting and How Does it Fit in SOC Operations? | Author/Organization: Expel | URL: https://expel.com/cyberspeak/threat-hunting-soc/ | Description: This guide explains threat hunting's role in SOCs, alignment with MITRE ATT&CK for TTPs, its symbiotic relationship with monitoring, and AI/ML applications for scalable anomaly detection. https://expel.com/cyberspeak/threat-hunting-soc/

What Is SOC Threat Hunting? | Author/Organization: Wiz | URL: https://www.wiz.io/academy/detection-and-response/soc-threat-hunting | Description: This overview defines SOC threat hunting as proactive searching for evasive threats, with best practices like blast radius prioritization, compliance alignment (NIST, ISO 27001, SOC 2), and metrics for MTTD/MTTR improvements. https://www.wiz.io/academy/detection-and-response/soc-threat-hunting

The Security Operations Maturity Model | Author/Organization: Exabeam | URL: https://www.exabeam.com/resources/ebooks/the-security-operations-maturity-model/ | Description: This white paper provides a framework to assess and advance SOC maturity in threat monitoring, hunting, investigation, and response by aligning technology, people, and processes. https://www.exabeam.com/resources/ebooks/the-security-operations-maturity-model/

A Framework for Cyber Threat Hunting | Author/Organization: Sqrrl Data, Inc. | URL: https://www.threathunting.net/files/framework-for-threat-hunting-whitepaper.pdf | Description: This white paper introduces the Threat Hunting Loop (hypothesis, investigation, uncoordinated, feedback) and Hunting Maturity Model (HM0-HM4), with strategies for scaling via analytics and the Hunt Matrix. https://www.threathunting.net/files/framework-for-threat-hunting-whitepaper.pdf

SOC Maturity - Setting Standards for Your SOC | Author/Organization: LRQA | URL: https://www.lrqa.com/en/insights/articles/soc-maturity-setting-standards-for-your-soc/ | Description: This article presents a four-level SOC maturity model developed with CREST and industry partners, focusing on threat landscape understanding, log management, and progression from preventative to high-capability operations. https://www.lrqa.com/en/insights/articles/soc-maturity-setting-standards-for-your-soc/

Practical Guide to the Threat Hunting Maturity Model | Author/Organization: Hunt.io | URL: https://hunt.io/new-design/glossary/threat-hunting-maturity-model | Description: This guide offers practical insights into building a threat hunting maturity model to detect advanced threats missed by traditional defenses in SOC environments. https://hunt.io/new-design/glossary/threat-hunting-maturity-model

The Evolution of Security Operations and Strategies for Building an Effective SOC | Author/Organization: ISACA | URL: https://www.isaca.org/resources/isaca-journal/issues/2021/volume-5/the-evolution-of-security-operations-and-strategies-for-building-an-effective-soc | Description: This journal article discusses SOC evolution, emphasizing TTPs-based threat hunting for early detection and remediation to enhance overall security operations maturity.

https://www.isaca.org/resources/isaca-journal/issues/2021/volume-5/the-evolution-of-security-operations-and-strategies-for-building-an-effective-soc

Hunting Maturity Model (as referenced in threat hunting frameworks) | Author/Organization: David J. Bianco / Sqrrl | URL: https://www.threathunting.net/files/framework-for-threat-hunting-whitepaper.pdf | Description: This model, integrated into broader frameworks like Sqrrl's Threat Hunting Loop, defines five maturity levels (HM0-HM4) for organizational threat hunting capabilities, from basic to advanced iterative execution. https://www.threathunting.net/files/framework-for-threat-hunting-whitepaper.pdf

Chapter 14: Incident Response, Crisis Management & Tabletop Exercises

NIST Special Publication 800-61 Revision 3: Incident Response Recommendations and Considerations | Author/Organization: National Institute of Standards and Technology (NIST) | URL: https://nvlpubs.nist.gov/nistpubs/SpecialPublications/NIST.SP.800-61r3.pdf | Description: This guide assists organizations in integrating cybersecurity incident response into risk management activities aligned with NIST CSF 2.0, covering preparation, detection, response, and recovery across Govern, Identify, Protect, Detect, Respond, and Recover functions. https://nvlpubs.nist.gov/nistpubs/SpecialPublications/NIST.SP.800-61r3.pdf

Computer Security Incident Handling Guide (NIST SP 800-61 Revision 2) | Author/Organization: National Institute of Standards and Technology (NIST) | Description: The foundational NIST publication outlining the four-step incident response lifecycle—preparation, detection and analysis, containment/eradication/recovery, and post-incident activity—with best practices for policies, teams, and exercises.

NIST Cybersecurity Framework (CSF) 2.0 | Author/Organization: National Institute of Standards and Technology (NIST) | Description: This framework integrates incident response into its core functions (Govern, Identify, Protect, Detect, Respond, Recover), providing a flexible structure for crisis management and continuous improvement in cybersecurity programs.

NIST Incident Response Project Page | Author/Organization: NIST Computer Security Resource Center (CSRC) | Description: Official NIST resource detailing SP 800-61r3 updates, emphasizing incident preparation, detection, response efficiency, and alignment with broader risk management to reduce incident impact.

SP 800-61 Rev. 3 Final Publication Page | Author/Organization: NIST Computer Security Resource Center (CSRC) | Description: Hosts the latest NIST incident response recommendations, including guidelines for prioritizing incidents, recovery processes, performance measures, and testing procedures like tabletop exercises.

NIST Incident Response: 4-Step Life Cycle, Templates and Tips | Author/Organization: Cynet | Description: Explains NIST's four-phase incident response process with templates for policies and plans, stressing continuous improvement, lessons learned, and integration with frameworks like ISO 27001.

NIST Incident Response: 4-Step Process and Critical Best Practices | Author/Organization: Exabeam | Description: Details NIST SP 800-61's lifecycle with best practices for preparation, including incident response plan templates, employee training, and proactive defenses to minimize breach impacts.

NIST Incident Response Guide: Lifecycle, Best Practices & Recovery | Author/Organization: AuditBoard | Description: Covers NIST's incident response cycle, team models, roles, tabletop exercise scenarios, and updates in SP 800-61r3 aligning with CSF 2.0 for technology-agnostic crisis handling.

Incident Response Steps & Phases: NIST Framework Explained | Author/Organization: SentinelOne | Description: Breaks down NIST's core phases with guidance on developing plans, playbooks, team training via tabletop exercises, and comparisons to models like SANS for effective incident mitigation.

NIST Publishes Updated Incident Response Recommendations and Considerations | Author/Organization: Inside Privacy (Covington & Burling LLP) | Description: Analyzes NIST SP 800-61r3 changes, including mapping to CSF 2.0 functions, a restructured lifecycle for dynamic incidents, and advice for updating plans with new preparation and recovery guidance.

Chapter 15: Compliance, Audit & Regulatory Frameworks

**** | Author/Organization: Mark Francis, Holland & Knight LLP | Description: This article provides an overview of NIST CSF 2.0, offering guidance for managing cyber risks through a risk-based approach for developing comprehensive information security programs.

**** | Author/Organization: National Institute of Standards and Technology (NIST) | Description: This publication outlines a structured, six-step process for managing security and privacy risks in federal information systems under FISMA, promoting consistent risk management practices.

**** | Author/Organization: National Institute of Standards and Technology (NIST) | Description: This comprehensive catalog organizes security and privacy controls into 20 families, serving as the most widely adopted standard for compliance and risk mitigation.

**** | Author/Organization: National Institute of Standards and Technology (NIST) | Description: This framework guides organizations in managing cybersecurity risks with core functions including Govern, Identify, Protect, Detect, Respond, and Recover, plus implementation examples and profiles.

**** | Author/Organization: National Institute of Standards and Technology (NIST) | Description: This provides a flexible, 7-step process for organizations to manage information security and privacy risks, linking to NIST standards for FISMA compliance.

**** | Author/Organization: National Institute of Standards and Technology (NIST) | Description: This standard specifies cybersecurity requirements for federal contractors handling controlled unclassified information (CUI) to ensure protection and compliance.

**** | Author/Organization: National Institute of Standards and Technology (NIST) | Description: This draft guide offers actionable steps for implementing CSF 2.0, integrating it with enterprise risk management and transitioning from prior versions.

**** | Author/Organization: National Institute of Standards and Technology (NIST) | Description: These updated publications align cybersecurity risk management guidance with CSF 2.0, supporting measurement and integration of risk practices.

**** | Author/Organization: National Institute of Standards and Technology (NIST) / SailPoint | Description: This details the CSF's three parts—Core (activities and outcomes), Tiers (maturity levels), and Profiles—for strategic cybersecurity risk assessment and compliance.

**** | Author/Organization: National Institute of Standards and Technology (NIST) | Description: This collection includes key frameworks like RMF, CSF, SP 800-53, and SSDF, providing standards for risk management, controls, and secure development compliance.

Chapter 16: Vendor Risk Management & Third-Party Cyber Risk

NIST Cybersecurity Framework (CSF) 2.0 | Author/Organization: NIST | URL: https://www.nist.gov/cyberframework | Description: Updates third-party and supply chain risk management with specific Govern (GV.SC) controls for supplier prioritization, contract integration, due diligence, and ongoing risk monitoring. https://www.nist.gov/cyberframework

NIST SP 800-53 Rev. 5: Security and Privacy Controls for Information Systems and Organizations | Author/Organization: NIST | URL: https://csrc.nist.gov/pubs/sp/800/53/r5/upd1/final | Description: Provides Supplier Risk (SR) controls as a baseline for managing third-party relationships, including encryption, incident reporting, and access restrictions to prevent vulnerabilities. https://csrc.nist.gov/pubs/sp/800/53/r5/upd1/final

NIST SP 800-161 Revision 1: Cybersecurity Supply Chain Risk Management Practices for Systems and Organizations | Author/Organization: NIST | URL: https://csrc.nist.gov/pubs/sp/800/161/r1/final | Description: Offers tiered guidance for identifying critical suppliers, assessing supply chain risks, and verifying resilience across vendor dependencies in response to Executive Order 14028. https://csrc.nist.gov/pubs/sp/800/161/r1/final

NIST SP 800-30: Risk Management Guide for Information Technology Systems | Author/Organization: NIST | URL: https://csrc.nist.gov/pubs/sp/800/30/r1/final | Description: Outlines a nine-step process for risk assessments, including system characterization, threat and vulnerability identification, and control analysis applicable to third-party risks. https://csrc.nist.gov/pubs/sp/800/30/r1/final

NIST SP 1326 (Initial Public Draft): Cybersecurity Supply Chain Risk Management - Due Diligence Quick-Start Guide | Author/Organization: NIST | URL: https://csrc.nist.gov/pubs/sp/1326/ipd | Description: Proposes a resource-efficient approach to supplier due diligence based on SP 800-161r1, focusing on primary risk factors for quick evaluations. https://csrc.nist.gov/pubs/sp/1326/ipd

NIST Risk Management Framework (RMF) | Author/Organization: NIST | URL: https://csrc.nist.gov/projects/risk-management | Description: Delivers a 7-step process for managing security and privacy risks, adaptable for integrating third-party vendor assessments into organizational programs. https://csrc.nist.gov/projects/risk-management

Best Practices in Cyber Supply Chain Risk Management: Vendor Selection and Management | Author/Organization: NIST (Workshop Briefing) | URL: https://csrc.nist.gov/CSRC/media/Projects/Supply-Chain-Risk-Management/documents/briefings/Workshop-Brief-on-Cyber-SCRM-Vendor-Selection-and-Management.pdf | Description: Details supplier risk criteria such as financial, location, and business continuity risks for effective third-party selection and ongoing management. https://csrc.nist.gov/CSRC/media/Projects/Supply-Chain-Risk-Management/documents/briefings/Workshop-Brief-on-Cyber-SCRM-Vendor-Selection-and-Management.pdf

NIST Third-Party Risk Management: 800-53, 800-161, CSF | Author/Organization: SAFE Security | URL: https://safe.security/resources/nist-third-party-risk-management-800-53-800-161-csf/ | Description: Explains integration of NIST 800-53 SR controls, 800-161 supply chain tiers, and CSF for compliance, policy development, and risk assessment tools. https://safe.security/resources/nist-third-party-risk-management-800-53-800-161-csf/

How to Use NIST SP 800-53 for Improved Third-Party Supply Chain Risk Management | Author/Organization: Mitratech | URL: https://mitratech.com/resource-hub/blog/use-nist-sp-800-53-for-third-party-supply-chain-risk-management/ | Description: Examines SP 800-53 controls for supply chain risks, emphasizing formal plans, transparency, pre-assessments, and automation for vendor due diligence and contracts. https://mitratech.com/resource-hub/blog/use-nist-sp-800-53-for-third-party-supply-chain-risk-management/

Meeting the Third-Party Risk Requirements of NIST 800-53 in 2026 | Author/Organization: UpGuard | URL: https://www.upguard.com/blog/third-party-risk-requirements-nist-800-53 | Description: Provides a structured framework for maturing cyber supply chain risk management using NIST SP 800-53 to address evolving third-party requirements. https://www.upguard.com/blog/third-party-risk-requirements-nist-800-53

Chapter 17: Business Continuity, Disaster Recovery & Operational Resilience

ISO 22301: Societal security | Author/Organization: Business continuity management systems | Description: Requirements

International Organization for Standardization (ISO)**

Primary international standard for establishing | Author/Organization: implementing | Description: maintaining, and improving a business continuity management system (BCMS) to prepare for, respond to, and recover from disruptive events.

ISO 22313: Societal security | Author/Organization: Business continuity management systems | Description: Guidance

International Organization for Standardization (ISO)**

Provides guidance on the application of ISO 22301 | Author/Organization: explaining specific regulatory clauses and protocols for planning | Description: monitoring, and updating business continuity processes.

ISO 27031: Information technology | Author/Organization: Security techniques | Description: Guidelines for information and communication technology readiness for business continuity

International Organization for Standardization (ISO)**

Focuses on ICT planning requirements for disaster recovery | Author/Organization: including the four critical steps of planning | Description: doing, checking, and acting to ensure data security and operational continuity.

NIST SP 800-34: Contingency Planning Guide for Federal Information Systems

National Institute of Standards and Technology (NIST)**

Provides a framework for IT contingency planning | Author/Organization: including risk assessment | Description: business impact analysis, and recovery strategies to maintain operations during disruptions.

Chapter 18: Advanced Identity Security & Privileged Access Management

NIST SP 800-207 Zero Trust Architecture

Organization/Author: NIST**

This publication outlines strategies and components for implementing zero trust architecture | Author/Organization: emphasizing identity management | Description: MFA, and privileged access controls in IT infrastructure.

NIST Cybersecurity Framework (CSF)

Organization/Author: NIST**

A flexible | Author/Organization: high-level framework for managing cybersecurity risks | Description: with strong focus on identity, access management, continuous monitoring, and risk prioritization across business functions.

ISO/IEC 27001 Information Security Management

Organization/Author: ISO**

An international standard for establishing | Author/Organization: implementing | Description: and maintaining an information security management system, including formal policies for identity and access controls.

Chapter 19: Network Security & Zero Trust Architecture (ZTA)

NIST SP 800-207 Zero Trust Architecture

Organization/Author: NIST**

Provides an official | Author/Organization: vendor-neutral reference outlining core principles | Description: logical components, use cases, and migration paths for implementing Zero Trust Architecture (ZTA).

CISA Zero Trust Maturity Model (ZTMM) Version 2.0

Organization/Author: Cybersecurity and Infrastructure Security Agency (CISA)**

Outlines a phased roadmap for Zero Trust adoption across five pillars: identity | Author/Organization: devices | Description: networks, applications/workloads, and data, with maturity stages from traditional to optimal.

DoD Zero Trust Reference Architecture

Organization/Author: Department of Defense (DoD)**

Expands on Zero Trust tenets with seven guiding principles | Author/Organization: including network segmentation | Description: automation, and visibility, to support capability planning and IT investment decisions.

NSA Zero Trust Implementation Guidelines (ZIGs)

Organization/Author: National Security Agency (NSA)**

Consists of a Primer and phased guidelines (Discovery | Author/Organization: Phase One | Description: Phase Two) aligned with the DoD Zero Trust Framework, detailing 42 capabilities and 91 activities for target-level ZT implementation.

Chapter 20: Governance, Risk Management & Executive Security Leadership

NIST Risk Management Framework (RMF) | Author/Organization: National Institute of Standards and Technology (NIST) | Description: Provides a comprehensive, flexible, repeatable 7-step process (Categorize, Select, Implement, Assess, Authorize, Monitor) for managing information security and privacy risks in organizations and systems.

NIST Cybersecurity Framework (CSF) 2.0 | Author/Organization: National Institute of Standards and Technology (NIST) | Description: Guides organizations across all sectors to manage and reduce cybersecurity risks through desired outcomes understandable by executives, managers, and practitioners.

ISO 31000:2018 Risk Management | Author/Organization: International Organization for Standardization (ISO) | Description: Offers principles, framework, and process for integrating risk management into organizational governance, strategy, and activities, emphasizing continuous improvement and flexibility.

COSO Enterprise Risk Management Framework | Author/Organization: Committee of Sponsoring Organizations of the Treadway Commission (COSO) | Description: Outlines five core components—governance and culture, strategy and objective-setting, performance, review and revision, and information, communication, and reporting—for enterprise-wide risk management.

COBIT (Control Objectives for Information and Related Technology) | Author/Organization: ISACA | Description: Provides a comprehensive framework with 40 governance and management objectives across five domains, aligning IT with business goals, including risk management and information security.

ISO 27001 Information Security Management | Author/Organization: International Organization for Standardization (ISO) | Description: Serves as the international standard for validating cybersecurity programs through requirements for establishing, implementing, maintaining, and continually improving an information security management system.

NIST SP 800-53 Security and Privacy Controls | Author/Organization: National Institute of Standards and Technology (NIST) | Description: Defines minimum security requirements for federal systems under FISMA, widely used across industries to improve information security with derivable frameworks like NIST 800-171.

CIS Controls (Center for Internet Security Controls) | Author/Organization: Center for Internet Security (CIS) | Description: Offers prioritized set of actions to mitigate common cyber risks, used alongside other frameworks to formalize security programs and track maturity.

Governance | Author/Organization: Risk | Description: and Compliance (GRC) Framework, Trend Micro (general industry standard), Unifies governance, risk management, and compliance to align security practices with business objectives, regulatory standards like GDPR and HIPAA, and threat mitigation.

ACSC Essential 8 | Author/Organization: Australian Cyber Security Centre (ACSC) | Description: Specifies eight threat mitigation strategies with a maturity model tailored to organizational capabilities and threat actors for protecting against common cyber attacks.

Chapter 21: Security Metrics, Reporting & Executive Dashboards

Enhancing Cybersecurity Metrics: CISO Strategies | Author/Organization: EY | Description: Discusses shifting to risk-informed reporting aligned with NIST CSF, ISO 27001, SOC 2, and business strategy, including risk appetite indicators and compliance metrics for executive dashboards.

The 10 Most Important Cybersecurity Metrics & KPIs for CISOs to Track | Author/Organization: Secureframe | Description: Lists 10 key metrics like vulnerability risk scores and security awareness scores, with guidance on tailoring for executive and board reporting to demonstrate business value.

Cloud Security Metrics That Matter: A CISO's Reporting Guide | Author/Organization: Sweet Security | Description: Provides KPIs such as compliance coverage score (aligned with CIS, NIST, PCI), vulnerability signal-to-noise ratio, and industry-specific metrics for board assurance.

4 Cyber Security Risk Assessment Reports Every CISO Needs | Author/Organization: CyberSaint | Description: Recommends four reports (Executive Risk Report, Trend Report, GDPR Report, Overview Summary) using CyberStrong scoring for aligning CISO activities with enterprise goals like a CFO's financials.

The CISO's Guide to the Top Cybersecurity Frameworks | Author/Organization: AttackIQ | Description: Overviews frameworks including ISO 27001/27002 (with metrics for ISMS performance), NIST CSF, CIS Controls, COBIT 2019, Cyber Kill Chain, and MITRE ATT&CK for cyber defense measurement.

How to Create Meaningful Security Metrics and KPIs | Author/Organization: IANS Research | Description: Offers guidance on building KPIs using frameworks to measure risk improvement in vulnerability management and security programs for board reporting and decision-making.

Cybersecurity Metrics & KPIs: What to Track in 2026 | Author/Organization: SentinelOne | Description: Covers NIST cybersecurity metrics categories (operational, compliance like GDPR/PCI DSS, risk-based), with best practices for standardization and board-level risk scores.

SP 800-55 Rev. 2 | Author/Organization: Performance Measurement Guide for Information Security | Description: NIST - Provides guidance on using metrics to assess adequacy of security controls, policies, and procedures for reporting and dashboards.

Cybersecurity Metrics Reporting Model | Author/Organization: ComplianceForge | Description: Practical model (CMRM) for sustainable metrics reporting capability tailored to CISO needs in security metrics and executive communication.

Performance Measurement Guide for Information Security (SP 800-55 Rev. 2) | Author/Organization: NIST (via csrc.nist.gov) | Description: Detailed framework for defining, collecting, and reporting security metrics to evaluate control effectiveness, directly supporting CISO dashboards.

Chapter 22: Architecture, Engineering & Platform Security

OWASP Secure-by-Design Framework | Author/Organization: OWASP | URL: https://owasp.org/www-project-secure-by-design-framework/ | Description: Practical guidance to embed security into software architecture, including principles like least privilege, defense in depth, and vetted patterns for requirements such as MFA and encryption. -

Platform Security Architecture (PSA) | Author/Organization: Arm/Xenonstack | URL: https://www.xenonstack.com/blog/platform-security-architectu re | Description: Comprehensive framework for networked devices with threat models, hardware/firmware standards, APIs, test suites, and certification for IoT security. -

SABSA (Sherwood Applied Business Security Architecture) | Author/Organization: Sherwood Applied Business Security Architecture | URL: https://keystonecorp.com/cybersecurity/it-security-architecture-frame works-best-practices-phases/ | Description: Business-driven framework with six layers (contextual to operational) aligning security with organizational goals and risk management. -

TOGAF (The Open Group Architecture Framework) | Author/Organization: The Open Group | URL: https://keystonecorp.com/cybersecurity/it-secu rity-architecture-frameworks-best-practices-phases/ | Description: Enterprise architecture methodology with ADM for aligning security architecture to business strategies, standardization, and gap analysis. -

Common Criteria | Author/Organization: International standards body | URL: https://destcert.com/resources/domain-3-security-architecture-and-engineering/ | Description: Evaluation and certification process using Protection Profiles (PP) to define security capabilities for products like firewalls, including 2FA and encryption. -

Arm Platform Security | Author/Organization: Arm | URL: https://www.arm.com/architecture/security-features/platform-security | Description: Standard security model with threat modeling, TMSA documents, hardware/firmware specs, ABIs, APIs, and reference implementations for secure product design. -

NIST Cybersecurity Framework | Author/Organization: NIST | URL: https://www.nist.gov/cyberframework | Description: Framework to understand and improve cybersecurity risk management, applicable to security architecture design and controls. -

ISO 27001 | Author/Organization: International Organization for Standardization | URL: https://keystonecorp.com/cybersecurity/it-security-architecture-frameworks-best-practices-phases/ | Description: Information security management standard for risk assessment, controls, and compliance in security architecture. -

COBIT | Author/Organization: ISACA | URL: https://www.isaca.org/resources/isaca-journal/issues/2017/volume-4/enterprise-security-architecturea-top-down-approach | Description: Governance framework with processes for enterprise security architecture, including vulnerability management, PKI, and alignment with business needs via PAM. -

Zero Trust Security Principles | Author/Organization: Industry standard (multiple sources) | URL: https://www.future-processing.com/blog/security-architecture-101-understanding-the-basics/ | Description: Architecture model emphasizing continuous verification, least privilege, and no implicit trust, integrated into frameworks like NIST and DevSecOps. -

Chapter 23: AI Security, Governance & Responsible AI

NIST AI Risk Management Framework (AI RMF) | Author/Organization: NIST | Description: Foundational US standard for AI risk management with four core functions: Govern, Map, Measure, and Manage; provides guidance for identifying risks, implementing controls, and continuous oversight.

ISO/IEC 42001 | Author/Organization: International Organization for Standardization (ISO) | Description: First formal AI Management System (AIMS) standard for operationalizing AI governance, lifecycle oversight, risk management, and accountability across design to retirement.

EU AI Act | Author/Organization: European Union | Description: Regulatory framework driving mandatory compliance for AI systems, emphasizing risk-based oversight and integration with governance models like NIST AI RMF and ISO 42001.

OWASP LLM Top-10 | Author/Organization: OWASP Foundation | Description: Essential AI security framework listing top 10 risks for large language models, with practical implementation guidance for CISOs addressing the machine learning lifecycle.

Cisco's Framework for AI Security | Author/Organization: Cisco | Description: Comprehensive framework covering five domains: Securing AI, AI for Security, AI Governance, AI Safety, and Responsible AI, tailored for enterprise security.

NIST Cybersecurity Framework (CSF) | Author/Organization: NIST | Description: Core governance framework integrated with AI RMF and ISO 27001 for layered cyber risk management, operational resilience, and AI decision governance in 2026.

ISO 27001 | Author/Organization: International Organization for Standardization (ISO) | Description: Information security management standard anchoring AI governance, combined with NIST CSF for assurance, audits, and regulatory overlays like NIS2 and DORA.

The 2025 CISOs' Guide to AI Governance | Author/Organization: TrustCloud | Description: Practical guide for CISOs on building frameworks aligned with ISO 42001 and NIST AI RMF, including risk assessment, policies, and audit preparation with best practices from leading companies.

AI Governance for CISOs: Securing SaaS AI Deployment | Author/Organization: Tetrate | Description: Framework for CISOs with controls for SaaS AI, including approved tool management, accountability, audit trails, network security, and cross-functional governance structures.

A Practical Guide to Implementing the NIST AI Risk Management Framework | Author/Organization: A-Team (Oracle) | Description: Step-by-step implementation guide integrating AI RMF with corporate governance, including oversight committees, ethical guidelines, privacy measures, and risk mitigation processes.

Chapter 24: Quantum Computing, Post-Quantum Cryptography & Cryptographic Resilience

NIST Post-Quantum Cryptography Standardization | Author/Organization: NIST | URL: https://csrc.nist.gov/projects/post-quantum-cryptography | Description: Official U.S. government standards for post-quantum cryptographic algorithms, including selected winners like CRYSTALS-Kyber and CRYSTALS-Dilithium for key encapsulation and digital signatures. -

Migration to Post-Quantum Cryptography | Author/Organization: NIST IR 8413 | URL: https://doi.org/10.6028/NIST.IR.8413 | Description: NIST's detailed framework guiding organizations through inventory, risk assessment, and phased migration to quantum-resistant cryptography. -

Quantum Computing and Post-Quantum Cryptography: A CISO's Guide to Accelerating Quantum-Safe Readiness | Author/Organization: IBM | URL: https://www.ibm.com/think/insights/ciso-guide-quantum-safe-readiness | Description: Practical steps for CISOs including cryptographic discovery, risk assessment, and transformation using tools like IBM Quantum Safe Explorer for CBOM generation. -

CISO's Guide to Preparing for the Quantum Shift | Author/Organization: Encryption Consulting | URL: https://www.encryptionconsulting.com/cisos-guide-to-preparing-for-the-quantum-shift/ | Description: Roadmap with levels from assessment (crypto inventory) to implementation, emphasizing hybrid cryptography, governance, and NIST standards compliance by 2025-2028. -

A CISO's Guide to Post-Quantum Readiness: How to Build Crypto-Agility Now | Author/Organization: CyberArk | URL: https://www.cyberark.com/resources/blog/a-cisos-guide-to-post-quantum-readiness-how-to-build-crypto-agility-now | Description: Step-by-step guide covering inventory, PQC algorithm selection, secrets rotation automation, and just-in-time access for cryptographic resilience. -

Quantum-Safe Cybersecurity: Essential CISO 2025 Guide | Author/Organization: CybelAngel | URL: https://cybelangel.com/blog/quantum-safe-cybersecurity/ | Description: Recommendations for CISOs including NIST-approved algorithms, risk prioritization, supply chain interoperability, and early PQC initiatives. -

A CISO's Guide to Quantum-Resistant Key Exchange Algorithms | Author/Organization: Gopher Security | URL: http://www.gopher.security/post-quantum/quantum-resistant-key-exchange-cisos-guide | Description: Overview of quantum-resistant key exchange protocols, their implementation, and preparation strategies for enterprise cryptographic resilience. -

Rise of the Quantum CISO: A Guide to Prepare CISOs and Technical Teams for the Quantum Era | Author/Organization: The Quantum Insider | URL: https://thequantuminsider.com/2024/02/12/rise-of-the-quantum-ciso-a-guide-to-prepare-cisos-and-technical-teams-for-the-quantum-era/ | Description: Strategy for quantum-inclusive IT, PQC education, infrastructure assessment, NIST standards tracking, and industry collaborations. -

8 Tips to Prepare for Quantum Computing and Post-Quantum Cryptography | Author/Organization: IANS Research | URL:

https://www.iansresearch.com/resources/all-blogs/post/security-blog/2025/10/07/8-tips-to-prepare-for-quantum-computing-and-post-quantum-cryptography | Description: Actionable tips for CISOs like assessing data value, building cryptographic inventories, and planning PQC transitions. -

CRYSTALS-Kyber (Post-Quantum Key Encapsulation Mechanism) | Author/Organization: Google/Broadcom/IBM/Royal Holloway (ML-KEM) | URL: https://pq-crystals.org/kyber/ | Description: Academic paper on NIST-selected lattice-based algorithm for quantum-resistant key exchange, with implementations and resilience proofs. -

APPENDIX E

About the Author

Cristian Ruvalcaba, CISSP, CCSP, MFA is a cybersecurity professional and strategist with over 20 years of experience spanning the corporate, government, energy, and fintech sectors. He is also the founder of and head researcher with Saluca Labs, a privacy first and compliance drive AI and cybersecurity research organization. Throughout his career, he has collaborated with CISOs, directors, and senior engineering leaders on detection strategy and maturity, incident response, security architecture, and SOC operations; helping organizations across four continents think more clearly about risk.

Cristian began his cybersecurity journey at Intuit in 2003, where he would eventually serve as a founding member of the company's Security Operations Center, building the operational processes and global incident response frameworks that would set the tone for the rest of his career. He went on to lead SIEM engineering teams at Optiv Security, where he drove detection strategy for multinational enterprise environments and reduced time-to-production for managed security customers by 75%. At IBM, he served as a Senior Cybersecurity Specialist in Threat Management, advising organizations on long-term security strategy, influencing the QRadar product roadmap through practitioner insights, and supporting over $30 million in influenced revenue across three years. His contributions earned multiple awards, including the IBM Golden Circle, two years in a row, and Entrepreneur Award.

A published author and thought leader, Cristian contributed an opening chapter to Advances in Security Information Management, 2013, and authored a SANS Gold Paper that reached the SANS Reading Room Top 25. He has spoken on panels alongside leaders from major cybersecurity organizations on topics including security architecture, MSSP evolution, SOC strategy, and SIEM modernization. As a lead instructor with ThriveDX, he also mentored the next generation of cybersecurity analysts and engineers through university bootcamp programs.

Cristian holds a Bachelor of Science in Computer Engineering and a Master of Fine Arts in Film Production, both from San Diego State University, a combination that reflects his belief that effective security leadership requires both technical rigor and the ability to communicate and tell a story. That creative background isn't just a footnote: he spent years performing improv and stand-up comedy and produced an award-winning short film, experiences that sharpened his ability to think on his feet, read a room, and deliver a message; skills any CISO will tell you are just as critical as understanding a kill chain.

www.saluca.com

Acknowledgements

This book is the outcome of decades of collaborations, friendships and common goals around security, with a bit of fun. I am grateful to those without whom my career would not have been possible. I have learned a great deal from dozens of close colleagues and hundreds of customers, clients and peers and look forward to continuing my professional education in hopes of honoring the relationships and shared knowledge I've picked up along the way. Special thanks to Jamie Jaworski, Tim Deloach, Chris Denton, Tirano Graham, Geoff Poer, Pete Hennis, Chris Debbas, Andy Myers, Dave Webb, Fran Malloy, Michael McCracken, Sylvia Henson, Markwayne Javier, David Stanislawski, Ed Renales and the late greats Dean Curry and Mario Rodriguez.

There are dozens more I have not listed, you are not forgotten, each connection has been a grain of sand on the beach of life.